Predicting the Behavior of the Educational System

Predicting the Behavior
of the Educational System

Thomas F. Green
with the assistance of
David P. Ericson and Robert H. Seidman

 Educator's International Press, Inc.
Troy, NY

Green, Thomas F.
Predicting the Behavior of the Educational System

Published by Educator's International Press, Inc.
18 Colleen Road
Troy, N. Y. 12180

Previously published by Syracuse University Press © 1980 (previous ISBN 0-8156-2223-6)

Library of Congress Catalog Card Number: 97-61631

ISBN   0-9658339-2-5

Manufactured in the United States of America

02 01 00 99 98 97   1 2 3 4 5 6

CONTENTS

LIST OF TABLES

LIST OF FIGURES

REINTRODUCTION

Reintroducing a book of one's own after nearly twenty years offers a rare opportunity to correct all kinds of mistakes. It calls to mind a prerogative of Congressmen, (and women) who, thinking through today's speech offered on the floor of the House or Senate, can return tomorrow and submit a motion to amend the record. Thus, do we construct the fragile face of wit and wisdom. The passage of time, of course, offers its own amendments to which no author need submit additions. The extensive time-series data that provided hints on the structure and behavior of the educational system, for example, will necessarily have changed, if only by the addition of a dozen data points. Yet, even a fairly extensive inspection of those series will show remarkably little need to alter our account. Suppose the result had been less satisfactory. Even then, the wiser course would be to turn away from cosmetic efforts to "put on a pretty face" and let things stand as originally published, leaving all the blemishes in place. Still, there may be some value in fresh reminders of some central points which experience suggests the reader is likely to misconstrue. Mistakes in the text ought to remain, but mistakes in reading ought to be avoided if possible. A fresh introduction might help.

Let's begin with the title. The book was first called *Rationality and Structure in the Educational Enterprise.* But that title seemed too static, too abstruse, too academic; unconnected to anything familiar and concrete. The title needs an active verb, I thought, and must at least convey some hint of the effort running throughout to discern the future of our educational arrangements and, therefore, of educational policy. It was from such thoughts that the reference to predicting and to system emerged. The earlier title made no mention of a "system." If that original title were allowed to stand, readers might have grasped more easily what kind of system we had in mind. It was certainly not the "school system" that seems to surface instantly in the minds of most when they hear the words "educational system." It was not merely a system of schools, but a system for educating, including—in the American case—both private and parochial schools along with provisions for home-schooling, the educational efforts of business and industry, and even programs provided by the armed forces and voluntary agencies. The idea was that all these arrangements must be construed not as an amorphous unorganized mess, but as a single system having a definite shape and its own kind of rationality. How is that system structured? What is central and what peripheral to it? How is it controlled? Catholic and other parochial schools are as much a part of that system as are the public schools. In fact, were it not for the existence of such parochial schools, the educational system that we set out to study—in its American form—would surely have become nowhere near as universally available nor as inclusive as it has come to be. Such schools do not constitute a separate system. They are included in the educational system that we intended to describe.

Repeated reference to "the system in its American form" hints further at our meaning. The American educational system was not the object of our study. It was only the most accessible specimen, simply one example of an educational system. Only in the twentieth century have systematic arrangements for education emerged in one society after another aimed at making intentional education both comprehensive and universal. Our conjecture was that we shall come to speak of this movement as the rise of "the educational system" much as we have learned to speak of "the market" as a quite particular arrangement for production, exchange, distribution, and investment that has emerged everywhere in the world, but only in the present century. The American educational system was not the object of study, only a specimen of that object.

Other misreadings stem either from confusion or indifference to the question: "What is a good or worthwhile education?"; or if not from indifference to it, then from incredulity that such a question might warrant a carefully reasoned discussion. The current movement of school reform seems peculiarly barren of attentive and thoughtful public discussion on the question as to what a good education would look like. Instead of a debate on the question, we seem to have a growing consensus upon a single answer virtually never doubted—a good education is one that prepares persons to fit the demands of a transforming employment system.

Predicting does little to remedy this defect. It is a formal account of the educational system in the sense that it lacks any discussion of the content of education. Emphasis falls upon what makes the system a system, not upon what would make it a system of educational excellence. This formal approach stems in part from an observation common among social forecasters of the late sixties that the educational system seems remarkably impervious to change. Alter its course by some reform and, unless you sustain the effort for a very long time, the system will soon return to its established ways. Why does it seem so impervious to change? The answer in *Predicting*, crudely put, was that the system, as we have come to know it, answers fairly well to human basics of such simplicity that to depart very substantially from its arrangements would be to attempt something like a reformation of human nature itself. Those basics we framed in such simplicities as "learning takes time", "it takes twelve months to get a year older", "every society must empty the nursery and none can be entirely indifferent to how it is done." How such simplicities shape the foundations of the educational system is just what the composition of *Predicting* was designed to show. But in doing so, it reveals a system in which, as it were, there are no persons. All is shape and form, with no content. This problem was acknowledged, and a path beyond it sketched, as far as I could discern the path, in the penultimate paragraph of the text.

> Any adequate account of the content of policy for the system must treat the relation of education to work life, and also its relation to civic life. And if that, then it must deal in some depth with the nature of "membership" and, therefore, with the place of history in the formation of a social memory. For without a social memory there is none of that attachment to the present or through time to underwrite either social membership or the existence of the system itself. Dealing with the educational content of the system leads one then to a treatment also of the moral emotions and the problems of public choice in the direction of the system in ways without which it cannot lay claim to be an educational system. (p. 169).

Such a reintroduction does not correct any errors of the past, but this restatement might add some clarity.

Thomas F. Green
Pompey, NY
December, 1997

ACKNOWLEDGMENTS

THE UNREMITTING LONELINESS of composition is made bearable and becomes possible to endure only by the continuing encouragement and interest and by the unbridled criticism and shared reflections of colleagues. And so, with the passage of time, one's indebtedness grows, extending to larger circles, including more persons than can be listed. Such indebtedness not only widens, but also deepens and is transformed from debt to gratitude. And from gratitude it often ripens into a kind of kinship seldom found outside the academic community. For such friends and teachers, it is easy to voice thanks.

Among them I include Robert Lynn, currently of The Lilly Endowment and formerly Dean of the Auburn Program of Union Theological Seminary in New York. His encouragement, patience, and critical wisdom over many years has been invaluable. To his associate, Ralph Lundgren, for his intelligent interest and concrete support I voice my thanks, and also to Charles Willis and the Kettering Foundation for the opportunity to frame the initial statements of many matters that remain within the text.

Under grants from these foundations, Robert H. Seidman and David P. Ericson assembled much of the time-series data on which this work is based; but also, and from their separate and disciplined perspectives, they provided continuous and cogent argument through nearly three years of discussions. Robert Seidman was solely responsible for assembling nearly one hundred years of data on nearly a hundred different dimensions of the American educational experience. Without that material, and without his careful judgment in its use, this work would have been impossible. David P. Ericson was solely responsible for the assemblage of historical data on school enrollment, attendance, and on statutes of compulsory attendance in every state and territory of the United States. But his philosophical sensibilities also figured prominently in framing the arguments on the connection between primary and secondary educational benefits as well as on the arguments concerning the dynamics of educational expansion. The total volume of research reports completed by these two scholars would come to more than double the size of the final study, and without those efforts no part of this work would have been completed.

Emily Haynes also has read the entire manuscript in several of its versions. Her acuity of judgment and her careful reading have guided me away from more outright errors than I would dare confess. The very conception of this work arises substantially from an unpublished but widely circulated paper that we did together years ago entitled "Notes Toward a General Theory of Educational Systems." Vincent Tinto and Gerald Grant have contributed in similar ways.

To James E. McClellan I wish to express a special kind of thanks and not only for his friendship and his integrity. He read an earlier version of the manuscript in fine detail and was repeatedly able to discern the central thread of argument even where I had not discovered it myself. I owe a similar special debt of thanks to Jesse Burkhead. As friend, colleague, and teacher, he has read the entire manuscript from the perspective of an economist, a scholar of public finance, and a student of both government and education. His decency, patience, and tenacity have been sorely tested. Most of what I have learned about economic theory and much that I have learned about government practice I learned under his guidance.

I must acknowledge also an enormous debt to the good offices of Marshall Smith, John Williamson, Hunter Moorman, Harold Hodgkinson, and their colleagues at the National Institute of Education for the opportunity to spend several months in the planning office and other divisions of that agency listening, observing, and exchanging ideas. If, in this work, there is some fidelity to the practical tasks of administration and planning within the limits of federal policy, that fidelity arises in large part from the opportunity to work within the National Institute of Education.

It was through the Country Planning Program of the Organization for Economic Co-operation and Development, and especially because of Beresford Hayward, that I was able to meet with and learn from the major educational planners of the OECD countries. His is an especially valuable imagination to encounter. As facilitator, guide, creative listener, provocateur, and host, Bere Hayward's contribution to scholarship on educational systems has gone too long without public acknowledgment. My debt to him is large. His contribution to this work is thankfully remembered.

I owe a debt to my students at Syracuse University, and to D. B. Gowin and a group of students he assembled in seminar at Cornell University. Students have listened for years to halting, partial, often confused attempts of mine to grope for the ideas here set forth. They have contributed more than they can possibly realize. Then there are my colleagues at the old Educational Policy Research Center at Syracuse, including James

Byrnes, currently of the Division of Income and Wealth of the Department of Commerce in Washington. He first introduced me to the data. Also A. Dale Tussing, Robert Wolfson, Manfred Stanley, and Warren Ziegler, each, in his own way, have given me encouragement and helpful guidance.

In the collegial arrangements of the academic institution one's friends and teachers share in the development of thought. But they do not share in bearing the burden of error. For their sake, I hereby enter the usual caveats of absolution.

Although this work has been many years in preparation, none of it, with one exception, has previously appeared in print. Chapter VII, severely shortened and without context, was delivered as an address to the Thirty-Fourth Annual Meeting of the Philosophy of Education Society in 1978. In that form, it appears in the Proceedings of the Society.

Pompey, N. Y.   TFG
Fall 1979

PREFACE

THIS IS THE FIRST VOLUME in a larger plan of two. In this first one, my purpose has been to describe both the structure and the dynamics of what I have chosen to call "the educational system," and to do so in a way that will capture the essential rationality of that structure and those dynamics. But I have had a further aim. It has been to give an account of that rationality so that the behavior of the system, its inherent processes, may become intelligible in a way that is *independent* of differences in political and economic ideology. It follows that the account of the system given in these pages is a formal account. It deals with the rational form, structure, and behavior of the system, but it makes no reference to its educational content.

In any specific society the *practice* of education is a moral enterprise. It has a content. It is one way that each generation expresses its moral intentions toward the next. In its practice of education, every society gives voice to its collective beliefs about what has worth. And so, in a second volume, I intend to deal with this educational content, with the moral and civic foundations of policy for the system and how those foundations may instruct us in the rudiments of moral education.

In this first volume, however, I have tried to sustain attention on what makes the educational system a *system*, and everywhere the same system, rather than on what makes it an *educational* system. I have tried to speak of "the educational system" as we sometimes speak of "the market" or "the nation state." There are different nation states — the French, the German, the Italian, the United States. But when we use the phrase "the nation state" we refer to something of which these are instances. The nation state burst upon the world out of the turmoil of the eighteenth and nineteenth centuries. It emerged in many places. It is a form of political, legal, and social organization. It is the expression of a certain kind of consciousness. It is a presence, perhaps a dysfunctional one, in our own day, but an undeniable part of the reality with which we live and from which we cannot escape.

xvii

The thought that I have tried to grasp is the possibility that the educational system, in like fashion, is an important aspect of the modern world, a kind of social organization, a presence, a new reality that has emerged only in our own century and virtually without notice. Though the system is instantiated in many places, it is *"the* system" everywhere in precisely the same way that though the nation state is exemplified in many places, it is the *same* reality in each that we point to with the phrase *"the* nation state."

In order to grasp such an idea, it may be useful, from time to time, to think of "the educational system" together with such phrases as "the multinational corporation" or "the capitalist system of economy" both of which refer to undeniable realities of, perhaps, decisive importance, and both of which can be described independently of particular instances. I have chosen to study the system in its American expression, partly because that is the example that I know best, but also because it may well represent the system in a mature form. I hope that the foreground presence of a single instance will not obscure the larger picture.

In the beginning, I had in mind no such expansive notion. My purpose was merely to patiently and quietly gain a better understanding of the specific and practical problems of educational policy that so dominated the 1960s. It was a sobering experience, this confrontation with the need to translate ideals and visions of the future into such mundane matters as budgets, buildings, regulations, legislation, and all the rest in the apparatus of public policy. Everywhere, it seemed to me, there were those convinced that we were caught up in a movement of pervasive social change. They said it was radical change and that from it there was no retreat. I felt constantly surrounded by those who seemed disposed to hitch their wagon to a trend and to ride it all the way into some brave new world in which pain, sorrow, inequality, failure, injustice, and even plain human cussedness would be banished. It seemed to me then, as it seems to me yet, a certainty that no such future will occur. For every trend there is a counter-trend. For every pleasant vision of the future of education there are unpleasant sacrifices. How large are they? How much do they matter? These seemed to me the important questions. On what grounds should we expect a counter-trend? How will it appear, and when?

The sustained and scholarly pursuit of such counter-questions has extraordinary consequences. It certainly heightens one's sense of irony. But anyone with a boundless taste for irony will appear perverse to others. I drew some satisfaction from the principle that whatever you think the future will be like, I will show you why it won't happen that way, or, if it does, then why it shouldn't. It is hard to prevent such practiced skepticism from lapsing into an unbecoming kind of automatic cynicism.

The supreme irony, however, is that in the attempt to study the future, I discovered most of all the obligation to revisit the past. If this disposition to find the counter-trends in every vision of the future is to be more than sheer perversity, then it must rest in a carefully documented study of those stabilities that being discoverable in the past are, therefore, likely to persist. In the midst of a concern for change and endless happy visions of the future, I began to search for what, in the world of education, does not change, and what is unlikely to change because of its rootedness in realities more fundamental than can be touched by so crude an instrument for change and control as public policy. The system began to announce itself! For if the system exists at all, then it will consist of those relationships, those structural necessities, and arguments of behavior that endure and remain unaltered no matter what results from the hard-fought but short-term battles that are waged over the formation of educational policy. *The system, whatever it is, is precisely what doesn't change* in the established arrangements of educational institutions and in the reiterated arguments that guide their behavior.

But what exactly is the system, and by what method can we identify its stabilities? These questions of definition and procedure deserve explicit treatment even before the inquiry begins, and not merely because one's conscience of craft and composition demand it, but because the approach followed here will seem unconventional to some, and, therefore a due respect for the reader requires at least a note on these fundamental matters. Yet, the issues are large and basic. Any truly adequate treatment of them would require the full exposition of a theory of definition, a theory of functional explanations, a discussion of the problems of methodological individualism, and a detailed exploration of the problems of practical inference. Such a treatment would be a plain distraction. Let me merely record here some of the more essential decisions of method implicit in the text and to acknowledge the difficulties.

It is among the first principles of philosophical method in conceptual analysis that one does *not* begin by defining those terms that are most centrally to be studied. Their definition, after all, is what we seek. We cannot, therefore, begin with definition. Hence, in this study I do not begin with a definition of "the system." Accordingly, in the text I have also tried to avoid all temptations to impose any predetermined and procrustean definition of the system on the data. Instead, I am content to rely upon the fact that the reader will bring to the text an adequate conception of what is meant by "the educational system." The domain of common discourse — the kind that we expect from well-educated persons — includes a great deal of talk about the educational system. Admittedly, the idea found there is vague. Its boundaries are ill-defined. Although "the educational system" can be given a technical definition, nevertheless, it is not a technical term, and there is nothing to be gained by providing a definition that establishes clear boundaries of meaning where there are no clear boundaries. In this case, as in the study of ethics, we can do no better than to follow the advice of Aristotle and refrain from asking for more precision than the subject will permit.

I believe it is enough, therefore, to let our quite ordinary, unreflective, and even vague conception of the educational system provide a test, for example, as to what the system includes and what it does not. The reader will, therefore, discover innumerable points where the essential and accidental properties of the system are measured against that quite ordinary and commonsense conception of the educational system. All that we require, by way of definition, is to consult that conception and we shall discover that it refers (1) to a set of schools and colleges, (2) related by a medium of exchange, and (3) arranged by some principles of sequence. The best we can say, at the outset, is that "the system" is a social structure and, at the same time, a kind of social process the rationality of which is heavily circumscribed by that structure.

This reference to the rationality of the system leads to a second and more important matter of method about which the reader should be forewarned. In the effort to let the structure and behavior of the system emerge out of our most common and ordinary use of the term, I have adopted what might be called the method of practical rationality. Though this inquiry emanates from an interest in educational policy, it is also rooted in a persistent concern with the nature of practical reason and practical argument. Human beings are rational creatures, even when, on other grounds, their behavior is construed as pathological.[1] In like manner, I construe the educational system as a rational system. That is to say, I construe it to be guided by rational arguments. That is the fundamental claim on which the theory of action implicit in the following account is made to rest. The structure and behavior of the system will be discovered if we can expose the practical arguments that explain its behavior.

The nature of practical inference, however, remains among the most debated problems of contemporary philosophy. Nevertheless, there is agreement, I believe, on at least two points. The first is that the conclusion of a practical argument is a proposition of the form "Do X." It is not a theoretical conclusion of the form "P is true." Aristotle claimed that the conclusion of a practical argument is an act.[2] Reasons for believing some-

---

1. This claim is formulated in more detail in Thomas F. Green, "Teacher Competence as Practical Rationality," *Educational Theory* 26 (3) (Summer 1976): 249–58.
2. The relevant passages are *De Motu Animalium*, Ch. 7, and *Nicomachean Ethics* VII, 3:1147a; VI, 2:1139a, 20; 11:1143b; *De Anima* III, 11:434a, 16–22; and 9:432b, 27.

thing are theoretical reasons, and their corresponding arguments are theoretical arguments. But reasons for doing something are practical reasons. Their corresponding arguments are practical arguments, and they always end in either an action or a conclusion of the form "Do X."

The second important feature of practical reasons is that they always presuppose the existence of some kind of human interest. "Do X because . . . " The "because" statement *becomes* a reason for doing something only for a person who already has some practical interest or concern. "Mark your letter to Australia 'Air Mail' because otherwise it will go by surface and will be delayed for weeks." If I did not *already* have an interest in the speed of mail delivery, then the reason given would be an interesting fact about the world, but would not constitute a reason for me to *do* anything. "A man who had no practical concerns would have no reasons for doing anything, no matter how wide his knowledge of the world and its ways might be."[3]

Thus, if we wish to explain why a certain person did X, we may find an answer by formulating the practical argument of his act and by identifying his corresponding practical interest. The method of practical rationality is simply the attempt to explain why A did X, or analogously, why the system does Y, by searching for the practical argument, or range of practical arguments, whose conclusion is "Do X" or "Do Y."

It is important to note also that whatever the relation between the premises and the conclusion of a practical argument may be, that relation is one of inference and not causality. It follows that to describe the behavior of the educational system by the method of practical rationality is to describe a system with persons or agents, but without any reference to causality. How is that done? We take the observed behavior of the system — its pattern of expansion, for example — to be the conclusion of a practical argument or series of practical arguments. The task then is to state the premises. Those premises may consist of social beliefs, general principles, and even judgments about the relative worth of different things. We do not care whether those premises are true or whether the principles they express are good. We are concerned only to make explicit the rules, beliefs, or principles that are required as premises in the system so that its observed behavior becomes rationally intelligible. The premises of such practical arguments are the reasons for the behavior of the system. They explain its behavior even though they do not explain it causally.

This is the approach that I have followed throughout. It will seem unorthodox to many, and so it may be worth a reminder that such an approach is not unlike the method of thinking commonly employed in the

3. Wm. Hay, M. G. Singer, and Arthur Murphy, *Reason and the Common Good* (Englewood Cliffs, N.J.: Prentice-Hall, 1963), p. 37.

study of micro-economic theory. But even if such an approach were wholly conventional, it would be subject to certain serious formal objections. The most important of these are considered in Appendix B.

There remains one final prefatory point. We must distinguish between a theory of the educational system and the theory of education. Whether the educational system is educationally valuable or effective, good or bad, to be preserved or abandoned — these questions I propose to leave open. In short, I have tried to avoid confusing the description of the system with its educational or social criticism. But neither have I made any attempt to endorse the system. The reader is free to extract from this account whatever moral, whatever educational lesson, whatever critique of the system he or she may find; but the author disclaims having put it there.

If there is any lesson at all to be learned from this investigation, it would be the simple claim that the system is likely to prevail. In recent years, it has been something of a fad to attempt constructing visions of alternative educational systems and such efforts have emphasized with considerable imagination how we might change things through public policy even to the point of attaining a different kind of system. I suspect, however, that there are no alternatives *to* the system as we know it, and that what are often proposed as alternatives *within* it are in reality proposals that would merely extend the power and reach of the system we already have without significantly changing it at all. But whether this somewhat cynical suspicion is more than mere conjecture is something we are not in a position to evaluate unless we can grasp more fully how the system works. In like manner, I am content to let evaluation of the strategies of definition and the method of practical rationality rest entirely upon the fruitfulness of the arguments that result from their application.

Predicting the Behavior of the Educational System

·∘[I]∘·

THE EDUCATIONAL SYSTEM
Primary and Derivative Elements

SINCE THE LAST QUARTER of the nineteenth century, virtually all "advanced" regions of the world have witnessed a development of unusual importance: the emergence of national educational systems. They are rooted everywhere in an earlier age, yet their full development, as we have come to know them, is recent. And their maturing as relatively independent sectors of modern societies has taken place only within the past one hundred years. This fact deserves more sustained attention than it has so far received.

Consider a parallel case. Human societies probably cannot exist without markets; still, the market *system* of economy is recent. It did not emerge until the seventeenth and eighteenth centuries. And the market *society* was not full-born until well into the nineteenth century. Its appearance was so transforming that it reshaped all of our most elemental social relations. It required a redefinition of time, of labor, and even of nature itself.[1]

The market society was struggling to be born through a period, rich in speculations about its theory, from Smith, Ricardo, and Malthus to Jeremy Bentham, John Stuart Mill, and Karl Marx. Throughout that period there was an acknowledged need to develop a theory that would render the behavior of the market rationally intelligible, even in its apparently irrational aspects.

The emergence of educational systems, however, has been accompanied by no such acknowledged need. Still, it may be possible to construct a theory that will render the behavior of the educational system rationally intelligible. To do so, even in an incomplete and highly debatable form, is the aim of this extended study. The attempt is firmly rooted in a concern with educational policy. For if there is indeed an educational system, then just as economic policy is policy to govern the economic system — the market society — so educational policy is policy for the educational system.

1. Karl Polanyi, *The Great Transformation* (Boston: Beacon Press, 1957).

1

But what is that system? How does it behave? Why do we expect to frame wise educational policy in ignorance of the educational system any more than we expect to frame wise monetary policy in ignorance of the monetary system? Not only do we lack any carefully constructed theory of the system, we also lack even a body of related propositions drawn with sufficient rigor to provide an adequate *descriptive* account of the system so that we can reasonably monitor the effects of policy. A theory of the educational system is at once what we clearly need and what we most transparently do not have.

Educational policy is always policy for the educational system. This proposition is the starting point. It is therefore taken not as a claim in need of demonstration, but as a claim in need of understanding. Of course, we do not entirely lack an understanding of educational systems. We can recognize their presence or absence in other countries and at other times. It is possible to find accounts of the *legal* structure of the American educational system including the formal and constitutional limits of state and federal participation, the creation of local school boards, the relations of professional associations, and so forth. We can even give a diagrammatic account of the relations between elementary and secondary schools and various kinds of post-secondary institutions. Such accounts give us little help in understanding how the system actually works. They give us little insight into how it has grown, why, or in what sectors it is likely to grow next, how its bases for support may change, how the political issues surrounding educational policy can be expected to change, or a thousand other important questions. Such structural descriptions tell us practically nothing that we really need to know about the dynamics of the educational system.

What we lack can be more vividly understood from the following conjecture. Let us suppose that in the United States there is no basic national educational policy. Certainly educational policy does not exist in the sense that monetary policy, fiscal policy, or defense policy exist. If we ask who is responsible for formulating and implementing monetary policy in the United States, we can give a fairly precise answer. We may point to the Federal Reserve Board, the Secretary of the Treasury, the Council of Economic Advisors, and to their joint powers to determine the availability and cost of money. And if we ask who forms basic defense policy, we may turn to the Joint Chiefs of Staff, the Secretary of Defense, the relevant Committees of Congress, the Secretary of State, and the Office of the President. But we have a different problem if we ask about basic educational policy in the United States. What is the locus of its enactment? Who formulates it? There is no place to point. Not even the formation of a cabinet-level Department of Education in the case of the United States will seriously change this situation.

Still we must admit quite another set of facts. It is possible to move from Bangor, Maine, to San Diego, California, or from Miami, Florida, to Seattle, Washington, leave the schools in one locality, enter those in another, and find approximately the same procedures, the same curriculum, and even strikingly similar facilities. It is possible to go to nearly any city or town, locate the local university or college by sight and even identify particular buildings — graduate student housing, the science laboratories, the chapel, the dormitories, and so forth. How does such uniformity arise in the absence of any basic policy requiring it?

Clearly, there is a system of some kind. Furthermore, it is in many respects a national system, a national system, however, that cannot be described merely by giving an account of the legal arrangements for education and the gross general structure of elementary, secondary, and advanced schools. By "the educational system" we refer to something more like a social system only a small part of which is captured by an account of its legal organization.

Such a system has a structure. There will be certain units or elements that are parts of the system and they will stand in certain relations, constituting the parts of a whole. The whole is the system, and the parts are the units of the system. Such a system will also have a culture. There will be rules or principles of conduct, a configuration of interests, and a set of shared beliefs that characterize the behavior of the units in the system and of persons who relate to the units of the system. These elements we may call the primitive, as opposed to the derivative elements of the system.

PRIMARY ELEMENTS

Schools

When we think of the educational system, we do not refer simply to the total arrangements for education in some society. We know that no society can exist beyond a single generation without providing some arrangements for children to grow up into that society. There must be some pattern, some way, by which the young become adults. That pattern, whatever it is, might be described as the system for educating the young. The word *system* in that context means something like "the way" or "the pattern" or "the accustomed procedures for growing up." No society can exist without some ways of growing up, but many have persisted without arranging that process into something that we would call an educational system.

Thus, we might agree that a particular social order includes provisions for growing up, but that it does not include an educational system. And there is no contradiction in these two claims. The educational system tends to emerge only when a portion of the total process is distinguished and assigned to special kinds of institutions. This development corresponds to the emergence of schools.

The point may seem a small one, but it is not. Without a distinction between the system for education and the educational system we would be unable to raise some of the most important questions that need to be raised about educational policy. Why? Because even though there is a difference between the educational process of growing up and the activities that go on in the educational system, still they are presumed to be related. And so one of the most significant questions for basic policy that can be asked about education is whether, and in what degree, the educational system advances or inhibits the process of education. The mere possibility of asking this question presupposes a distinction between the educational system, on the one hand, and the social arrangements for growing up, on the other.

By "the educational system" we refer then to a system of schools and colleges. Wherever educational systems exist, however, there may also exist schools that are not themselves part of the system. There may be schools — like the Henry George School in Philadelphia or the schools that Ayn Rand supports — that exist, but without any ties to other schools. There is no point in denying that they are schools, that they are educational institutions, or that they are a part of the total arrangements for education. There is a point, however, in denying that they are a part of the educational system. You may take a course at the Henry George School, and success will earn you a certificate entitling you to take another course in the Henry George School. And completing that course will entitle you to take still another. But you cannot take those certificates to the University of Maryland and gain credit for anything. This fact alone counts against the claim that the Henry George School is a part of the educational system that includes the University of Maryland. Thus, the educational system, in our normal conception of it, includes schools and colleges, but not all schools and colleges.

The Medium of Exchange

It seems intuitively clear that, in order for an institution to be a part of the educational system, it must stand in some relations of mutuality with other schools or colleges. There must be that part-whole relationship that arises from some discernible connection of the parts. The required forms of interdependence are expressed through such things as certificates, diplomas, and transcripts, which though different in many ways, are alike in one important respect. They are all instruments by which activities carried on in one school or college can be recognized, and, in a sense, exchanged for activities of a similar sort that might have been carried on within another institution. These instrumentalities of the system are its media of exchange. Their existence permits us to speak of a single educational system just as our capacity to exchange dollars for francs and marks for pounds permits us to speak of a single monetary system. They establish the sort of interdependence or mutuality that permits a person to complete the fifth grade in one part of the country and enter the sixth grade in another or to receive the B.A. degree from one college with reasonable assurance that it will be recognized by another college.

Whether there can be instruments of exchange other than diplomas, transcripts, and certificates remains an important problem in any attempt to construct alternatives to the system. For the moment, however, it is enough to note that by the phrase "educational system" we refer not simply to institutions called schools or colleges, but to schools and colleges that stand in relations of mutuality expressed through a medium of exchange.

The claim is that something like the medium of exchange is a necessary condition for the existence of an educational system. But is it really necessary? Can we be sure that there is no way to establish a system without creating such a medium of exchange? Consider the following conceptual experiment. Let us imagine two colleges existing in the same geographical neighborhood, but under different sponsorship with slightly different educational missions, and authorized under different governmental provisions. Imagine further that no activities carried out in either college are recognized as equivalent to those carried out in the other. We are to suppose, in short, that there is no way for a person to go from Alma Mater to Alma Pater and have it recognized that "I don't need to take that course, I already had it at Alma Mater." Under those conditions, it would be difficult to imagine on what grounds these two colleges could be regarded as part of the same educational system. But despite their substantial independence, we might argue that they are part of the same system provided they are both subject to the same agency of government, such as a licensing board or state education department. Thus for example, a school of cosmetology and a school of mortuary science may recognize no common medium of exchange, but we may still regard them as part of the same educational system if both are chartered by the same authority and subject to the same regulatory agencies. Thus, it does not seem true that a medium of exchange is necessary to what we mean by an educational system.

The example shows that there is more to our conception of an educational system than just the medium of exchange permitting the substitution of activities. If two schools are responsible to the same legal authority or, in some other way are part of the same legal structure, then we might say they are part of the same educational system even though there is no exchange of activities between them. On the other hand, if we imagine one of the states in the United States in which all schools operate under the authority of the same state agency, and if we imagine further that there is no medium of exchange between *any* of the schools, then, in one sense, we might say that there exists an educational system in that state, but, in another sense, we would be justified in claiming that in that state there is no educational system at all. What exists instead is simply a legal system and a legal procedure for the establishment of schools, a loose aggregation of totally independent schools having nothing in common except their bare legal relation to a single agency of government. We would be warranted in saying in one sense that such a state has an educational system, but in another sense, we could claim that it has no educational *system* at all. Both senses of the phrase "educational system" are included in our ordinary conception, but it is only the second of these two senses on which I mean to focus.

This emphasis is no mere expression of preference. The fact is that the second sense of the phrase "educational system" is the more fundamental. It is quite conceivable, though rather unlikely that there might exist an educational system without anything resembling a common legal authority. Such a state of affairs would probably be inconvenient or inefficient, but it would lack nothing needed for us to say that an educational system exists. The same kind of argument, however, cannot be mustered in support of the conceptual necessity for a common legal authority. We may have a common legal authority for all schools, but if there is no medium for the exchange of activities among them, then we cannot say unambiguously that they constitute an educational system. A recognized medium of exchange is sufficient for the existence of an educational system. A common legal authority for schools is neither necessary nor sufficient.

This conception of a medium of exchange raises other questions. How does it operate to shape our judgment that some kinds of institutions are included in the system and others are not? For example, how does this second feature of the educational system help us to understand the position of accrediting institutions? The answer is that the answer cannot be very clear and probably should not be unambiguous. Accrediting associations function primarily to assure that there is an effective medium of exchange between the schools and colleges of the system. To whatever extent they are needed to maintain an effective system of exchange, then to that extent and in that respect, accrediting associations are part of the system even though they are not educational institutions.

This idea of a medium of exchange is not to be taken as providing a precise criterion for deciding what is within and what is without the system. Any accurate analysis of the system will probably have to confront again and again examples of institutions that are within the system in some respects and not in others. Nonetheless, what counts to support the inclusion of any institution is its relation to the creation, maintenance, and employment of some medium of exchange.

Consider, for example, the kind of education often conducted by industrial firms — career training, on the job training, or management training. Are we to regard such activites as part of the educational system and does their existence make a firm like General Electric Corporation a part of the educational system? The answer, again, must be both yes and no. The idea of a medium of exchange gives no decisive answer to the question. Nonetheless, *it does provide a relevant clue.* Can an employee take evidence of what he has done in educational programs conducted by his employer and present that evidence to a college, a business school, or some agency in lieu of similar activities performed in a school or college that is part of the system? If the answer to that question is "yes," then we have evidence that, in certain respects and for certain purposes, there exists a medium of exchange permitting the substitution of certain activities performed within General Electric for certain activities that would have been performed within a school or college of the system. It follows that for certain purposes, and to a definite extent, General Electric is a part of the educational system.

On the other hand, if the answer to our question is "no," then we have evidence that General Electric, even though it conducts educational programs and establishes schools, is not a part of the system. The concept of a medium of exchange does not yield a clear-cut definition of the boundaries of the system, but it provides a relevant test in determining the boundaries. Furthermore, it provides a test that leaves the boundaries fluid, and that does no violence to our ordinary understanding of what we mean by an educational system. In short, the requirement that there be some capacity for substituting activities is no mere stipulation. It reflects what in fact we ordinarily mean by an educational system even to the point of preserving our ordinary judgment that the boundaries of the system are vague.

The Principle of Sequence

We now have two primary characteristics of the educational system. The first is that it consists of schools and colleges. And the second is that they are related by a kind of connective tissue so that activities performed in one institution may be substituted for the same activities as if they had been performed in another. I wish now to introduce a third feature. By the phrase "educational system" we mean to refer not to any system of schools and colleges, but only to those in which the system of such institutions is arranged on the principle of sequence. The *principle* of sequence is to be contrasted, however, from any particular *rule* of sequence. The principle can be given precise definition. It states that the system of schools is organized into levels, so that if a person has completed the nth level of the system, that will constitute a sufficient reason for concluding that he has completed the level of $n-1$, but not a sufficient reason for concluding that he has completed or will complete the level of $n+1$.

There are many versions of the relevant levels, and therefore there may be different rules of sequence reflecting the same principle. The levels may be, and typically are, grades. But even in a non-graded school, there are different levels through which students are expected to progress. And within any system viewed as a whole there are typically different levels of schools arranged on a principle of sequence — elementary schools, secondary schools, academies, trade schools, colleges, and so forth. No matter what the rule of sequence is, no matter what definition the different levels receive, the *principle* of sequence will apply. If there were *no* rule of sequence, we would be unable to speak of persons passing through the system, or progressing within the system. There are many other things that it would be impossible to say if educational systems were not arranged according to some rules of sequence.

The principle of sequence may be the most counter-intuitive of the three primitive properties of educational systems. Is sequence as necessary to educational systems as a medium of exchange? That question must be left open. The fact is, however, that all existing educational systems employ some rule of sequence. Perhaps the necessity of such a principle stems not from the nature of educational systems, but from the more primitive fact that there is always a definite sequence in what is to be learned or a definite sequence in human growth and development (see Chapter IV).

The principle of sequence is a necessary presupposition of some observations to follow in this exposition. Furthermore the existence of some rule of sequence is presupposed in practically all policy proposals. No great harm will result from including it as an essential feature of all educational systems. Still, I wish to leave it an open question as to whether there can be an educational system that does not employ such a principle. It may be that denying the principle of sequence in all of its forms would result in a different kind of educational system. It may be instead that it would result in a system for education, but no educational system at all.

DERIVATIVE ELEMENTS

Since every educational system will have these primary characteristics — schools, a medium of exchange, and a rule of sequence — it follows that they will have certain secondary properties. The system will have some definite size. It will have some system of control. And finally, it will produce some distribution of results. There is nothing extraordinary about such a claim. Every social system, or for that matter, every institution, will have some size, some system of control, and will create some distribution of goods. But *it is a central thesis of this study not simply that educational systems have these secondary features, but that the policy agenda for the system is created largely by their interaction.* This additional claim is no mere truism. It is sufficiently complex to require detailed examination.

Size

Obviously, every educational system has some size. But if we try to be definite and precise about how the system *changes* in size, we shall be led quickly into unexpected complexities and be confronted with interesting fundamentals. There are different kinds of size; therefore there are different modes of expansion and contraction for the system. It will be susceptible to expansion in at least eight different ways.

The different modes of growth are identified on Table 1.1 only to identify the different dimensions of size. Since the system, presumably, may either increase or decrease in size, it follows that for every mode of growth there is a corresponding mode of contraction. Expansion and contraction are both changes in size. If the system may grow in response to a growth in the school-age population, it may also shrink in response to a diminishing population. Since it may grow by adding responsibilities, it may contract by discarding them. If the system may expand by lengthening the school year, then it may contract by shortening it.

Two points concerning this list deserve extended treatment. The first arises from the claim that in listing the modes of growth we have not listed

TABLE 1.1
The Modes of Growth

---

1. The system may expand in response to increases in the school-age population either by increasing the number of units in the system, or by increasing the number of students in units of the system, or both.
2. The system may expand by increasing rates of attendance and survival. *Growth in attainment.*
3. The system may expand by adding levels either at the top or at the bottom. *Vertical expansion.*
4. The system may expand by assuming responsibility for educational and social functions that are either new, that have been ignored, or that have been carried out by other institutions. *Horizontal expansion.*
5. The system may expand either by differentiation of programs or institutions or both. *Differentiation.*
6. The system may expand by intensification, that is, by attempting to do more in the same time or the same in less time. *Growth in efficiency.*
7. The system may expand by extending the school year or the school day.
8. The system may expand by increasing the number of persons needed to staff it *independently* of the number of students and number of its units, the magnitude of the school-age population, rates of attendance, survival.

---

the causes of growth in the system. The second arises from asking what kinds of relations exist between the different modes of growth. What is the logic of their connection? If one of them occurs, will it follow that some other will also occur? If the system contracts in one of its dimensions, will it also shrink in others?

Consider, first, the matter of causality. It may seem, on the surface at least, that in identifying the modes of growth in Table 1.1, we have identified the causes of expansion in the system. What could be clearer than the claim that what *caused* or *produced* educational expansion in the United States during the sixties was an enormous increase in the size of the school-age population (Mode #1) together with an increase in the participation rate (Mode #2)? There were more people to be educated and more people stayed longer in the system. If we discover that more people are participating in the system *or* that a greater proportion of a certain age cohort is participating at one time than at another, then, indeed, we could say that the system had expanded. Furthermore, we could say, with considerable precision, in what ways it had expanded. But nevertheless, we would be unable, with any completeness, to give the causes or reasons for that expansion. To do that, we would need considerably more information.

Imagine a society confronted with a substantial increase in the number of young children fairly uniformly distributed throughout its social structure. Imagine further that the increase in the school-age cohort is far beyond the capacity of the educational system to serve. Ordinarily, under those conditions we would expect the system to expand by the addition of more schools or larger schools and more teachers in order to accommodate more children in the system. Thus, we would expect the system to expand in the number and size of its units and in the number of people needed to staff it. But the mere increase in the number of children of school age does not constitute, by itself, a sufficient reason for that expansion. The demographic facts need to be accompanied by certain other assumptions or social beliefs.

Actually, when faced with such demographic changes, a society may have several choices. It could choose simply to educate a smaller proportion of the school-age population. By incurring a decline in the participation rate, expansion of the system can be avoided. If such a decision were made, however, the system would have to become more selective. The society would have to determine, *in a new way,* on what grounds it will decide who is admitted to the system and who is not.

Ordinarily, we would expect no society to exercise this choice. But, on what foundation does this expectation rest? What is it — we may ask in Humean fashion — that disposes the mind in its passage from the fact of an increase in the school-age population to the practical conclusion, "Expand the system"? The answer must lie in the acceptance of the belief that *it is better that all children have some education within the system, however defective, than that some have none at all.*[2] The acceptance of this belief will permit the mind to negotiate the inference from the facts of demographic growth to the directive, "Expand the system." Such a belief is one way to formulate the conviction that the opportunity for *some* education, at least at certain levels of the system, should be universal. When we reason that the system will expand when faced with an increase in the school-age population, we are in fact adopting the belief that the system at certain levels must serve all children, or, in other words, that the system, at certain levels, should not be selective.

Now I recognize, of course, that more than one belief will suffice to negotiate the inference from an expansion of the school-age population to an expansion of the educational system. Instead of adopting the belief that

2. Note the formulation of this belief. It does not advance the claim that it is better *for the child* to have some education in the system rather than none. Whether it is better for the child or only better for the society is a matter left open. The answer to that question makes no difference to the logical function of this belief in the argument. All that matters is that some education in the system is believed to be better than none, for all children.

the system must be universal, one could simply adopt the view that it is less trouble to expand the system than to develop a workable means for selecting which children will be admitted to school and which will not. Therefore expand the system. The same practical conclusion, in short, can be reached by more than one set of premises. And in this discovery there is no surprise. Indeed, were it not the case, political coalitions would be rendered all the more difficult to create. Political coalitions, and in fact policy decisions generally, are often possible only because different persons, for different reasons, may nonetheless, agree on what to do. One may vote to increase school taxes because failure to do so will produce a decline in real estate values. Another may do so because it will benefit his own children. That is to say, they may reason to the same practical conclusion from quite different premises.

But secondly, we should observe that of these two different beliefs, the first is a belief about what is good and should be done, and the second is merely a belief about what is convenient.[3] Only the first of these beliefs — that it is better that all children have some education in the system than that some have none — could be regarded as a normative principle of the system. And that, indeed, is precisely the point. Given a widespread acceptance of this belief in some society, *together* with the demographic facts of rapid population growth, we may conclude that the educational system will expand. We can negotiate that inference because we know that, given such a belief, the society will reject any choice making the system more selective than it has been. Only by eliciting this underlying belief—and by making the hidden premise explicit — can we understand the reasons or causes for expansion in the first mode. Indeed, only if we adopt this belief can we reason from an increase in the school-age population to the facile conclusion that the educational system will expand. This belief then, is a fundamental part of the reason or cause for expansion of the system in the first of the modes of growth. It is among the premises of the practical arguments of the system.

And therein lies an important lesson. Each of the modes of growth is like a jack-in-the box. Each conceals an important social belief. If you press the mode of growth in the right place, its implicit social belief will pop out.

3. In the interests of methodological precision, it is worth noting, at least in passing, that no practical argument, strictly speaking, can be valid unless its premises include a statement of the form "Do X." Otherwise the premises could not yield a conclusion of the form "Do X." Therefore, in addition to the beliefs identified, there is in each of these cases yet another suppressed premise. In the first argument, it is the premise "Do what is good" and in the second it is "Do whatever is the easier thing." These imperative premises are required by the strictures of logic. But they are also, and nearly always, so easy to identify that I shall be content to record here my awareness of their necessity and henceforth let the practical arguments of the system remain in the incomplete form of enthymemes.

Each of these beliefs is, in effect, a premise in a practical argument of the system. It is a premise in an argument whose inference moves from the existence of a certain state of affairs in the society to a conclusion directing the system to do X or Y. What is vital to our understanding of the system is not the study of the modes of growth. They are merely dimensions of size. What is vital is the system of beliefs concealed in our *inferences* about the modes of growth.

These premises of belief, however, are by no means always of uniform weight. The same belief may count more heavily at one time than at another. As we have already observed, the policy agenda for the system is created largely by the interaction of size, distribution, control, and hierarchy (see p. 9). Imagine, for example, a society, like Bolivia, in which only 5 percent of the school-age children persist in the system to the end of the sixth school year. In such a society there is unlikely to be a widespread conviction that it is better that all children have some education within the system than that some have none. Thus, in such a society, it would be relatively easy to survive a sudden expansion in the size of the school-age population without any expansion of the system.

In short, the credibility of the social beliefs implicit in our reasoning about the expansion of the system is itself effected by the size of the system along several dimensions. A rapid increase in the population of school age is more likely to produce expansion in a system that already has reached a certain stage of growth because only beyond a certain stage of growth is the necessary social belief likely to be sufficiently widespread. To identify that stage is, of course, a problem for empirical research. But the immediate point is to note that the causes or reasons for growth of the system are likely to have different relative strength at different stages in the expansion of the system. The distributive behavior of the system, in short, will be influenced by its size.

And therein lies a second lesson. If we begin to examine the structure of the system—even though limited to the three primitive elements already introduced — we shall be confronted immediately with the reality of its culture. The social beliefs implicit in the reasons for each mode of growth are beliefs about some good or about the relative importance of different goods and the trade-offs between them. Such social beliefs enter into arguments about policy for the system because they are presupposed in our reasoning about "how the system works," and how the system works is precisely what we are attempting to influence and use in formulating educational policy.

Given this axiomatic social belief about the universality of the system together with the demographic conditions of growth, it follows that the educational system will expand. But it need not expand by increasing the number of its units. Instead, the society might experiment with intensification; that is, it might attempt to accomplish the same in less time or more in the same amount of time. If whatever is to be accomplished by the system can be accomplished in half the time currently devoted to it, then the capacity of the system could be doubled without any increase in the number of its units.

Such a decision might be implemented by that familiar, but rapidly fading practice of multiple school sessions. From the point of view of any child within the system, such arrangements attempt to accomplish the same with less time, but from the point of view of the system itself, the attempt is to accomplish more within the same time. Under these conditions, there would be more students within each unit of the system, and, as a practical matter, there would probably have to be more teachers and administrators. But there would be no need for more students, more teachers, or more administrators engaged in activities within the system *at the same time*. Thus, by expanding in the sixth mode, intensification, to accommodate more students, the system will expand also in its first mode by increasing the size, but not the number of its units.

Relations between the Modes of Growth

Thus, we arrive at the second major point to be derived from Table 1.1, the claim that there are important relations *between* the modes of growth. If the system expands in one of its dimensions of size, then it might also, and as a consequence, expand in another. But this suggestion may be deceptive; the relations between the modes of growth are not logically determined in any strict sense. Expansion by intensification does not *entail* expansion in the first mode, although, as we have seen, it can produce it. As far as I can see, neither does expansion in any mode logically require expansion in any other. Still, it may be true that some kinds of growth, for reasons other than sheer logic, are likely to occur only in conjunction with others, or perhaps only in succession to others. If there are such mediated relations between the modes of growth, then what is it that mediates the connection? Here again, in reasoning from the occurrence of one mode of growth to another, we are reasoning through a suppressed premise of a practical argument. It is the suppressed premise that mediates the relations between the modes of growth, and therefore, it is the suppressed premise of the practical argument that we must identify if we are to understand the relations between the modes of growth.

It can be argued, for example, that for any system, if there is a steady and significant expansion in the participation rate (Mode #2), then the system will expand also by differentiation (Mode #5). But this relation does not arise because differentiation is a part of what we *mean* by an increase in the participation rate. If we reason thus, we do so through a suppressed premise that makes such an inference possible, and that premise is simply that any curriculum adequate for a small portion of the population is unlikely to be adequate for all. No society is likely to succeed in increasing the participation rate of the system from, say, ten percent to seventy-five percent, unless it is also successful in providing a range of different curricula. If this premise is accepted, then we can reason that if the system expands significantly by an increase in its participation rate, then it will have expanded also by differentiation. It should be noted, however, that the converse is both unlikely in fact and unlikely by this analysis. That is to say, any society might create many curricula either in the same or in different institutions without expanding the participation rate of the system. Thus, when our formulation of the principle of curricular differentiation is understood as a premise in a practical argument of the system, we are permitted to reason from increases in participation to increases in differentiation, but not conversely.

By way of further illustration, consider the kinds of relations that might exist between intensification (Mode #6), expansion by growth in population (Mode #1), and expansion by differentiation (Mode #5). Intensification, under whatever circumstances it occurs, is always an increase in the technical efficiency of the system.[4] But it is possible for a society to increase the capacity of its educational system without using that capacity. There are no a priori grounds to reject the possibility that every society could intensify the activities of its educational system so as to accomplish whatever it accomplishes in half the time that it normally takes, and that it could do so without using that increased capacity to accommodate more students. Intensification would then occur, but it would not result in an expansion of the system in the first mode.

But why would any society do such a thing? Why would any society increase the capacity of the system without using it? When we say that it *could* be done, we express a mere conceptual or logical possibility. But is there any reason to suppose that it *would* be done? Is there any practical argument of the system that would direct that it be done? The question is

---

4. Here, as well as elsewhere, the concept of technical efficiency is used in the standard sense of a low input to output ratio. Economic efficiency is defined in a manner more closely related to "effectiveness." In the lexicon of welfare economics, the economic efficiency of the system is its capacity to produce what the consumer wants. Some such distinction is clearly needed, since no system can be regarded as efficient, in one sense, if it is technically efficient in producing what nobody wants.

important. It is to ask, in effect, whether there is anything in the nature of the system itself that would suffice to make efficiency a goal to be sought?

Consider an analogy. In the housing industry the price of the product is established by the least efficient producer. Why? By producing housing in the most efficient way that it *can* be produced, it may be feasible to market good housing for thousands of dollars less than is currently done. But the incentives of the market are such that all the most efficient producer is likely to do is to offer his product at an attractive, but still marginal, price below the least efficient or the next least efficient producer. In doing this, his margin of profit is increased. So the incentive for efficiency in the housing industry is real, not because there is inducement to produce housing for the lowest possible price, but because anyone who can increase his efficiency by a significant magnitude can also increase his margin of profit *without* reducing his price to the consumer. There is a constant incentive toward efficiency as long as increased efficiency is a means toward increased margin of profit. Efficiency in such a system, is an instrumental value constantly present provided the incentive to enlarge profits is constantly operable.

Now, we may ask whether there is anything comparable to this incentive for efficiency in the case of the educational system. The answer, I believe, is that there is not.[5] Indeed, we shall see that *strong incentives are created by the nature of the system itself for it to be as inefficient as it is permitted to be* (see Chapter IV). There is nothing in the normal operation of the system that would create incentives to maximize efficiency. But what does this claim really mean? It means that whether the system *can* be more efficient than it is, whether it *can* accomplish whatever it is supposed to accomplish in less time, is a question that will arise only when increased efficiency is believed to provide the answer to some problem that does not itself arise from *inefficiency*. In the behavior of a firm, there is a *constant* incentive to increase efficiency even when things are going well. In the

---

5. We need not be concerned for the moment to understand *why* there is no such incentive in the case of the educational system. We need only recognize, for the moment, that efficiency is not a constant, operable, value in the behavior of the educational system. It can be argued that the concept of technical efficiency makes no sense except in a system where clear and measurable definitions can be given to inputs and outputs, and that since this cannot be done in the case of the educational system, therefore, technical efficiency cannot operate as a normative principle in the behavior of the system.

On the other hand, it might be argued that the reason efficiency is not a primary value in the behavior of the educational system is that the system itself is not a market. Schools do not operate as firms. And efficiency becomes an operable value only within the setting of a market system. If the latter argument is the correct account of the matter, then it would follow that efficiency would not be part of the normative structure of the system *even if inputs and outputs could be exactly defined and measured.*

educational system, on the other hand, there are incentives to find out how efficient the system *can* be only when things are *not* going well.[6]

What kinds of "going badly" will suffice to make efficiency an important concern? Consider two illustrative possibilities. First of all, *if* the system is faced with needs for overwhelming expansion, then it might be important to test how efficient the system can be as an alternative to costly expansion. The purpose of increasing efficiency would then be to accomplish as much in less time or more in the same time. Secondly, *if* the costs of the system become so large that only constant or declining levels of resources can be available to it, then there might be strong incentives to test the capacity of the system for efficiency in order to avoid cutting back in the number and size of programs. Here the incentive is to accomplish at least as much, but with fewer resources, and without any reduction in time.

In this last possible incentive for efficiency, there is concealed another principle, another premise in the practical arguments of the system. It is that when faced with static or declining resources, the system will rank an increase in efficiency as more desirable than a decrease in differentiation. That is to say, instead of reducing the number of its programs by consolidation, the system will seek to maintain them with diminished resources. If this principle is correct, it follows that differentiation of the system is ranked as a higher value than efficiency. It follows also that there is no monotonic relation between a decline in resources for the system and a decline in its size. As we shall see a bit later (Chapter IV), there are reasons to believe that the system will expand, even when there is a decline in resources for it and a decline in the demand for its services.

These illustrations strengthen the claim that maximizing efficiency is unlikely to enter into the practical arguments of the system except in response to problems that do not themselves arise from a lack of efficiency. But furthermore, they establish some of the ways in which the modes of growth are related to one another. There are connections between the modes of growth, but they are not logical relations of necessity. Rather, one mode of growth may implicate another, but always through the mediation of some belief about the good of the system, what it is good for, how its goods are ranked, or about the nature of social causation.

---

6. The budget process in an educational institution and in the system itself comes as close as we can to a structure of incentives for efficiency. Yet, as we shall see subsequently, that process is more aptly described as a set of incentives for the system to be as inefficient as it is permitted to be.

Summary

The educational system is to be distinguished from the system for education, and, therefore, the theory of the system is to be distinguished from the theory of education. The system is essentially a system of schools and colleges, related by a medium of exchange, and ordered by a principle of sequence. But because the system has three primary features, it has also certain derivative properties — a definite size, a system of control, a set of distributive principles, and some hierarchical order. Of these derivative properties, we have so far considered, and only in a perfunctory way, what flows from the fact that the system must have some definite size and that that size may change.

·•৩[II]৩·•

THE EDUCATIONAL SYSTEM
Control

Every educational system will have some definite size. There will also be some arrangements for its social control, and those arrangements can be discovered in the structure of the interests whose presence makes the system arise in the first place, and those whose advancement fires the engines of change within it.

But why seek the control of the system in the structure of interests? Why not turn directly to the distribution of power and authority or to the legal regulations that guide the system? The question is important. The major outlines of its answer are implicit in the preceding chapter. We seek a description of the educational system and how it works through an explication of the practical arguments of its behavior. That is to say, we seek the kind of explanation that consists in exposing the premises of the practical arguments or range of practical arguments that constitute the practical reasons for the system's behavior.

But practical reasons always presuppose the existence of some kind of human interest. A practical reason is always the practical reason *of* some agent (either literally or metaphorically), and it *becomes* a reason for that agent to act in a certain way only because that reason is related to some already existing interest.

Thus, if we are concerned to describe the behavior of the system by seeking its practical reasons, then we are presupposing that those reasons are connected with pre-existing interests. My interest in making the wall last is what makes the reason given, a reason for building the wall in a certain way. The curriculum appropriate for a few is unlikely to be appropriate for everyone. It is our interest in extending the benefits of education to everyone that makes this principle a reason for behaving in certain ways. Given that interest, then that principle becomes a practical reason for differentiating curricula. *The reasons for acting in a certain way become the practical reasons for an agent because they are connected to an already existing practical interest.* And, correspondingly, if the practical

19

interests of two agents are different, then they will have different practical reasons for acting, whether in the same way or in different ways. Thus, we discover how the system is controlled by examining first the different practical interests imbedded in the system and secondly, by identifying the practical reasons connected with those different interests.

Such an analysis should not be confused with the familiar view that in the "liberal" state the course of policy is determined by the interplay of conflicting interests, and that those interests that prevail are the interests of those who have the most power. Interests are important to identify not because they determine the course of the system, but because they determine what can count as a practical reason. And we are interested in relations of power not because we believe that certain agents are more powerful than others, (although they are) but because we believe that certain practical reasons are more weighty than others.

In seeking to understand the control of the system through the structure of interests, neither do I mean to suggest in any anthropomorphic sense, that the system itself has interests, nor that only one set of interests is expressed in the educational system. The system is not always of one mind. And neither are human agents. We may have conflicting interests. And therefore, we may receive conflicting directives about what to do. As practical agents, we seek some adjustment of the conflicting interests, and we do that by seeking to balance the competing practical arguments by other practical arguments. In an analogous way, the educational system is presented with conflicting interests resulting in opposing practical arguments. Those practical arguments must be weighed and balanced, and in that weighing and balancing we discover how the system is controlled.

THE STRUCTURE OF INTERESTS

To describe the control of the system, it may be sufficient to identify four sets of interests. They are the interests of (1) the state, (2) parents, (3) the society, and (4) the incumbents or occupants of positions in the system.

There are two immensely important points to be noted about this enumeration. The first has to do with the concept of "interests" itself. Interests, it may be argued, are always identified as the interests *of* some persons or group of persons. They are never disembodied. Thus, it may seem that we cannot be clear in identifying any interests unless we can be quite precise in identifying the persons or groups of persons whose interests they are. We can speak of the interests *of* parents, and the interests *of* the incumbents of the system because we know roughly what persons are referred to by the words *parents* and *incumbents*. But how, in this way of thinking, can we refer to the interests of the state or the interests of society? Where are such interests lodged? What persons or groups of persons are referred to by the words *state* and *society?* The critical claim I wish to examine is the claim that we cannot have identified a set of human interests unless we can identify the human beings whose interests they are.

As a kind of slogan, or practical guide to sociological method, such a claim has much to recommend it. But as a matter of logic, it constitutes a mistake. The mistake arises from a failure to distinguish between the phrase "interest *in*" and the phrase "interest *of.*" When we ask "Who has an interest *in* maintaining the present tax laws?" or *"In* whose interest is it to maintain the present tax laws?" we are identifying a potential human interest and we are asking where it is lodged. And the very possibility of asking such a question presupposes that we can identify human interests without being able to specify precisely the persons whose interests they are. We do not ordinarily suppose that our failure to identify such persons constitutes a failure to have identified an interest. Furthermore, we can ask such a question and receive the answer "It is not in the interest of anyone to maintain the present tax laws." Thus, the very possibility of asking such a question presupposes the intelligibility of replying that such an interest is not lodged anywhere in anyone. Still by asking the question we have identified an interest. Thus, we can and do identify interests *in* x without in the least having to identify x as the interest *of* any specific persons. It is the case that human interests are always interests *in* such and such. It is not the case that they must always be identified as the interests *of* so and so particular persons or groups.

Thus, in the enumeration of interests, our concern is to identify and to distinguish certain sets of interests, not certain sets of persons. How such interests are distributed is an important, distinguishable question. Thus, the interests to be considered may be identified as (a) state interests, (b) parental interests, (c) societal interests, and (d) incumbent interests. Just as parental interests may be lodged in persons who are not parents, so also state interests may be lodged in persons who are not part of the government.

The second point is that this enumeration includes no mention of the interests of children. There is a reason, however, for this omission. In the first place, we are concerned here with giving an account of the system of control. For this purpose, it seems to accord with common sense and with experience to take the position that the interests of children do not enter significantly in the system of control *except* when those interests produce practical reasons for action that are also produced from some set of interests that is on this list. Childrens' interests, in other words, enter into the control of the system only when they are advanced either as the interests of the state, parents, the larger society, or the incumbents of the system.

Furthermore, children will have a stronger *moral* claim against the state, the society, their parents, and possibly the system itself, if we speak of their possessing *rights* rather than merely interests. Human beings may have interests where they have no rights. When a person has a right to (do) X, it follows that someone else has a duty either to do or to forbear doing something. Interests have no such consequences. Their possession does not generate corresponding duties on the part of anyone. If some individual or group of parents claim that they have an interest in "getting a good education" or "in assuring that their children have a certain kind of education" it does not follow that they have any right to what they claim. On the other hand, if they have an acknowledged right to a certain kind of education, then it follows that the state, parents, some agency of the society, or perhaps even the system itself has duties to do or to forbear doing certain things. Thus, to describe the control of the system as a structure of interests is a *morally* weaker account than would result from describing the arrangements of control as a system of rights. On the other hand, to describe the arrangements for control as the structure of interests is a stronger account than would result from describing it in relation to rights, because it is more inclusive. Such an account is more inclusive because the concept of "interest" includes the notion of moral interests, but also because it takes account of circumstances in which issues of control arise, but no moral claims are made.

We may rest then, for the moment at least, with the view that the arrangements for the social control of the system are found in the structure of interests, and the interests to be considered are those of (1) the state, (2) the society, (3) parents, and (4) the incumbents of the system itself.

State Interests

The interests of the state are of two sorts, compelling and derived. The compelling interests of the state can be summed up in two requirements — that (1) each individual attain economic independence, and (2) that each grant minimum obedience to civil law. We could say, in more colloquial terms, that the compelling interests of the state are that children grow up so that they are neither on the dole nor in prison.

Though I have stated these compelling interests as belonging to the state, we should recognize that, in fact, they add up to the most basic interests of any human collective to reduce dependence of a certain sort, not independence of friends or independence from participation in cooperative activities that the community requires. Indeed, were we to establish a new and independent community, then, provided that we had any aspiration for that community to continue beyond our own lives, we would confront immediately the task of deciding how to educate the children so that they will continue the community and grow out of the necessity of being wards. We would have to decide how to empty the nursery and how to do so in a way calculated to continue the community of adults. To suggest then that the compelling interests of the state are the attainment of economic independence and adherence to civil law is merely to acknowledge the basic interest of any human collective in its own survival. Education, like the provision of food and clothing, is a survival function.

These interests, of course, are never fully satisfied, nor is there ever an expectation that they will be satisfied in every individual or all the time. No community is ever totally without crime. None is ever totally successful in the socialization of the young. None is ever totally without dependence of various sorts. It is sufficient that these interests be satisfied, on the whole, in general, and most of the time.

The state's compelling interests are minimal in relation to educational ideals and maximal in relation to power. That is to say, such compelling interests neither define nor encompass what anyone would regard as a good education. They extend only to what, in general, is necessary. In that respect they are minimal. But, on the other hand, they are maximal in the sense that if they ever conflict with the rights or interests of individuals, then the compelling interests of the state will prevail. Thus, they are minimal in their scope and maximal in their power.

However, the state's interests are not limited to its compelling interests. If these interests are indeed compelling, then it follows that the state will have derived interests arising from the effect to secure them. The state may have no interest in defining for each the best education for his children. But, by the same token, the state does have an interest in assuring that children are not educated in ways that will threaten its continued existence. The state may have no interest in how lavishly a community cares to support the education of its young, but it will have a strong and fundamental concern that the problem not be ignored altogether. Nor can it be attended to only a little. The community must give the education of the young enough attention to secure the compelling interests of the state.

Thus, in consequence of its compelling interests, the state has certain derived or secondary interests including the determination of who can teach, who will be educated for how long, what will be taught under what conditions, and what will constitute an acceptable level of attention to these problems on the part of the family and the local community. Thus, the derived interests of the state can extend to the control of finance (both capital and operating), the licensing of teachers, the specification of curriculum, and standards of attendance.

These derived interests, like the compelling interests from which they stem, remain minimal. The principle is that they can extend only so far as is necessary to secure the compelling interests of the state. But the compelling interests of the state are at the same time maximal in respect to power. They can prevail. And so, in principle, there is no limit to how far the derived interest of the state may extend into the regulation of education. Power does not impose its own limitations. If the acceptable minimum is suitably interpreted, then the derived interests of the state can be extended to the most minute regulation of curriculum, school organization, support, licensing of teachers and so forth. What is initially a concern with bare essentials can become all-inclusive in its reach. How far the derived interests of the state can reach remains an open question. The "open" question is closed, however, by specifying an acceptable level of probability that the compelling interests of the state in education are being secured.

Parental Interests

If the path of this analysis were to remain unabridged, it would produce a system of control with a single dynamic of change. Because the compelling interests of the state are never fully secured in every respect and all the time, it follows that there always remain grounds for the continued extension of the state's derived interests into a more and more detailed control of the system. If there were no other interests than those of the state, or if there were no *rights* to limit them, then education could become totalitarian in the strict sense. Fortunately, however, there are parental interests, and they are given weight in the system of control.

The interests of parents begin by being identical with the compelling interests of the state. No state, nor any human collective, could be satisfied if large numbers of its youth grow up to be either economically noncontributing or in jail. We may be assured, however, that neither would parents be satisfied if that is the way their children turn out. So there seems, initially at least, to be no conflict whatever between the state's compelling interests and fundamental parental interests.

There is a difference, however. The state's interests in these matters are satisfied if they are satisfied in the aggregate, and on the whole. But parental interests will not be satisfied by success in the aggregate or on the whole. Parental interests are identical with those of the state in substance. But the state's compelling interests are minimal in degree and the parents' are maximal. The state's interests are aggregate. Parental interests are not. The state may wish to insure the minimum that is essential, but parents typically aspire to the best that is possible; and they seek not simply the best that is possible on the whole, but the best th.t is possible *for their own children*.

This difference between parental interests and state interests is vital. Its implications are enormous. For example, the state may have an interest in securing equal educational opportunity for all children within its jurisdiction. Indeed, in many modern states, the advancement of such an interest may be deemed a fundamental duty. Parents, however, (with notable exceptions) are unlikely to have such an interest even as a proximate goal, and no parent whatever is likely to view equal opportunity as an ultimate goal or interest. What parents want is not that their children have equal opportunity, but that they get the best that is possible, and that will always mean opportunities "better than *some* others get."

The exceptions to this principle should be noted. The first is that those parents who view their own children as disadvantaged may see the assurance of an equal chance at education to be an improvement. Thus, they may have an interest in promoting equal opportunity as a proximate or temporary step toward securing the best that is possible for their children. The second exception is defined by that group of parents who see themselves and their children as secure in their advantages. In truth, however, these parents are not so likely to see it in their interests to promote equal opportunity as they are likely to find no interest in opposing it. They may have nothing to gain from the *attainment* of equal opportunity, but by the same token, they may have nothing to lose in the *attempt* to achieve it. In neither of these cases, however, is equal educational opportunity likely to be an ultimate parental interest. Nonetheless, it may be a strong derived interest or even a fundamental duty of the state.

Thus, by distinguishing parental interests and state's interests, we begin to see how the control of the system, the formulation of its practical reasons for acting in one way or another, is shaped. Parental interests begin by being substantively identical with the compelling interests of the state. They end by being very different and perhaps even in conflict. The compelling and derived interests of the state, though minimal in scope and maximal in power are always and necessarily aggregate. Parental interests, by contrast, have to do always with what is best and not merely necessary, and they are never aggregate.

Societal Interests

To distinguish between state interests, parental interests, and societal interests is to presuppose a distinction of some kind between state and society. By the state I mean simply the legal organization of society. The state is simply the society viewed from the point of view of its legal order. It is not the same as "the government," since the state may continue even though the government is drastically changed. But neither is the state the same as "the society." In any society, there may be many human affairs of broad social interest, but without direct government control — the creation of symphony orchestras and museums, for example. These are interests whose advancement benefits everyone in the society, but which do not themselves fall directly under the jurisdiction of the state. They are examples of those interests that are important not for the continuation of society, but for its improvement. Such interests belong neither to parents nor to the state. They are societal interests.

The interests of society, like the interests of parents, are, at first, identical with those of the state. Still, they should be distinguished both from those of the state and from those of parents. They are unlike the interests of the state since they extend far beyond what is needed in general as a minimum; but they are unlike the interests of parents since they fall short of the best that anyone would desire in particular. Since they are interests in aggregate goods, they are unlike the interests of parents, and since they are more than minimal in scope, they are unlike the interests of the state.

They might be clearly identified by a fundamental principle. *If* it can be shown that not everyone benefits from X, then it cannot be justified that everyone should be taxed to support X. On the other hand, *if* it can be claimed that everyone benefits from X, then it can be argued also that everyone *can be* called upon to support X. One or another version of this principle will suffice to distinguish between state's interests, parental interests, and societal interests. If it can be shown that everyone benefits from X, and that X is not a compelling interest of the state, then the promotion of X is a societal interest. The state clearly has the power to advance such interests although it has no duty to do so and no compelling interest in doing so.

From this principle it is possible to generate an enormous number of specific arguments each identifying a particular societal interest. The full range of such arguments can be reduced, however, to three classes exemplified by three equally specific, kindred, though different claims. The first is the claim that everyone benefits from the development of an educated elite whose skills and judgment will contribute to the good conduct of government and therefore to the preservation of an orderly society. The second is the judgment that everyone benefits from the expansion of skills and talents that contribute to the continued advancement or development of society. The third is the claim that everyone benefits from the widest possible distribution of certain minimal skills, like reading, certain dispositions, like respect for craft, and certain personality characteristics, like punctuality and tenacity.[1]

The first of these claims can be expressed by saying that everybody has an interest in advancing the development of a few on the grounds that it is best to be governed by the "best" if not "the brightest." Any social process or any social institution that can present a *prima facie* claim to select "the best" in this respect will have also a *prima facie* claim that it advances a social interest. The second illustrative claim can be expressed in the rather mundane thought that it is better that the plumbing work than that it not work, and that it remains better even if securing that good means that only a few are trained to be competent plumbers. Any social process or social institution that can claim *prima facie* to be necessary for creating the pools of knowledge and skill required for the continued advancement of society can present the *prima facie* claim to represent the interests of society. The third claim can be expressed in the specific observation that if everybody can read, there are likely to be more books, newspapers and publishers. Any institution or social process that can claim to advance the skills of inquiry and judgment can lay a claim to represent a social interest.

In short, social interests are (1) interests in those goods that benefit everyone directly even if their distribution is restricted to only a few, as well as (2) interests in those goods, like orderly government and good roads, that cannot be possessed by anyone unless they are secured for everyone. Thus, social interests are aggregate rather than specific and in that respect they are like the interests of the state and unlike the interests of parents. We do not really care who *in particular* is a good plumber as long as somebody is and as long as there are enough of them. Social interests are also more than minimal. They go beyond considerations of mere independence and civil obedience. They are interests not in what is essential for society, but in what is essential for a *good* society. In that respect they are like the interests of parents and unlike the compelling and derived interests of the state.

The very possibility of "manpower planning" rests upon the assumption that it is a fundamental interest of society that there be enough plumbers to keep the plumbing working. Insofar as such planning is supposed to have consequences for the system, it assumes further that the

1. Each of these claims appeals to the *social* value of increasing the spread of knowledge, skill, or expanded human sensibilities, which, as we shall see, turn out to constitute the definable group of "educational benefits." See Chapter III.

The strength of these claims however, rests upon the existence of *social* interests and the existence of those interests produces an endless variety of what I shall refer to later as "social benefit arguments" for the support of the system. The nature of these interests and their resulting arguments are more fully considered in Chapter VIII, Arguments of Public and Private Benefits: The Political Support for the System.

educational system is a primary means of advancing that social interest. To the extent that the results of manpower studies can be implemented in policy, the further assumption is uniformly adopted that quite individual parental interests can be leashed in the service of aggregate societal interests.[2] Thus, if a shortage of engineers is imminent, then policy-makers might seek to (1) make that fact as widely known as possible and thus influence the advice that youth receive, or they may (2) seek to increase incentives for youth to enter engineering by selective scholarships or other forms of student aid or social privilege. In either case, a fundamental social interest is being pursued through the educational system by enlisting parental interests in the service of social interests. If this chain of assumptions, or any assumption within the set, were abandoned, we might continue to have "manpower studies," but they would have no point. We see once again that the control of the system is discovered in the structure of interests, and that we exercise control over the system by advancing those interests, adjusting their conflict, and establishing connections among them so that multiple interests can be pursued jointly in the same course of action. That "adjustment" of interests is what we describe from another perspective as political compromise or political negotiation.

The Interests of Incumbents

In seeking to discover the control of the system in the structure of such interests, I have not meant to suggest that these different interests are always found in different persons. Parents, of course, may have social interests, and any agent of the state may have parental interests. Any natural individual, that is to say, any actual living and breathing real person may have many kinds of interests including moral interests. I have been concerned merely to identify different kinds of interests and their different properties. What distribution they receive or where they are lodged is an entirely different matter. This conceptual point is vital if we are to understand the interests of the incumbents of the system. Their roles are complex. They may be parents, and they are always both members of the society and agents of the state. They are also, we may presume, moral individuals.

The difficulty in describing the interests of teachers and administrators in the system arises, however, from another kind of complexity.

2. I have defined parental interests as the interests that parents typically have *for* their children. I am now assuming that precisely those *same* interests can be the interests *of* youth and adults *for* themselves. I shall continue to refer to them, however, as parental interests, on the analogy that just as parents can express a care for their children so can their children, as they mature, express a care *for themselves*.

Insofar as teachers and administrators are salaried, their interests are those of employees. Insofar as they are practitioners of an art aimed at promoting the welfare of clients and insofar as they are members of an association of peers, then their interests are those of professionals. And insofar as they practice a craft of "making something happen," they are technicians. Different, and even conflicting interests emerge from these different perspectives on what it means to occupy a position in the system. Because the interests of the incumbent arise partly from the role of employee, partly from the role of professional and partly from the role of technicians, they must be treated, as we say, *passim*. They cannot be identified with quite the singularity that is possible in identifying state's interests, parental interests, and societal interest.[3]

THE SOCIAL LOGIC OF SYSTEMIC GOALS

The system is "not of one mind." It includes different sets of interests, and therefore it receives different directives to guide its behavior. Further, there is no single set of interests that can be advanced without limit. Different interests, moreover, may clash or harmonize, and some may be advanced in the pursuit of others. We should not be surprised to discover in addition that these sets of interest stand in some dynamic not only among themselves but also in relation to the systemic properties of size and distribution. We should not anticipate, in other words, that the interests prevailing in a small system will remain unchanged as the system expands. This problem concerning the relation between control and the properties of size and distribution must be deferred (see Chapters VI and VIII). But, in the account given to this point, there is one other deficiency that can be remedied now.

　　The interests entering into the system of control have been identified without applications. It is well enough to say that the interests of parents are maximal rather than minimal and individual rather than aggregate, and that they seek the best that is possible for their children rather than the minimum necessary. But how, within the system of control, do we define what is best? How does the state identify what is necessary? And how do the state's interests and parental interests change in these details? To this problem we may find a proximate solution in understanding the social logic of educational goals.

3. The interests of the incumbents of the system, as employees, are considered in detail in Chapter IV. Their interests as professionals are examined also in Chapters IV and VIII.

General Goals and Specific Goals

Let us observe a distinction between general and broad goals, on the one hand, and specific goals or targets, on the other hand. By general goals I refer to such aspirations as the intention to educate each child to the fullest of his potential; and by specific goals I refer to such concrete declarations as the intention to increase the reading scores for children in a certain school by one grade point within one year. Specific goals always designate a time when the goal is to be attained. They are also expressed so that what constitutes their attainment is clearly specified and so that the magnitude of any "falling short" can be determined. General goals, in contrast, are never formulated so that it is possible to tell when the goal has been attained, how far we are short of its attainment or when it is to be achieved. There is, *in principle,* no way that any school can tell that it is producing (now) good citizens (for the future) or that it is educating children to their fullest potential. The first of these goals is indefinite in specifying the relevant future and there is nothing that could constitute the attainment of the second because presumably there is nothing anyone has learned, about which one cannot have learned more. No conceivable improvement in the techniques of measurement will suffice to transform either of these general goals into specific targets.

Because of these intrinsic difficulties in the formulation of general goals, it has sometimes been argued that they are useless in providing practical guidance either for schools or school systems. All such goals, it is suggested, should be replaced by specific targets that can be monitored and that can be known to have been achieved or to have remained unattained by some definable margin. That intellectual move is basic to some versions of the accountability movement in American education, and also to the development of state-assessment programs and the effort to introduce the techniques of modern management into the educational system.

I wish to suggest, however, that this move rests on a mistaken conception of the logic of general goals and their function within the social control of the system. We may not know when we are educating children to their fullest potential, but there are circumstances in which virtually everyone will agree that we are failing to do so. It may seem that if we can agree on when we are failing, then we should be able to agree on when we are succeeding. That inference, however, simply doesn't follow. It rests upon an erroneous view of the social function of general educational goals, their relation to specific goals, and their relation to the different and conflicting interests reflected in the system.

It is not the function of general educational goals to establish what we are to count as a good, much less the best, state of affairs. *It is their function to tell us what we are to count as relevant in advancing the judgment that things have gotten intolerably bad.* If we are able to view the social utility of general educational goals in this way, then we shall see that they serve their function tolerably well. They are usually invoked, and perform their function, not when we have fallen somewhat short of what is "good" or "best," but when we have fallen short of what is acceptable. That is the time when general goals are invoked, and at such times they suffice to establish quite specific targets. The general principle that we should educate each child to his fullest potential means that the curriculum should not be too narrow, the facilities should not be too impoverished and standards should not be too low. Never mind that the phrases "too narrow," "too impoverished," and "too low" are left undefined. They will be defined differently in different circumstances. But the point is that they *are* defined, they are defined in specific settings, and they are defined always in respect to what falls short of the acceptable and not in relation to what falls short of the best. When the interests of parents are provoked they will be saying things like "Add a French class" (the curriculum is too narrow) or "Add a science lab" (the facilities are too impoverished) or "Don't underestimate our kids" (the standards are too low).

Such appeals are specific enough. They are about as specific as anyone can reasonably expect from the expression of generally informed and benevolent parental interests. And they constitute a covert formulation of the general criticism to the schools "You are not doing as much as you should for our children." And this, in turn is only another way of saying "You should seek to educate our children to the fullest of their potential." It is not the import of such a message to say to the schools, "You are not doing the best that can be done" since presumably that is *always* true. Rather it is the import of such a message that what is being done is unacceptable and unacceptable in quite specific ways. In short, general goals operate effectively in the establishment of specific targets provided we recognize that their function is to provide criteria for determining what kinds of arguments will constitute serious charges of failure. *Specific educational goals are derived from general educational goals through a social process in which there is produced a definition of what constitutes not the best, but the worst that is acceptable.* To suppose that specific goals for the system can or must be generated independently of general goals is to succumb to a most fundamental misunderstanding of the nature of educational goals.

It is important to keep in mind that in this analysis, I am concerned with the nature of *systemic* goals, not the goals that particular individuals, or even small academic departments might set for themselves. Individuals and even small groups of people may set goals for themselves on the assumption that they are doing fairly well already but can undertake certain steps that will result in doing somewhat better in the future. But the sum of all such individually established goals do not add up to the goals for an entire school or college, to say nothing of the system as a whole. The claim being advanced here is that specific goals for a large unit or for the system as a whole are derived from shared or general goals through a social process in which various interests are expressed in ways that define the threshold of the unacceptable.

Note: Nowhere is there an educational institution or an educational system whose members could not, of an evening, by simply taking thought, develop a rationally intelligible and socially defensible set of goals for the institution. The task, viewed as an intellectual problem, is not difficult. But it is also futile unless there is a social process by which the goals that each individual sets for himself and for the institution can be translated into the goals of the institution. The argument advanced here is that that process will either be the expression of a single will, and therefore the product of strong, central, and authoritative leadership or it will be a process in which the interplay of interests is permitted to define objectives through the detailed specification of what is unacceptable. The claim is that even within the most centralized systems there are few opportunities for the mere imposition of goals upon the system. There are no kings and queens of education. Even the gods of government bestow their blessings upon the various tribal enclaves of the system not by some mere impulse of whimsy, but to accord with how they view the shifting interplay of interests.

Specific goals for the guidance of the system are thus dependent, in a way, upon the general goals of the system. But in what way? If we suppose that specific goals are dependent upon general goals as the conclusion of an argument is dependent upon its premises, then we are immediately presented with certain problems that defy solution. That is to say, if we suppose that the specific targets for the system are to be *derived* from certain general propositions expressed in general goals then we must seek agreement upon the premises, and we must discover some kind of tight *logical* relation between our general goals and specific courses of action. Such an understanding of the relation between general and specific systemic goals is part of the underlying motivation that often leads schoolmen to express the need for a philosophy of education. Philosophical claims, it is true, often have a certain air of generality about them. But it is the kind of generality shared by the claims of logic and mathematics and not the kind expressed by general educational goals.

If we were to derive specific directives from the general goals of the system by a strict logical process, then the first thing we would need is agreement on the general goals. This perspective immediately coverts the philosophy of education into a kind of modern, secularized, evangelical enterprise. It represents a perverse conception of the nature of philosophy and what it might contribute to the cause of education. It may also explain why the literature on educational goals is so uniformly dull. On the whole, it contains neither good philosophy nor useful advice. But even were it possible to surmount this problem there would remain the difficulty that from the general goals of education there is *no* direct and rationally persuasive path to arrive at specific directives for action. This claim may seem odd, but it will seem less odd when we recognize that neither will the principles of moral theory suffice to determine our moral duty in specific circumstances. Specific goals for the system simply do not stand in that kind of dependence to general goals any more than moral decisions stand in that kind of relation to moral principles.

The view presented here is that the dependence of specific systemic goals upon general goals is not a logical dependence, but a kind of dependence that emerges from the social process by which specific targets are set. The function of general goals in that social process is to provide the criteria of relevance in arriving at any judgment that the system in some respect is doing badly. From this perspective it turns out that such generally accepted aspirations for the system as developing good citizens, stimulating creativity, developing economic independence, encouraging all the potentialities of children — these aspirations do get translated into specific goals. It is a relevant criticism of the schools to say that the curriculum is too narrow, the facilities too impoverished, or the standards too low, because such criticisms can be linked to an appeal to general goals. But it is not a relevant criticism of the schools that they do not assure election to public office for students of political science nor financial security for students of business. That is *not* a criticism that can be linked to any general goals of the system and therefore cannot be regarded as a relevant *failure*.

It may be a peculiarity of educational goals for the system that they are defined not out of agreement on what is good, better, and best, but out of agreement on what is bad, worse, and absolutely intolerable. The irony is that currently in the United States there are extensive efforts to secure better sources of information about schools and their performance (state assessment) in order to establish more rational decision making, especially in the allocation of resources. Insofar as those efforts contain reference to goals, they are usually defined along the continuum of good, better and best in ways appropriate to an industrial management system. If I am correct in these observations about educational goals, then this movement will, in the end, simply provide more effective means of monitoring the minimal standards. They will begin in an effort to move from good to better to best, and end by merely defining more clearly when and where things are bad, worse, and absolutely intolerable.

The Hierarchy of Minimal Standards

In respect to standards, the interests of the state are minimal in scope, but maximal in power and aggregation. By contrast, the interests of parents typically, in respect to standards, are maximal in scope, and minimal in power and aggregation. In short, from parental interests comes the desire that things go very well indeed *for their own children,* but the interests of the state result in the desire that things simply not go very badly, on the whole. But how can such phrases as "very well indeed" and "not very badly on the whole" be defined? Obviously, the specific content given to these phrases must change through time.

Though it is in the interests of parents to secure the best that is possible for their children, and in the interests of the state to secure the minimum necessary for everyone, still, the specific meaning of *best* emerges from reflection on the minimum tolerable. But here again the conception of that minimum may change in time and place. If we have a society or a community in which everyone learns to read, then the fact that few find pleasure in it, may be regarded as intolerable. In those circumstances the schools might be urged to undertake the responsibility of teaching so that reading is enjoyed. Such a goal is not required to meet the compelling interests of the state, though it may clearly accord with the interests of parents. It can be viewed as a societal interest.

But if we have a society in which substantial numbers of students are penalized because they do not learn to read even in the literal sense of functional literacy, then the fact that few enjoy reading is likely to be regarded as tolerable and the minimal responsibilities of schools are unlikely to include such a goal either for parents or for the state. And if children in school have neither security of person nor property, then even the teaching of basic literacy is likely to give way to other goals, although in these latter circumstances it may be doubted whether the goals can be construed as educational goals in any sense at all.

The Transformation of Goals to Functions

Thus, we see that what constitutes the minimum acceptable standards for either parents or the state may change. But is there some underlying principle that serves to establish that progression or hierarchy of minimal acceptable standards?[4] The underlying principle is that nothing can be a goal in education, or in any other precinct of life, if it is already attained. It cannot be my goal to get up this morning. I have already done it. On the other hand, it might be my goal to go to bed early tonight. However obvious this point may seem, it is important nonetheless because it helps us to understand why the function of educational goals is to define the terms of failure rather than success. This is one of the reasons why the general goals of the system are stable. No matter how well the schools may do, they will never attain their general goals. Such goals always assure us that there is more to be done.

There is, however, a second principle in this dynamic relationship of goals and interests, and it may be decisive for understanding the control of the system. The compelling interests of the state are limited to minimal needs, although we recognize also that the derived interests of the state can be extended indefinitely. Similarly, though the interests of parents are always more than minimal, likewise there is no limit to their extent. Whatever is achieved, they can always seek to achieve more. But now we see that what parents regard as the threshold of the intolerable may also change.

Within the United States I suspect that the three R's plus a certain kind of citizenship education fall within the set of minimal skills. They are the skills and dispositions that, on the whole, are most central to the interests of the state, the society, and parents, as well. But there is some evidence that a substantial part of the American people believe that in these basic areas of education, the schools can be successful. *Thus, these attainments get transformed from goals for the system into functions of the system.* This principle that goals get transformed into functions is a direct corollary of the analytic principle that nothing can be a goal if it is already attained. The importance of this corollary lies in the fact that the failure to perform the functions of the school will be uniformly regarded as more serious than a failure to meet the goals of the system. Failure to discharge its functions will imperil the legitimacy of the system itself whereas failure to meet its goals is unlikely to have any such serious consequences.

This last observation is of exceptional importance. Both the goals of the system and the functions of the system are likely to be raised as the system becomes more and more successful. And although it may be in the interests of parents to seek the best they can secure for their own children, it is not in their interests to permit the state to define that "best." Yet, as goals for the schools become the functions of the system, the discharge of

---

4. There was a time in the history of American education when it would have been regarded as absolutely intolerable that people complete their schooling without a working knowledge of the scriptures.

those functions tends to fall more and more within the legitimate reach of the state's interests to secure because their attainment becomes more serious, more compelling, more minimally necessary. Meeting the basic functions of the system is a requirement that falls within the compelling interests of the state to assure. Meeting the goals of the system has no such serious consequences. Thus, as the system grows, as it becomes more successful, the reach of the state is likely to extend more and more into the areas characteristic of the interests of parents. There is likely to emerge a conflict of interests. The adjustment of that conflict is likely to extend the role of the state in proportion as it results in an extension of the state's legitimate and compelling interests.

·∘[III]∘·

THE EDUCATIONAL SYSTEM
Distribution

T HE THIRD DERIVATIVE FEATURE of all educational systems stems from the fact that they are all systems of distribution. (1) There will be a distribution of resources within the system, (2) a distribution of benefits resulting from the system, and also a relation between the distribution of resources and benefits warranted by (3) some presumed distribution of educationally relevant attributes in the population served by the system.

Resources, benefits, and educational attributes — these are the elements that enter into the distributive behavior of the system. Furthermore, they are related, and their relationships will change depending upon different rates and magnitudes of change in the size of the system. The kinds of distributive behavior interact not only with each other, but also with the modes of growth and contraction.

DISTRIBUTION OF RESOURCES

In the politics of the system, problems concerning the distribution of resources are the most evident and the most frequently discussed. Thus, they appear to be the most fundamental. Within the logic of the system, however, these problems are less fundamental than either the distribution of benefits, or the distribution of educationally relevant attributes of the population.

There are several grounds on which this claim rests. The first is that all rationally satisfactory arguments supporting a particular distribution of resources rest either upon views concerning the desirable distribution of benefits or upon views concerning the actual distribution of educationally relevant attributes or both.[1] We may distinguish, in short, between three quite different sorts of questions. There are (1) those concerning the *appropriate* distribution of resources, (2) those concerning the *desirable* distribution of benefits, and (3) those concerning the *actual* distribution of educationally relevant attributes among the persons served by the system. We cannot answer questions of the first sort except by appealing to answers to the second or third sorts of questions. In other words, any rationally satisfactory argument offered to support a particular distribution of resources in the system will contain a suppressed premise setting forth either an assumed view concerning the proper distribution of benefits or an assumed view concerning the actual distribution of educationally relevant attributes.

Now it may be true that all arguments concerning resource distribution are dependent upon prior arguments concerning the distribution of benefits and educationally relevant attributes. But the converse is not true. That is to say, we may argue satisfactorily in support of a specific distribution of benefits without appealing to any particular view about the distribution of resources. And similarly, we may argue in support of a particular view of the distribution of educationally relevant attributes without assuming any particular view about the distribution of resources.

These observations, if true, are sufficient to establish the claim that questions of resource distribution may be the most important distributive questions in the politics of the system, but nonetheless, they are least fundamental in the logic of the system. Such a claim requires decisive proof.[2] It may be enough at the moment, however, to offer a second

1. Distinguish between arguments concerning the *magnitude* of resources *for* the system and arguments concerning the *distribution* of resources *within* the system. I am concerned here only with an important feature of arguments concerning the distribution of resources *within* the system. Questions about the magnitude of resources *for* the system are, of course, allocational questions also, but at a different level. Such questions concern the appropriate division of the total public budget and not simply the distribution of that share going to the educational system. The *division* of the public budget reflects a social decision to buy more or less in the way of public goods as contrasted with private goods. Such a decision does require a political argument rather than an educational argument. How that political argument can be framed within the interests reflected in the system is the subject of Chapter VIII.

2. The demonstration of this point would require a constructive proof designed to establish that a particular class is empty. In the present case, *as a minimum*, the demonstration would have to establish the claim that the class of arguments (1) that are rationally satisfactory, i.e., sound, (2) that seek to establish the acceptability of a particular distribution of resources *within* the system, and (3) that make no appeal to any view about the appropriate distribution of benefits or the actual distribution of educationally relevant attributes, is an empty class. Such a claim cannot be established by our mere failure to find such an argument. That would demonstrate only that our ingenuity is limited. What needs demonstration is that there cannot be such an argument in principle. That is to say, what is required, is a constructive proof.

observation to help reduce the counter-intuitive appearance of the essential point.

Why is it, we may ask, that in the politics of the system questions concerning the distribution of resources appear to be more basic than they are in the logic of the system? Two points are important. The first is the simple fact that at the level of legislation there are really only two things that can be accomplished in any case. The first is to establish the magnitude of resources *to* the system; and the second is to establish guidelines either for the distribution of those resources *in* the system or for the conduct of other affairs, like the requirements of curriculum and the licensing of personnel, that do not primarily involve the allocation of resources. Determining the magnitude of support for the system is the only one of these two tasks that is raised regularly because it is the only one that requires attention in relation to the *size* of the total public budget related to public goods. At the level of state or federal government — at least in the United States — nothing more is regularly done that directly effects the conduct of the system. Large changes in the guidelines, such as would occur with fundamental alterations in the formula for state aid to schools or in the requirements for the design of school buildings, or in the requirements of curriculum, are rather rare occurrences. The problem that appears most regularly and most frequently in the politics of the system is the determination of the *size* of the educational system's share of the public budget according to a rarely altered formula for its distribution.

It took forty years, for example, for any significant change in the state-aid formula for schools to reach the legislature in the State of New York. And even then, it was raised only after the report of a "Blue-Ribbon Commission" and an extended and lavishly supported program of research. The size of state aid to schools, however, is an annual issue in the politics of New York State since together with costs of welfare and programs of retirement, it constitutes the most significant factor in the total size of the state's budget. The constant and most recurring problem in the politics of the system concerns the magnitude of resources allocated to it and not the distribution of resources within it. That the distribution of resources within the system is so infrequently raised may help to persuade us that such a problem may be less than fundamental in the logic of the system.

But there is more. Why is it that questions concerning the allocation of resources within the system are so seldom raised? The answer is fairly easy to discover. They are so seldom raised not merely because they are difficult, but because raising them is so divisive. It is politically useful to avoid such questions. But this confession seems to contradict the claim that such questions are not really fundamental. Only the most sensitive social questions are so divisive that there is any political merit in seeking to avoid them. But one must press the question. Why are issues of resource distribution within the system so divisive? The answer is clearly that they are divisive because there is no way of raising them without raising questions about the appropriate distribution of benefits and the actual distribution of educationally relevant attributes in the population, and those are the questions that are divisive.

We cannot suggest alternative ways of distributing resources within the system without suggesting that different persons should share differently in the benefits of the system than they now do. For example, we cannot claim that the disadvantaged should receive greater resources because they have greater needs unless we are prepared to advance the view that the benefits of the system should be distributed more evenly than they are now. If such a proposal is socially divisive, as many think it is, then it is divisive not because it advances a fresh view about how resources should be distributed in the system, but because it rests upon a particular view concerning the proper distribution of benefits. If it is socially divisive to suggest that no school or school district should be permitted to spend more per pupil than any other, then it is not divisive because it suggests a different view of the distribution of resources, but because it rests on the view that the children of the wealthy should not be permitted to share disproportionately in the benefits of the system. That would be viewed by some as a step toward a more just distribution of benefits and by others it will be viewed as a fiscally imposed limitation on their capacity to love their children in ways that demonstrate a concern for their future.

In reality, nobody cares how resources are distributed within the educational system except those who spend the resources in the system and those who receive salaries from the system. What people do care about is how and on what grounds the *benefits* of the system are distributed, and *they care about the distribution of resources only to the extent that they believe the distribution of benefits is effected by the distribution of resources.* Thus, to the belief in the efficacy of education we must add the belief in the efficacy of resources in the system. Without that belief, the system would still have to distribute resources in some way, but that problem then would no longer even appear to be basic to the behavior of the system. We may therefore pass on to a more crucial set of questions, namely those dealing with the distribution of benefits.

DISTRIBUTION OF BENEFITS

Educational Benefits

All educational systems are implicated in the distribution of three kinds of goods or benefits: (1) educational benefits, (2) non-educational social goods, and (3) second-order educational benefits. The three can be distinguished on quite precise grounds, although it is somewhat more difficult to establish just what subsets of goods fall within each category. Educational benefits are such things as knowledge, skills, perhaps certain kinds of taste, and certainly standards of civility or manners. These goods are often distributed, of course, in other ways than through the educational system. They need not be learned in schools. Still, they are so intimately connected to the educational system that *if they were not distributed to anyone in any degree, by the system,* then we would be puzzled by the claim that the system is an *educational system.* If no one ever learned through the educational system to read, to calculate, or to exercise any number of other skills, then we might continue to say that the system is a means of child custodianship or that it is a device for controlling the size of the labor force, but we could not give any clear sense to the claim that it is an *educational* system. *Educational benefits then, are those goods whose distribution by the system is a logically necessary condition for the system to be regarded as educational.*

In calling these things "goods" or "benefits," I am departing from the language usually employed by economists in speaking of public goods and private goods or in speaking of economic commodities. This usage also departs, though less severely, from the terminology often used in systems analysis to speak of "outputs" or "outcomes."

The difference of usage is to be found, partially at least, in the following points. First, the concept of an economic good is often construed to be value neutral. That is to say, an economic good, or, for that matter, a systems output can be something that is generally, or even universally, agreed to be bad. Neither concept implies *benefit* in the etymologically literal sense in which the term is here used to suggest something that is good or valuable. Secondly, there are many outcomes or results of the system that are in no way logically essential to its being an educational system. For example, it is sometimes suggested that the American system produces in children the anxiety that comes with the need to achieve and the lack of curiosity and wonder that comes from being subjected to an externally determined order of learning. These may be outcomes of the system, but they are not educational goods or benefits in the sense intended here. Indeed, if these, and other outcomes like them, were no longer produced, we would not cease referring to the system as an educational system. We would say it is a better educational system, not that it had ceased being an educational system. Such outcomes are dispensable. They are inessential to the claim that the system is an educational system. Although they may be outcomes of the system, nonetheless, they do not satisfy the definition of educational goods.

The connection that I am trying to describe between the system and the distribution of educational goods is a logical or conceptual connection and not a factual one. Somewhere, there may be a system that, in fact, distributes no educational benefits to anyone whatever, but it cannot be an educational system. There cannot be an educational system that does not claim to distribute such goods because the set of benefits that we are concerned with may be defined as just those goods or benefits —*whatever they are* —that must be distributed by the system if it is to make good on the claim to be an educational system. Therefore, that there are such goods and that they are distributed by every educational system, is a claim that turns out to be analytic. That such goods are distributed by an educational system is strictly entailed by the assumption that it is an educational system and not a penal system, a monetary system, or an employment system.

Non-Educational Social Goods

By non-educational social goods, on the other hand, I mean to refer to certain social goods that are often treated as though they were distributed *by* the educational system even though in fact they are not. They are such social goods as income, occupational opportunity, status, prestige and power. Such goods are never distributed *by* the educational system; and that is the primary reason why they are not here regarded as educational goods. Still, there are societies in which these social goods appear to be distributed on the basis of the distribution of educational goods that the system does distribute.

The phrase "on the basis of" in this formulation deserves special attention. What does it mean? I do not mean, by this phrase, to suggest the existence of a mere correlation between the distribution of educational goods and the distribution of non-educational social goods. I do not mean to suggest, in other words, that those who, on the whole, have greater knowledge and skill just happen to be those with greater income, status, and occupational opportunity. On the contrary, I mean to suggest a social state of affairs in which such persons are awarded greater income, opportunity, and status on grounds of their greater knowledge and skill, as attested to by the educational system.

It is easy to imagine a society in which such non-educational social goods are distributed on some other grounds altogether than the possession of educational benefits. Such a supposition is quite consistent with the further supposition that, in such a society, there may be a strong discoverable correlation between the distribution of educational benefits and the distribution of non-educational social goods. Yet, in such a society we could not say, from the mere observation of this correlation, that non-educational social goods are distributed on the basis of the possession of educational benefits.

Thus, in suggesting that there might be some society in which social goods are distributed on the basis of educational benefits, I do not mean to suggest the existence of a mere correlation between the distributions of these two kinds of benefits. On the contrary, I mean to refer to the grounds on which an inequality in the possession of social goods might be justified. If an inequality in the distribution of social goods is justified on grounds of a corresponding inequality in the distribution of educational benefits, then we could say, in a quite precise and literal sense, that such a society distributes social goods to its people on the basis of their possession of educational goods. Such a state of affairs would produce a correlation, say, between education and income, but the correlation itself would not have the slightest tendency to reveal the basis for that distribution. Its basis would be found not in what produces it, but in what justifies it. Thus, when we suggest that non-educational social goods might be distributed on the basis of the distribution of educational benefits, we are suggesting the existence of a normative principle that is essential to the structure of the system and especially to its relation to the surrounding social system. That normative principle is that *those having a greater share of educational benefits merit or deserve a greater share of non-educational social goods.* That is the normative assumption concealed in the harmless looking phrase "on the basis of."

Having stated this principle, however, one must press on to make two limiting points. The first is that this formulation should not be confused with the formulation of a moral principle. The principle is not that persons distinguished by their possession of educational goods are better human beings. Such a view is possible, of course, but it is no part of the principle that those having a greater share of educational benefits merit a greater share of non-educational social goods. That principle states only that such individuals have a special, important, but nonetheless limited kind of merit that is believed to justify their also having a greater share of non-educational social goods. They are not, by that token, better human beings in any moral sense whatever.

The second important limiting point arises from the fact that there can be other normative principles that would suffice to establish a connection between the distribution of educational benefits and the distribution of non-educational social goods. The principle that I have identified would establish a strong positive correlation between the distribution of these two kinds of goods. There are other normative principles, however, that would establish a negative correlation or none at all. What is there to recommend this particular formulation?

The answer is, that though there are other principles that can be identified, for the union of these two sets of goods, they are unlikely to be adopted in a system that is very large, and, if adopted, they are unlikely to exclude the principle identified. We can imagine, for example, a society in which there is a strong negative relation between the distribution of educational benefits and the distribution of non-educational social goods. That would mean, for example, that there is a negative correlation between education and income. Such a state of affairs would roughly correspond to what Plato recommended as best for the rulers in his ideal polis. He thought that the rulers, the best educated, should be without either wealth in property or in income that leads to wealth in property. Under these circumstances, it is highly unlikely that many would be motivated to undertake the effort necessary to secure much in the way of educational benefits. Some would, but most would not. The system would be small and very elite. If the system becomes very large, both in absolute numbers and in proportion to the school-age population, we may assume that the correlation between the acquisition of educational goods and the acquisition of non-educational social goods is positive, or at least, that it is believed to be positive. If the system is large, there may be other normative principles operating, but that they would operate instead of this one, rather than only in addition to it, is most doubtful.

Of course, we could adopt the view that no normative principle is needed because no justification is needed for the relation between these two kinds of goods. There simply is no justice in their relation because no question of justice is involved. Such a view may be consistent with a strong connection between the distribution of educational and non-educational social goods, but it is neither necessary nor does it justify such a connection. Therefore, it might be argued, the principle that those who have more in the way of educational goods merit more in the way of non-educational social goods, is not a necessary principle in the structure of the system.

Against such a view, we may make the following points. In seeking an account of the system, we are concerned not merely to describe its structure or its organization. We are concerned as well to give an account of the sources of its legitimacy. In denying that the link between the distribution of educational and non-educational social goods needs any justification, we are denying that it requires any social legitimation. The point is that no society, nor any social institution, is likely to persist unless people believe it to be in their interests to support it, and not in their collective interests only, but in their individual and quite personal self-interest. It would be hard to understand how the system could grow very large unless it is believed to be in the interests of people to acquire the benefits of the system, and believed to be in their interests because it is a legitimated way to secure a greater share of non-educational social goods than they would otherwise be likely to secure. This suggests a condition in which the relation between the acquisition of educational and non-educational social goods is (1) strong, (2) positive, and (3) authorized or justified. If the system is large, in short, then the normative principle that I have been discussing will be an essential part of the structure of the system.

The system does not itself distribute non-educational social goods. Nonetheless, if it is to expand very much, there must be propagated the belief that a legitimate connection exists between the acquisition of educational benefits and the distribution of non-educational social goods. That connection provides the link between the educational system and the allocation of social goods in the society. It is also what provides one version of the belief in the efficacy of education. Were there no such link, there would be no grounds for a belief in the efficacy of education.

This entire discussion of the relation between educational benefits and non-educational social goods, up to this point, has been focused on a connection that is ideal only. If any society is actually to allocate social goods on the basis of the distribution of educational goods, it needs more than a mere principle. It needs some social invention through which it can make that connection specific, concrete, and knowable. It needs some means of determining who has secured the benefits of the system. And with this necessity we come to the third aspect in the distribution of benefits, the distribution of what I shall call second-order educational benefits.

Second-Order Educational Benefits

By second-order educational benefits I mean such goods of the system as certificates, degrees, diplomas, in special circumstances transcripts, and, in an extended sense, such things as occupational licenses. Such tokens are distributed *by* the educational system. Therefore, they differ from non-educational social goods. Neither are they educational goods in the strict sense in which we defined that term. We have already seen (in Chapter I) that such things as certificates, degrees, transcripts, and the like serve an essential role in establishing the "medium of exchange" that permits activities performed in one institution of the system to be substituted for the same activities as if they had been performed in another. Perhaps some other devices could serve the same function but not be recognized as degrees, certificates, diplomas or transcripts. It is hard to imagine what that social invention might be. But the point is to recognize that the distribution of such second-order educational benefits by the educational system is essential to what we mean by calling it a *system*. However, they are not essential to our meaning in calling that system educational. They are not themselves educational goods; they are surrogates for the possession of educational benefits, i.e., substitutes for knowledge, skill, taste, etc. But, in serving as surrogates for educational benefits, they also serve the system as a medium of exchange.

Finally, by being surrogates for the real educational benefits of knowledge, skill and taste, such devices provide the needed practical and socially workable tool for actually implementing the normative link between the distribution of educational benefits and the distribution of non-educational social goods. Certificates, diplomas, degrees, and the like, when distributed *by* the system, make it practicable for the society to allocate non-educational social goods on the basis of the distribution of educational benefits. If they were perfect surrogates for educational goods, then the implementation of the connection between these two sets of goods through the use of such certificates would be perfectly rational and without fault.

Just how this works can be illustrated in an interesting way by the behavior of the system itself. For the system allocates access to its benefits largely through the use of second-order educational goods. That is to say, the system cannot avoid distributing access in some way to its own services and resources. Access to education is a good of some kind. What kind of good is it? To which of the three categories does it belong?

Typically, the system itself allocates access to places within it. Thus, access to the system itself appears to be an educational good, since, like them, it is distributed by the system. On the other hand, the actual distribution of access to the system is carried out in practical terms through the distribution of second-order educational goods, i.e., certificates, diplomas, credentials and transcripts. Access to the services and resources of the system, in other words, appears to be an educational good, but it functions as a non-educational social good. Thus, the behavior of the system itself beautifully illustrates what it means to say that non-educational social goods are distributed on the basis of the distribution of educational goods *through the instrumentality* of second-order educational benefits.

We have then three kinds of goods whose distribution implicates the educational system (see Table 3.2).

TABLE 3.2
Distributive Benefits

1 Educational Benefits	2 Non-educational Social Benefits	3 Second-order Educational Benefits
Knowledge	Income	Certificates
Skills	Occupational opportunity	Diplomas
Taste, manners,	Status	Transcripts
standards of civility	Prestige	Licenses

The first and third groups of benefits are distributed *by* the educational system. The second group is not. Yet the most important relations between these groups of benefits are those that exist or can be made to exist between the first group, which the system does distribute, and the second group, which it does not distribute. The third group of benefits is merely the socially practical means of implementing the normative principles that establish a socially legitimate relation between the other two. Important and interesting consequences for our understanding of the system flow from the ways that these groups of benefits are distinguished. These consequences will be explored more fully in other chapters, but their salient features should be sketched here. For, without exception, they establish the kinds of approaches that can be reasonably used in the formulation of policy for the system.

It follows from the distinction between these different sets of goods that the *value* of second-order educational benefits is *exclusively* instrumental. Educational goods, on the other hand, may have either intrinsic *or* instrumental value.[3] It is perfectly rational for a person to value his knowledge, his skills, his familiarity with tradition and standards of civility for their own sake, and to seek to enlarge those capacities for the sheer pleasure of it. Indeed, the more of these goods that one can secure — beyond a certain point of basic familiarity — the more one is likely to value additions to these goods for their own sake. We would recognize a certain pathology, however, in the behavior of a person who covets degrees,

---

3. By this remark, I do not mean to deny that there are persons who *desire* diplomas and credentials *as though they were intrinsically* valuable. But, as we shall begin to see in Chapter VII that desire is in many ways pathological. Its widespread acceptance would be symptomatic of a kind of social pathology induced partly by the creation of a very large system and partly by a *very* strong and socially rationalized link between educational benefits and non-educational social goods.

diplomas, and educational certificates for their own sake. Such behavior would stand in relation to the worth of second-order educational benefits in the same way that miserliness and greed stand related to the worth of money. Both constitute misunderstandings of the value of a certain good.

This point will turn out to be of extraordinary importance for the following two reasons. First of all, the instrumental value of second-order educational benefits stems entirely from their utility in providing the socially practical link between the first group of goods and such other goods as income, status, and occupational opportunity. Suppose that that utility were to decline precipitously. Then it would follow, simply as a matter of logic, that their remaining instrumental value would be their value within the system itself. Such "tokens" would then have worth only for distributing access to the resources and services of the system. Such a state of affairs is the functional equivalent of a situation in which the primary instrumental use of second-order educational goods is to afford opportunities for more education.

Secondly, because the value of second-order educational goods is exclusively instrumental, it follows that, unlike the connection between educational goods and non-educational social goods, there are no normative principles essential to the legitimation of their distribution except those requiring them to be rationally valid surrogates of educational goods. The legitimacy of second-order educational goods is limited entirely by the extent to which they accurately indicate the possession of those particular educational goods that warrant access to certain non-educational social goods. To the extent that this claim cannot be rationally defended, second-order educational goods lose legitimacy, and the system loses whatever instrumentality it has to deliver on the claim that doing well in the system is necessary for doing well in securing the social goods of life.

The remedy, for the system, consists in restoring the rational validity of second-order educational benefits as surrogates of educational benefits. In short, what must happen is a renewed demonstration that those educational goods distributed by the system and attested to by certificates, diplomas, and the like, are, in fact those educational benefits on the basis of which we may determine the legitimate distribution of non-educational social goods. The claim that second-order educational benefits have lost their validity, or never had it, is a first premise in the reform movement called competency-based education; and the attempt to restore that validity is its central objective. Competency-based education is one of three movements attempting to reform the distributive behavior of the system by creating a more rational link between the distribution of educational benefits and the distribution of non-educational social goods through the distribution of second-order educational benefits.

DISTRIBUTION OF EDUCATIONALLY RELEVANT ATTRIBUTES

The educational system will distribute its benefits unequally, and it will do so no matter how the system is organized and no matter how "benefits" are defined. The fact is that some people will do well in the system and some will not do so well. They will reach different levels in the acquisition of knowledge, skill, taste and the standards of civility, or they will achieve the same level at different rates.[4] We do not ordinarily regard this result as unjust. We do not, for example, suppose that there is anything inherently unjust in the fact that some children are better at reading than others, that students of history learn more literature than others, or that students of physics know more mathematics than others. These inequalities in the distribution of educational benefits are inevitable, purposeful, and unobjectionable.

On the other hand, if we find that children who read poorly are almost always from a certain social class, or of a certain sex or race, then we might wonder whether such a distributive result is acceptable. We would wonder on what basis the system distributes its benefits unequally. That they are unequally distributed is inevitable, but that their unequal distribution should stem from irrelevant attributes like sex, race, or social class, does not seem inevitable. Neither does it seem justified. And such a distributive result seems unjustified because attributes like race, sex, and social class, are usually regarded as inappropriate grounds on which to justify an unequal distribution of benefits. They are, or one might say, educationally irrelevant attributes.

In short, *the system must distribute its educational benefits on the basis of the distribution of the educationally relevant attributes in the population.* What does this mean? The phrase "educationally relevant attribute" can be defined by the following criterion: If X is an educationally relevant attribute of persons, then no educational system can be charged with injustice on the grounds that it distributes its benefits to accord with the distribution of X in the population. Thus, by "educationally relevant" I do not mean "relevant to the successful conduct of the educational pro-

---

4. Levels of *achievement* in securing the goods of the system are not to be confused with achieving different levels of the system. I shall adhere to a strict distinction between educational achievement, on the one hand, and educational attainment, on the other. One's educational attainment is defined as the last level *of the system* reached. Educational achievement, however, is defined as the level of mastery of knowledge, skill, or the acquisition of taste. The two are related, but only contingently and only very roughly. Children at the same level of attainment, say, the fifth grade, may achieve at a variety of levels. Indeed, the different levels of their achievement will roughly approximate a range of five grades. There is no way to reason from the level of attainment to the level of achievement or conversely.

cess." On the contrary, I mean relevant to the grounds on which a particular distribution of educational benefits might be regarded as just or unjust. For example, social class origin may be relevant to consider in designing successful educational activities. So is ethnic origin. But if it is claimed that a distribution of benefits to accord with ethnic origin is unjust, then ethnic origin is not being regarded as an educationally relevant attribute in the sense defined here.

There are only three educationally relevant attributes of the population in this sense. They are (1) choice, (2) courage, and (3) ability. No inequality in the distribution of educational achievement can be regarded as unjust if it results from the exercise of choice, courage (or other virtues) or ability in the population. These are educationally relevant attributes for the distribution of educational benefits. On the other hand, race, sex, and social class are never the result of choice, and we assume that they are unrelated to the possession of courage — or any other virtues — and that they do not determine ability. It may be that Amish children, for example, when compared with others, achieve at a lower level. I am not sure that this is so. It is so however that, as a group, they choose not to participate in the system beyond a level somewhat lower than is typical of the rest of the population. If this results in lower levels of achievement, we would not regard it as unjust since it is a consequence of the exercise of choice.

Similarly, if someone, or some group were to benefit disproportionately from the system as a consequence of being more courageous, more persistent, more hard-working, we would not regard the resulting inequality as unjust either. On the other hand, if it could be firmly established, or if it is merely believed, that a particular class, sex, or race is specially endowed with tenacity (or other good virtues), or with ability, then it would not be regarded as unjust if they benefited disproportionately from the system. The point is not that such claims of a disproportionate concentration of educationally relevant attributes can be established. Probably they cannot. The point is rather to note what would be accomplished by such a demonstration. An educationally irrelevant attribute would then become an indicator of the presence of an educationally relevant attribute.

I am not concerned, for the moment with the *truth* of claims that blacks are less well endowed than whites, or Jews more than Gentiles. The point is rather to observe the function of such claims in the logic of the system's distributive behavior. And that function is to convert an educationally irrelevant attribute of the population into an indicator of an educationally relevant attribute. The logic of this thinking shows that we normally regard choice, tenacity, and ability to be educationally relevant attributes of the population in the sense defined and that we do not regard class, sex, and race in the same light. Even racists, sexists, elitists and egalitarians would agree with this claim.

We thus arrive at two further principles of the system. The first states that *the system must distribute its benefits to accord with the distribution of educationally relevant attributes in the population.* This statement I shall refer to henceforth as The Principle of Fair Benefit Distribution. The second states that *those attributes referred to in The Principle of Fair Benefit Distribution as "educationally relevant" are choice, tenacity and ability.*

The most important of these is ability. How shall we define it? If ability is an educationally relevant attribute, then it seems vital that we be quite clear about what ability is and what kinds are to count. We must keep in mind, however, that our purpose is to understand the structure of the system. For this purpose, it is enough to understand that however ability is defined, its distribution must be regarded by the system as a determinate factor in the fair distribution of its benefits. The actual definition of *ability* will be a frequent point of controversy. The purpose of our analysis is not to resolve that controversy, but to understand the point of it. The term may be left undefined.

This step might be viewed as an inexcusable evasion. It will seem so, however, only if we fail to understand the further fact that the system will define the term "ability" even if we do not. The point to observe is that the system, in giving an operational definition of the term "ability," will simultaneously give a more precise, and also operational, definition to what will count as educational benefits. In the operations of the system the terms *ability* and *benefit* are correlative. *Ability* will be defined as whatever it is on the basis of which the system distributes its benefits. And *benefits* will be defined as whatever it is that is distributed on the basis of ability.

As definition, such a move has the logical fault of circularity. But, nonetheless, it is a circularity that describes the behavior of the system. For example, if we think of intelligence either as an endowment or as an acquired trait, we may regard its distribution as relevant in determining the appropriate distribution of educational benefits by the system. Intelligence is one component in the definition of ability. But what is intelligence? How shall we define it?

Controversy currently rages over the use of IQ tests in determining the placement of individuals in the distribution of intelligence. It is widely agreed that intelligence tests do not measure intelligence in any large and inclusive sense of the term. But the use of such measures is often defended on the grounds that they *do* measure the abilities needed to do well in school. And being able to measure *that*, it is argued, is no small matter. In such a defense, ability — in this case intelligence — is defined as whatever it is on the basis of which the system distributes its benefits. This is a perfectly reasonable operational definition of one part of ability. But the further assumption is implicit that whatever benefits are distributed by the system can be defined, partly, at least, as those that are distributed on the basis of ability.

This logical circularity, in other words, reflects a social reality. Understanding it is absolutely vital to understanding the system. It explains, for example, why no system is in serious trouble as long as only one of these terms is opened for redefinition. The system can always provide an operational definition in terms of the other. It also explains why no policy proposal for the system would be truly radical if it seeks redefinitions of either *ability* or *benefit* as though they were independent terms.

Summary

Thus, the distributive behavior of the system is determined by the value of educational benefits, the instrumental utility of second-order benefits for the distribution of non-educational social goods, and finally, by the relation between these benefits and the distribution of educationally relevant attributes of the population through the operation of the Principle of Fair Benefit Distribution. The dynamics established by the relations between these different goods are complex in the extreme. They will necessarily occupy a central position in any effort to describe the behavior of the system.

·◦[IV]◦·

THE EDUCATIONAL SYSTEM
Hierarchical Principles

T HE SYSTEM HAS A STRUCTURE. Parts of it can be discovered in the dynamics of its control; others in the need for some medium of exchange; still others in the social beliefs implicit in the modes of growth, and in the principles of the system's distributive behavior. But, figuratively speaking, these are all features of the system's horizontal structure. We know, however, that the system is also organized hierarchically. The principle of sequence is among its most fundamental features (see Chapter I).

This layered structure is more complex, however, than is suggested by any simple rendering of the principle of sequence. It is found not only in the existence of grades within schools, and in the presence of higher and lower schools, but also in the fact that the system has a status structure. Among higher and lower schools, there are schools of higher and lower status, and furthermore, among the various curricula of the schools, there are differences of status reflecting status differences among positions within the society. So the hierarchical structure of the system is complex. It includes properties captured by the principle of sequence, but it includes much more than that.

That the system has such features may seem self-evident, yet neither their consequences nor their origins are self-evident or well understood. They deserve a considered examination; for, at least in certain of their features, they rest upon quite intractable facts of logic and of human nature. They are therefore likely to be among the most durable features of the system even if the system undergoes drastic and rapid change. We may identify the hierarchical principles of the system under three major headings: The Hierarchies and Downward Drift of Learning, The Self-Regulating Hierarchies of the System as Employer, and, finally, The Hierarchies of Status.

53

THE HIERARCHIES AND DOWNWARD DRIFT OF LEARNING

Learning and Time

Consider, to begin with, the obvious fact that learning takes time and that learning some things takes a long time indeed. Learning is *never* instantaneous.[1] It follows that if some skill is to be learned by a certain time, then we must begin learning it at some earlier time. And if somebody learning it requires somebody teaching it, then if we want a certain skill to be developed by the time a certain level of the system is reached, we must start teaching it at some earlier level. Differences of level, viewed in this way, are differences in time. The result is that the specification of the curriculum moves downward in the system. That is one of the ways that the levels of the system are connected. The connection arises from the undoubted fact that learning takes time. It is worth noting, moreover, that those skills whose acquisition we construe to take a very long time indeed are those that tend to recur in teaching at every level of the system, such things as reading, writing, computing, the principles of science, their application, and other subjects deemed essential in the cultivation of thought.[2]

Consider, secondly, the obvious fact that for anything that can be learned, there will be different levels of mastery. This is the truth that we presuppose in every setting where we speak of elementary, intermediate, and advanced levels of achievement in the acquisition of any skill or in the mastery of any subject. It is a corollary of the proposition that learning takes time. These two propositions, taken together, suggest that there is a rough, but important, connection between the amount of time spent in learning and the levels of achievement reached. And this suggestion is correct, as far as it goes.

But there is this difficulty. Though it is true, without exception, that learning takes time, it is not true, conversely, that if more time is spent, more will be learned. If we continue to construe the levels of the system as different levels of time spent, then there will be a connection between the levels of the system and levels of achievement reached. But that connec-

1. This observation does not exclude the possibility of the so-called "Ahah! phenomenon," the occurrence of sudden insight, which may *seem* to be instantaneous. The concept of learning is ambiguous, however. Sometimes it refers to a process and sometimes to an achievement. Learning, as process or activity, is never instantaneous, and learning as achievement -- as the occurrence of sudden insight, for example -- is always the terminus of an activity that does take time.

2. Note, furthermore, that these are the skills and competencies that tend to be associated with the higher status positions in the society and the higher status curricula in the school.

tion must be weak. The connection arises from the fact that learning takes time. The weakness of the connection arises from the fact that though learning takes time, it does not follow that more time spent will necessarily result in more learning.

The more important implications of this second obvious fact are to be found, however, in another direction. We assume that higher levels of mastery are preferable to lower levels. Nobody favors incompetence. If higher levels of achievement in any skill or subject can be attained by starting earlier, then it is preferable to start earlier. And if they can be attained by keeping at it longer, then it is preferable to keep at it longer. Of course, starting earlier can be a way of keeping at it longer. If mastery takes time, and higher levels of mastery are preferable to lower ones, then there is reason, in the practical argument of the system, to start earlier and earlier in the mastery of any subject or skill that takes a long time. Again, the practical reasoning of the system reinforces the downward drift in the specification of what is to be learned and at what level of mastery.

The Imperatives of the Technological Market

This downward drift has its sources also in the imperatives of the technological market. If there is to be a continuing market for any technology, that technology must be used. If its use requires the exercise of new and specialized skills, then those skills will have to be acquired and widely shared within the population or there will be no market for the technology. In a society where people lack the skill of reading time, there is unlikely to be a large market for clocks and watches. The mere creation, and even perfection, of computers is an insufficient condition for the existence of a market for computers. They must be used, and for their use there must be a rather widespread familiarity with the principles and operation of computers.

It is vital here to distinguish between a new technology and a new invention. A new technology is a fairly rare kind of invention. But we must further distinguish between those new technologies whose use requires the acquisition of particular skills and those whose use does not. The creation of the wireless is the invention of a new technology; indeed, it is the prelude to an entire family of new technologies. But no special skills are needed to operate a radio receiver. Hence, the market for radio receivers requires the spread of no new skills. In contrast, the operation of telegraphy or of typewriters does require special skills. Therefore, the market for such devices is limited by the spread of certain skills.

But how do such skills become widespread? For this, the producers of the technology must either rely on some other existing institutions, or they must undertake to do it themselves. Where schools exist, it will either be done in schools, or else those who market the technology will have to do it through schools or programs of instruction of their own. The preferable solution is for the system to take on the task of developing the skills needed for the creation and maintenance of the technological market. In short, we expect the system to be the primary agency for developing an expanding pool and array of skills. If "the system" fails, then the society will not sustain a large and continuing market for technologies whose use requires the exercise of special skills and abilities.

This assumption about the social value of the system cannot be lightly abandoned. We are unlikely, even in an attentive study of this assumption to discover any alternative. Yet, the fact that we rely on the system for the sustenance of technological markets, can only be counted as prelude. What is the dominant theme?

The history of every new technology victorious in the market is the history of the downward drift in the social acquisition of its principles and the skills of its applications. The first computer programmers were the inventors and creators of the hardware. They were persons highly trained in mathematics and engineering. The next generation of programmers were doubtless possessed of training almost as advanced. But surely, the third generation were taught the art of programming without either prior training in advanced mathematics or engineering or in programs of the system designed to produce programming skills. They were trained either by the agencies who marketed the hardware or by those who wished to use it. They could not have been trained by the system because in the beginning of any new technology, there never are such programs in the system. But as the principles of the technology become better and more widely understood and as the required skills become more clearly identified, programs will develop first at the advanced levels of college and then will extend into the secondary and even elementary schools.[3] In 1840 there was only one

3. This downward drift may seem obviously applicable in the case of computer programming. But does it fit generally? Does it, for example, describe the process for the spread of typing skills and the creation of a market for typewriters? Consider a single case -- Syracuse, New York. The typewriter was first mass-produced in 1874, but there was little demand for it until the next decade. In 1881 only 1,200 typewriters were sold nationally. *Boyd's Directory of Syracuse* for the year 1876-77 lists the occupation of one William King as "typewriter," and until 1883, his is the only such listing. By 1890, however, the "typewriting" category of the business directory had come to represent only those individuals who were engaged in either selling typewriters or in giving lessons. Operators were listed under the heading "stenographer." In 1890, of the three kinds of listings under "typewriter" there were two dealers, three persons offering lessons, and one offering both sales and lessons. There were also two typewriter supply stores and two business colleges offering typing courses. In the actual spread of typing skills, the central question was not where or by whom the skill should be taught, but whether it needed to be taught at all. Typing by "hunt and peck" requires

textbook in calculus available in the United States, and it was used at advanced graduate levels of the system. Now there are 150, and the topic is taught in many high schools.

In short, if X is a technical capacity desired for the technological market, then that capacity will be sought first at a relatively high level of the system and then at successively lower levels. The path in the social acquisition of such technical skills is downward, and moreover, it is downward, eventually, within the system. Their social acquisition does not require the existence of the educational system. There are methods of accomplishing the same result by extended indenture, apprenticeship, or home study. But if the system is available, it will be used. And it is likely to be used, because it is the most efficient solution to the problem of creating and sustaining the market for any technology. The imperatives of the technological market reinforce, once again, the tendency for the curriculum to be defined in the downward drift of what is to be learned.

Given the principles already identified — that learning takes time, and that there are levels of mastery — it is easy to see how this downward drift is made to occur. Without our even having to think about it, the system mandates a kind of natural experiment in early learning. To see this, let us assume that a particular level of achievement in a given skill is desired by the end of level L, and that reaching that degree of mastery is believed to take more than one year.[4] It follows that we must begin developing the desired skill at a level of the system below L.

no teacher, but typing by "the touch system" does. The victory of the touch system made the machine more useful, but also created the need for instruction. It became necessary for the selling agent to provide training. William King was such a marketer-teacher. Individuals who had the skill began to offer instruction. Between 1885 and 1900 a number of such "informal" schools appeared and they were often associated with firms offering typing services. The next step was the introduction of typing into the business schools of the community. The first was in 1884. By 1900 five schools were offering such courses, and by 1910 there were eight. Finally, the public school system responded. In his annual report of 1898 the Superintendent of the Syracuse schools wrote, "It is wise, I think, to hold to a conservative position concerning innovations and fads that are receiving attention in some localities, and endeavor to eliminate rather than ingraft these features." And even after the development of a commercial high school in 1900, the principal complained in his report that many students were leaving the program before completion so that they could complete a typing course in the local business schools. And so, in 1908 typing was finally offered as an 11th grade elective. The following year it was made a 10th grade elective and a specialization in the 11th and 12th grades. By 1916, the schools in San Francisco and Los Angeles were offering stenography and typing at the 7th and 8th levels. The progression was from (1) skill development by the retailer, to (2) informal instruction, to (3) business schools, to (4) the public schools, and from higher to lower levels in the system. (*The Downward Drift of the Typewriter: 1874 to 1930*, Research Memorandum by Edward O'Neil, unpublished, December, 1977.)

4. These assumptions are by no means unusual. They are satisfied, in fact, more often than not in actual experience.

We are led, in short, to begin an experiment. Suppose it is *true* that the level of achievement desired in the wanted skill can be acquired earlier than L. We are likely to discover that truth because in order to get the desired result at the Lth level of the system we shall already have started *trying* to get it at L−1. If we discover that it is possible to get the desired *result* at L−1, then either we shall have discovered that no more than a year is needed, or else that we can begin at L−2 and reach a higher level of achievement at L. As long as we believe that attaining the desired skill and mastery takes more than one year, and that it is desirable to maximize achievement, then we shall be led, willy nilly, into an attempt to push its attainment to successively lower levels of the system. We are led, in short, by the logic of the hierarchical structure of the system, together with the exigencies of time, to test the possibilities of progressively earlier and earlier achievement.

Limits on the Downward Drift of Learning

Is there no limit to this downward drift? Does it have no practical terminus? Of course it does; and that limit has *at least* two conceivable sources. Suppose that, in the nature of things, there are prerequisites.[5] Suppose, in other words, that learning some things requires that other things be learned first. We are familiar with talk of basics. Of course, it may be doubted that there are certain things that must be learned in order that other things can be learned. What we sometimes think of as prerequisites in this sense may be, in reality, only different levels of mastery. Is the mastery of simple algebraic expressions a genuine prerequisite for the study of functions or is it merely a lower level of mastery in algebra? But whether the existence of such prerequisites is rooted in the nature of learning and development or in the nature of knowledge, the claim that there are such prerequisites provides one kind of meaning to the idea that there are basics in education.

In order to grasp the connection between the structure of curriculum, the downward drift of learning, and the hierarchical structure of the system, the concept of "prerequisites" is important. Its proper interpretation requires careful adherence to the ancient distinction between the order of being and the order of learning. By "the order of being" is meant the logical or ontological order of things. The word "order" in "the order of being"

5. "...in the nature of things." One wants to ask "In the nature of *what* things?" Are we referring to things psychological, logical, social or metaphysical? This question must be answered, but its answer is deferred. Nor do we assume, *at this point,* that there are any such prerequisites.

implies nothing about temporal sequence, nor, in the same context, does the prefix in *"pre*requisite" have the meaning of temporal precedence. Let us suppose, for example, that, as Russell and Whitehead attempted to establish, all of mathematics is deducible from logic. It would follow that in the order of being, logic is prior to, more fundamental than, or *pre*requisite to mathematics. It would not follow, however, that anyone does, should, or must learn logic before learning mathematics. Logic would then be understood as prerequisite in the order of being, but not necessarily in the order of learning.

What can come before what, in the order of learning, is always an empirical question; but what is more fundamental than what, in the order of being, is never an empirical question. Thus, when we know the logical or ontological structure of a certain field of human knowledge, it does not follow that we know anything about the pedagogical order or the order of learning. From the point of view of logic, trigonometry is an extension of geometry and algebra. It therefore comes after geometry and algebra. But, from the point of view of learning, it may be that one should learn algebra and geometry through the study of trigonometry. Similarly, moral theory is the account of the first principles of the moral life. But its study is not necessary, or for that matter even desirable, in the order of moral development. Indeed, it is only from "the moral point of view" that one can study moral theory at all. As Aristotle put it, first principles may be the last learned, but they remain first nonetheless. Thus, the order of learning can be, and often is, the converse of the logical order of things.

Curriculum is often constructed in an effort to make the order of learning reflect the order of being. But they are not the same thing, nor can one reason from one to the other. The failure to distinguish between these two senses of prerequisite goes far to account for the disposition of academics to discuss questions of course prerequisites — always an empirical matter — as though they were discussing a question that could be decided a priori from the lore of the academic guild. When we enter the domain of the order of learning, then the "pre" in "prerequisite" has the meaning of temporal precedence, and then also the temporal constraints arising from the hierarchical structure of the system become imposed upon the solution to problems of curricular sequence.

Without some version of the concept of prerequisite — whether rooted in the order of learning or in the order of being — we could make no sense of the idea that some things to be learned — reading and computation, for example — are more basic than other things. Let us recall, however, that learning takes time. Therefore, learning the basics, however defined, takes time. If learning X requires that one has already learned Y, then the earliest point at which one can *begin* learning X is the point at which one has learned

Y. This inference establishes a limit to the downward drift of the curriculum.

The second source of such a limit arises from the possible existence of a second kind of prerequisite. It may be that there are stages in the natural morphology of cognitive and physical development, and therefore stages at which certain kinds of learning cannot occur. Abstractions or symbol manipulation, for example, may not be "learnable" at certain stages in human development. The acquisition of physical skills may be similarly constrained. Their appearance may require the attainment of certain stages of physical maturation. Learning takes time, but so does passage through the various stages of physical and cognitive development. Thus, any stage theory in education will presuppose (1) that passage through the various stages of development takes time, and (2) that the stages are related so that later stages are reached only by passing through earlier ones.[6] We have here another view of prerequisites. Thus, if reaching stage X requires that one pass through stage Y, then the earliest time at which one can reach stage X is the time at which one has already attained stage Y. This inference sets a limit on the downward drift of what is to be learned. But it is a limit stemming not from the nature of the thing to be learned, but from the nature of the human organism and its physical or psychological development.

The layered structure of the system reflects these temporal, logical, and developmental considerations which, in turn, reinforce the assumption that the system will be hierarchically ordered. If we could start *do novo* to construct an educational system, we would end by constructing a system with levels precisely because we could not escape the weight of these considerations.

But nothing in these remarks implies that the levels need correspond in any strict way to chronological age. Even so, there is likely to be a gross and rough correspondence between the levels of the system and age, and there are reasons to think that that correspondence will tend to become dis-

6. There is a further logical requirement that must be satisfied, but is seldom acknowledged, by any stage theory of prerequisites in education. Consider the claim that children pass through certain stages in their cognitive, physical, and moral development, and that those stages are features of human morphology. Consider also the very different claim that in order to learn certain things, we must first have learned certain others, and that these prerequisites are epistemologically rather than morphologically rooted. They stem from the nature of knowledge rather than from the nature of human development. I know of no data that can be accounted for by one of these claims that cannot be accounted for by the other. In short, it is not easy to see on what empirical grounds it is possible to base a choice between these two claims. Yet, they have different meanings that are likely to be reflected in different pedagogical practices. Yet the adoption of a stage theory in human learning must rest either upon the demonstration that there is a clear empirical difference between these quite different claims, or else it will rest merely upon an understandable human preference for one pedagogy over another.

criminating and precise, especially at the lower levels of the system. Why? First of all, if it is discovered that the stages of human development correspond roughly to some modal period of time, then it will follow that the achievement levels will reflect age groupings even though the levels of the system are not *defined* by age. There are some periods in the life of an individual during which change is sizeable and rapid. We tend to think, for example, that the developmental distance between the ages of nine and sixteen is greater than between the ages of thirty and thirty-seven. Great change in physical, social and cognitive development can occur within a relatively small period of years or even months during the first two decades of life. Any educational system whose principles require no close correspondence between its levels and chronological age, but which defines the levels instead to accord with such developmental changes, is likely nonetheless, to produce age groupings and to produce them, for some periods of the life cycle, to accord with age differences of perhaps no more than three years.[7]

Furthermore, in giving institutional form to the definition of different levels in the system, these developmental considerations are likely to be more difficult to ignore than equally large differences in cognitive and intellectual development. For example, everyone is in favor of the young learning to care for the younger. It is part of growing up. Yet, the prospect that one's own children might be placed in the care of older youth or placed under their influence on a regular basis is enough to excite intense fear in the minds of most parents. In this respect parental interests enter strongly into the control of the system, and they reinforce the disposition to define the levels of the system — especially in its lower reaches — in ways that will accord with rather precise differences of age.

There are further, but less immediately powerful reasons why the system, having levels, will tend to implement its hierarchical structure in ways that make it, as we say, age-graded. If we attend to the incidence of high achievement in skills and subjects that typically take a very long time to master, there will, once again, be a kind of gross correspondence of achievement to age. Mastering the piano takes a long time. Thus, few accomplished pianists are children, and we acknowledge their rarity by referring to them as "prodigies" — a term that etymologically implies the idea of something done even before it can be thought. One can be a

7. This seems a reasonable estimate. How much truth is there to the assumption that the American system is rigorously age-graded? Answer: Quite a bit, but perhaps not as much as is commonly supposed. The decennial census reports the age distribution at each level of the system. The 1970 Census reports that of all those enrolled at the twelfth level of the system (a total of 3,311,982), 2.25 percent were age 16, 51.56 percent were age 17, 34.56 percent were age 18, and 8.54 percent were age 19. The total of these *four* years constitutes nearly 97 percent of the total enrollment at that level, and the age group of 17 and 18 year olds constitute 86 percent of the total. Is this a strict kind of age-gradedness?

beginner, of course, in any skill or any subject at any age. But one is highly unlikely to be a master at an early age in any achievement that takes as long as mastery of the piano. There is a correspondence between high achievement and age — both in the system and out of it — simply because learning takes time and because age is the inevitable accompaniment of the passage of time.

Conversely, if there are some skills, dispositions, or characteristics that are regarded as important for everyone to master, and if their mastery takes a long time, then one is likely to find a preponderance of the young among those at the lower mastery levels of such achievements. Besides, if there are any skills, dispositions, or subjects that are deemed by the society to be important for all, the disposition will be to start early with all. Thus, beginners in some things tend to be the young, and the accomplished in others tend to be the old, and this gross correspondence of the levels of the system to differences of age arises from quite intractable features of the hierarchies of learning and human nature. The levels of the system have been defined by the hierarchies of learning and not by differences of age. We see nonetheless that those levels will roughly, not precisely, correspond to differences in age — more at the lower levels of the system than at the upper.

THE SELF-REGULATING HIERARCHIES OF THE SYSTEM AS EMPLOYER

The System as its Own Market

There are other kinds of hierarchies and other resulting dynamics than those arising from the downward drift of learning. Consider an example of another sort. *If the system substantially and quickly expands its programs of early childhood education, then it will expand its graduate programs.* In short, expansion at the lower reaches of the system requires expansion at its higher reaches. The converse may also be the case. A substantial expansion of graduate programs in early childhood education may strengthen whatever interests exist to expand the system at a pre-school level.

I do not advance these conditional propositions as the expression of true causal claims. The point is rather to illustrate the kinds of claims implicit in our ordinary thinking about the system, claims that presuppose a connection between its different *levels*. In general if there is any change, x, at a given level, L, such that its occurrence produces or requires a change at

L±n, then we have strong evidence that the different levels are systemically related. This principle is merely another version of the downward drift of learning. This is the kind of relationship that we appeal to when we reason that expansion of the system at the bottom will produce or require expansion at the top. Any empirical evidence that such a relationship exists is added evidence that some kind of hierarchical system exits.

What is it then, that we presuppose, when we so easily reason from an expansion of early childhood education to an accompanying expansion of graduate education? This inference is perhaps as illicit as any we could invent. Yet, there is a certain initial plausibility about it. That plausibility can only be traced to the unstated principle that *programs of early childhood education must be staffed by persons who are specialists in early childhood education and that such specialists must themselves be the product of graduate programs of the system.* I know of no other premise that would suffice to establish the kind of connection between the lower and higher levels of the system exemplified in the example. Surely, if we believed, as a general rule, that programs of early childhood education could be staffed by *any* person who had completed high school or less in the system, then the inference that if they expand, then graduate programs will also expand would have no plausibility whatever.[8]

We may put the point quite generally. We see a connection between the upper and lower levels of the system partly because we assume that *positions in the system must be staffed by persons who are products of the system.* That is to say, qualifications for holding a position within the system include educational prerequisites. *The system is itself a part of the market for its own product.*

This principle is rich in implications. There are, of course, other institutions, sets of institutions, or sub-systems in the society that share this feature of being part of the market for their own product. General Motors, for example, undoubtedly owns cars, and they are unlikely to be Ford and Chrysler products. Thus, General Motors is a purchaser of automobiles as well as a producer. It is a part of its own market. But its role as consumer represents a small share of the total market for General Motors cars. If it were to become a large share, say, one-fifth of the total

---

8. It is worth noting other things presupposed in this inference. They include the claim that there are relevant differences stemming from the nature of child development so that we require specialists in early childhood to staff programs in early childhood education. That is to say, it presupposes that persons qualified as secondary teachers are not, *by virtue of their qualifications,* suitable also as teachers in early childhood education. There is something special about early childhood. The relation between levels in the system rests not only upon organizational principles of the system, but also upon considerations concerning the hierarchies of learning and the morphology of human development.

market, then General Motors, as producer, would be in a strong position to design its products to meet its own requirements as consumer.

By analogy, we are led to see the importance of asking what share of the total market for educated persons is represented by the educational system itself, whether the size of that share changes under conditions of expansion or contraction, whether it changes at different points in the total growth of the system, and finally whether there are any indicators of a point at which the system's share of the market makes it possible for the system, as producer, to define the educational process solely to meet the needs of the system as employer.[9] We can say, *a priori,* that *the educational system's share in the total market for educated persons will increase whenever the total number of positions within the system expands more rapidly than the number of positions in the employment system requiring an educational prerequisite.* Each of the modes of growth is likely to produce this state of affairs (see Chapter I). Thus, we arrive at the conjecture that as the system expands so will its capacity to define the educational process in ways designed to satisfy the requirements for assuming positions within the system itself.

Differentiation and Professionalization

When we recognize that the system is a part of its own market, we are also in a position to understand the importance of charting the differentiation of roles within the system and the consequences for the system of differentiating roles outside. Role differentiation within the system is one way of expanding the system's total share in the market for educated persons. The creation of a demand for guidance counselors will create a demand for graduate programs preparing such persons. And, in general, when new roles are created within the society — quality control engineers, social workers, communication specialists — those who first create the roles are unlikely to have been prepared by educational programs in the system. But, by the same token, they are also unlikely to permit their successors to be so ill prepared. Thus, role differentiation outside the system is likely to be accompanied by program differentiation within the system and by the establishment of educational prerequisites for admission to its practice.

9. It is significant, for these reasons, to note from 1931 to 1953, among all the different fields of study, the largest single proportion of bachelor's and first professional degrees awarded in the United States was degrees granted in education. It ranged from 14.8 to 23.1 percent of the total. See *A Statistical Portrait of Higher Education* by Seymour E. Harris (New York: McGraw-Hill, 1972), Table 2.3-4, p. 318.

We call this process professionalization. Role differentiation within the system is simply a special case of this same process by which educational prerequisites are extended to more and more social roles within the society. Thus, parents were the first early childhood educators. But as soon as a role is created in the system and distinguished not only from parental roles, but also from the roles of other teachers, then programs are established to prepare persons for such roles and educational prerequisites are created for their selection.

This process may seem to stand only in the most tenuous relation to the hierarchies of the system. Yet, I note it here because it is important in the general effort to account for our inference from an expansion of early childhood education to an expansion of the graduate levels in the system. It is an important process to note in trying to understand how the different levels of the system are related and how that relationship is, in turn, connected with the modes of growth.

We assume that positions in the system are to be staffed by persons who are themselves products of the system. But this formulation is still incomplete. The belief we are groping for includes the claim that the system must be staffed by persons who are products of the system at some level higher than the one to be staffed. Yet, even this version is incomplete. How much higher than a given level must a person have progressed in order to qualify? We cannot require positions at the highest levels of the system to be staffed by those who have completed still higher levels. Thus, if we imagine a system with twenty levels of attainment, we can staff the first level exclusively from those who have progressed nineteen levels higher, but we cannot follow such a rule in staffing the twentieth level.

Though we can staff the different levels of the system with those from the highest, it does not follow that we must or will do so. Nonetheless, we are likely to do so to whatever extent the supply of educated persons will permit. After all, we would not staff a first grade class with a first grade student, nor even, if we can help it, with an adult who had only completed the first grade. We would reach for a person who had attained a much higher level in the system. We would find no similar difficulties, however, in staffing an advanced graduate seminar with a person who has never completed the highest degree. We will tend to reach as far above the level to be staffed as we possibly can. The lower we go in the system the greater is the distance we seem to require between the level staffed and the level of the system attained by the person staffing it. The greatest such distance would occur at the lowest level of the system. Thus, we should not be surprised to discover that expansion of the system at the lowest level requires expansion at the highest level.

The Principle of Uniform Growth

The principle we are seeking then looks something like this: *The system will tend to require any level, L, to be staffed by persons who have completed L + n in the system so that n will decline as L increases.* This principle does *not* state that those who staff progressively higher levels of the system must have completed progressively higher levels of the system themselves. It focuses attention rather on the *distance* between the level of the system to be staffed and the level attained by the person who staffs that level. In fact, this principle would be satisfied even in a system where every position is staffed by persons who have completed the highest level. In that case, the distance between the level to be staffed and the level attained by the person staffing it would be a continuous slope function of the progressively higher levels of the system.

This state of affairs is, in fact, what the system tends toward, i.e., a state of affairs in which every position in the system is staffed by a person who has completed the highest level, which is to say, earned the highest degree. Why else would we so easily adopt the assumption that anyone who holds a regular position as undergraduate teacher must have completed a level higher than an undergraduate degree in the field that he is teaching,[10] and that that undergraduate faculty is best whose members have completed the highest level in the greatest numbers. No one doubts that the number of Ph.D.s on an undergraduate faculty is used as a measure of quality. And as the number of Ph.D.s approaches 100 percent at one level of the system, it is likely to be viewed as a more important measure of quality at the next lower level.

The long run tendency of the system is to continually expand and to reach toward a point where it is staffed entirely by persons who have completed the highest level of the system. This principle can be equivalently rendered in the claim that the system will tend either to expand or to raise the educational prerequisites for any position in the system or both *regardless of the supply of qualified candidates.* In order to grasp the importance of this claim, it will be helpful to consider in detail two quite contrasting sets of circumstances, *Model Case #1,* in which the supply of

---

10.   There are notable exceptions to this rule that an undergraduate teacher must have completed a level higher than an undergraduate degree in the field that he is teaching. There are institutions that do not exemplify the rule. But, as we shall see in the next chapter, these exceptions are most notable because of their tendency to cluster around the top and the bottom of the institutional status hierarchy of the system. An institution secure in its position at the top of the status hierarchy is less likely to demand the Ph.D. for undergraduate teachers than an institution somewhat lower and more insecure in status. And a low status institution is more likely to insist on a faculty of Ph.D.s but is also less likely to succeed in getting it.

qualified persons exceeds the demand, and *Model Case #2,* in which the demand exceeds the supply.

Model Case #1. Let us imagine a situation in which there are 100 positions to be filled in the system at level L, and 400 candidates with qualifications for positions at L or higher. How might the system respond *to these features* of the situation? It could respond either by (1) raising the qualifications until only 100 candidates remain, or (2) leaving the qualifications unchanged and simultaneously increasing the number of positions for persons with L qualifications, or (3) by a combination of raising the qualifications and increasing the number of positions available.

There are two points important to observe about these alternatives. First of all, we must admit that other things may happen in the system than those included in these three choices. For example, the qualifications might be lowered rather than raised or they might remain unchanged without any accompanying attempt to increase the number of positions for persons with L qualifications. Either of these is a logically possible course of action. They are both excluded, however, because neither can be regarded as a *response to* conditions of having more qualified persons than positions. Indeed, if either course of events were to actually occur, it would have to occur on some other grounds than as a response to an oversupply of qualified persons. We may put the point in another way. An oversupply of persons with L qualifications or better *can* constitute a good reason for either raising the qualifications of anyone to secure a position at that level or for increasing the number of positions or some combination. But such circumstances would not constitute a good reason for either lowering the qualifications or for leaving them unchanged. Hence, either lowering the qualifications or doing nothing may constitute courses of action in response to *some* situation facing the system, but they will not count as a response to an oversupply of qualified persons.

The second point is that these alternatives might be carried out in a variety of ways. Selecting what to do does not determine how to do it. For example, suppose we had a system (which we do not) in which the qualifications for positions at each successive level were higher than those for the level just preceding. Then one way to raise the qualifications for a position at L would be to simply apply the standards of each successively higher level until only 100 persons qualified.

But there are other ways to do the same thing. In any situation where there are 400 persons *equally* qualified for only 100 positions, it follows as a matter of mere logic, that the 100 selected will be selected on some other grounds than qualifications, i.e., they will be selected on the basis of friendship, preference, prejudice, convenience, or power. Introducing such factors into the situation is the functional equivalent of raising qualifications, even though the kinds of qualifications introduced are not *educational* qualifications and are not the kind that can be given any rational, meritocratic justification.[11]

Thus, there are multiple ways of raising qualifications. There are also multiple ways of increasing the number of positions for persons of L qualifications. The most obvious way is to increase the number of positions in the system at the level L. The arguments typically used to endorse this move are quite familiar. They illustrate, once again, a point touched upon earlier, namely that insofar as the system is an *educational* system, there are no operable incentives to maximize technical efficiency (see Chapter I).

Thus, if it is better to have only twenty students for each teacher in the system rather than forty, then it must be better yet to have only five students for each teacher. And if that is better, then presumably, it will be better still to have two teachers to each student. This is a powerful argument for increasing the number of positions at L in the system, even when there is an excess of qualified persons at that level. But it is an argument that rests upon educational grounds, and not on grounds of efficiency.[12]

It is worth pondering that arguments offered in support of reducing the number of students per teacher in the system always rest upon educational reasons, and arguments offered in support of increasing the number of students per teacher always rest upon claims of technical efficiency. In short, there are no educational limits imposed on the reduction of the number of students per teacher, and therefore, no educational arguments that, in respect to this particular problem, rest upon standards of technical

11. It might be objected that because such bases for choice as friendship and preference cannot be given a meritocratic justification, therefore, they should not be regarded as qualifications. There is warrant for this judgment in the ordinary use of the term "qualification." Nonetheless, I include them for two reasons. First, because they do constitute additional criteria that are employed when other standards do not suffice; therefore, they do function as qualifications function. Secondly, though they cannot be justified on meritocratic grounds they can often be justified on non-meritocratic grounds. For example, it probably is true that, to an extent lying just short of "cronyism," friends will work better together than strangers, even though, on other grounds, the strangers may be more qualified.

12. Does such an argument always rest on educational grounds? Consider how we might estimate the future demand for teachers. We may project a constantly growing demand by introducing the premise that a constantly decreasing ratio of students to teachers is educationally desirable. Whether such a premise can be given sound educational defense is something that can be doubted. It cannot be doubted, however, that it expresses the perceived interests of incumbents in the system, especially when the system is confronted with declining enrollments. Thus, what is offered as an educational argument may be grasped instead as simply the expression of the interests of incumbents. In general, for reasons made explicit in Chapter VIII, it is always preferable for the selfish interests of incumbents to be advanced through arguments that reverberate with a concern for educational excellence. The essential point, however, is to note that in neither construction of the premise will the argument rest on claims of efficiency.

efficiency. Insofar as the system is educational, incentives to efficiency do not enter significantly into defining the number of positions to be available in the system. Insofar as the system is a system, however, it must be managed, and, for that reason, some standards of technical efficiency will be imposed in determining the number of positions in the system. But they will be imposed always to be retracted whenever the educational issues again become serious.

There is a second way to increase the number of positions in the system for persons of L qualifications. We might adopt the assumption that anyone qualified to hold a position at L is qualified to hold one at any level lower than L.[13] A third choice would be to extend the qualifications for anyone at L within the system so that such qualifications become first sufficient, then necessary for anyone to qualify for certain positions normally regarded as outside the system. Thus, we might seek to create roles within the penal system, the medical system, or in industry to be filled only by persons who are qualified to fill positions *within* the system. This alternative amounts to an extension of the system into institutions where it had not extended before. It is a strategy for increasing the number of positions for persons with L qualifications in the system. It is that mode of growth, in short, that we described (Chapter I) as horizontal.

The main import of these observations may be summarized as follows. First, the conditions set in our model case are often believed to require a contraction of the system as opposed to expansion. Secondly, the terms of that model case do not specify the causes of a surplus of qualified persons for positions in the system. The surplus may result from a decline in the size of the school-age cohort at the lower levels of the system, or from an inordinately large number of persons preparing to assume positions in the system, or both. Or it may result merely from an unusually stable staff within the system together with a constant or growing number of persons preparing to enter that work force.

But the point is that whatever may be the sources of a surplus of qualified persons, and however much we may be inclined to view these circumstances as conditions of no-growth, the fact is that the tendency of the system, under these circumstances, will be to either raise the qualifications for positions within the system, to increase the number of positions within it, or to expand the system itself so that qualifications for its posi-

---

13. This is a choice that would be dysfunctional to adopt in the unqualified way in which it is stated. Nonetheless, it illustrates a possible systemic response to the conditions set in Model Case #1, and it is feasible within limits. For example, it is implausible to suggest that anyone qualified to teach in the ninth grade is *therefore* qualified to be a preschool teacher, though it is not implausible to suggest that such a one may be qualified to teach at the eighth or even the sixth levels.

tions will be increasingly required for assuming employment roles outside the system. In short, under those conditions that we normally think of as requiring contraction, the tendency of the system will be to expand or to raise its qualifications or both.

We need not persist, however, at this abstract level of thought in considering this rather counter-intuitive claim. The terms of our first model case describe some aspects of the situation actually faced by the American system at the moment, and they are likely to persist for some years to come. What do we observe happening? We observe, first of all, a movement, with wide support, to extend the system so that schooling begins earlier, and secondly, a correspondingly growing interest in extending educational opportunities to later periods of life, even to something called "life-long learning." But in addition to these movements — so evident to everyone — to extend the system beyond its highest levels and below its lowest, we need only wait for some thorough defense of horizontal expansion. And sure enough! In the *Teachers College Record* for May 1976, we find an example, an article by Robert Nash and Edward Ducharme called "A Futures Perspective on Preparing Educators for the Human Service Society: How to Restore a Sense of Social Purpose to Teacher Education." But the appearance of such articles is only a symptom. One will do well to ponder in the same context the rapid and recent increase in the number of college programs addressed to "new careers in education."

It is important to keep in mind, however, that the qualifications we have been considering are *educational* prerequisites or educational *attainment* prerequisites. *They are not standards of performance.* If we were to replace these educational prerequisites with performance standards, the hierarchical structure of the system would be drastically altered. In that case, we could no longer make the inferential leap, for example, from an expansion of early childhood programs in the system to an expansion of graduate programs in early childhood studies. If a person can qualify for a position in the system at level L entirely on the basis of performance standards, then it is a stark irrelevance to ask whether that person has attained at some level higher than L. Indeed, it is irrelevant whether he has attained at any level lower than L. In short, attainment, in that case, is irrelevant to qualifications for positions within the system.

It is equally vital to note, however, that if performance standards for securing positions in the system are used only as a supplement to educational attainment standards, and not as a substitute for them, it would still follow that expansion of early childhood programs in the system would lead to expansion of studies in early childhood at the higher levels. In short, *the different levels of the system, as we know it, are hierarchically connected not by the application of performance standards, but by the application of*

educational attainment qualifications in staffing the system. If performance standards are used as a supplement to attainment standards rather
than as a replacement for them, then the effects are likely to be quite
minimal. There are three reasons for this judgment.

In the first place, attainment within the system *is* a kind of performance standard. It is not a standard that offers strong assurance of excellence on the part of those who meet it. But, on the other hand, neither could
we argue that it is totally irrelevant to excellence. It is, after all, a kind of
demonstration of performance capabilities.

Secondly, I believe it is true that none of the professions employ
performance standards instead of attainment standards among the criteria
for admission to the profession. It is true that in medical and nursing
education there are strong components of internships and clinical practice.
But these are usually construed either as included in attainment standards
or else they are undertaken after admission to the profession. All of the
professions, however, employ performance standards in the formation of
peer judgments following upon admission to the profession. The profession
judges its own, as do colleagues and associates in any work setting. Typically then, among the professions, judgments of competence are warranted
by educational attainment criteria. But judgments of excellence are warranted by performance standards incorporated into peer judgments. This
difference between competence and excellence, between admission to a
profession and surpassingly good practice, is vital to the conception of a
profession. It is unlikely to be uniquely abandoned by the profession of
teachers.

Finally, it is probably true that if we start out to restructure the
system by replacing attainment prerequisites by performance standards,
we are likely to end, nonetheless, by employing them only in a supplemen-
tary way. But on what grounds does such a judgment rest? If competent
performance in any position in the system is something that must be
learned, then however it is learned, its acquisition will take time. If it takes
a long time, then those who have learned it will tend, in a rough way, to be
those who are older. Furthermore, if it is something that can be learned and
is something important to have learned for employment in the system, then
it is likely to be regarded as something important enough to be taught in the
system, and there will be levels of its achievement. Those levels are likely
to correspond, again in a rough way, to levels of the system. Thus, even if
we start out to replace attainment prerequisites for employment in the
system with performance standards, we are likely, nonetheless, to end by
reintroducing something roughly like attainment prerequisites for employment. The change is likely to be quite marginal, which is not to deny
that it could be educationally significant.

Model Case #2. Consider now the alternatives for the system when there are more positions at L than there are persons with L qualifications. Suppose, for example, that there are 100 positions and only ten qualified persons to fill them.

How might the system respond to these conditions? Here again, we may lower the qualifications, raise them, or leave them unchanged. The system may leave the positions vacant or fill them temporarily with unqualified persons. Those are the choices.

The most interesting, and in some respects the most reasonable combination of these choices is to simply lower the qualifications for positions at L until all the positions are filled. But however reasonable this choice may seem from certain points of view, it is unlikely to occur because *any* attempt to lower the qualifications for any position in the system is a tacit admission that the qualifications were unnecessarily high to begin with. Viewed from the vantage of parental interests, such an admission may be an easy one. It may even be elicited from some representatives of government. But it is likely to remain totally unacceptable to any incumbent of the system whether the incumbent views his interests as those of employer, employee, technician, or professional. We may doubt that any incumbent of the system would have an interest in lowering the qualifications for any position in the system except for one just higher than his own, in the hierarchy of qualifications. We may doubt further that anyone would have an interest in raising the qualifications for any position except for one just lower than his own.[14]

Of course, it is possible to lower qualifications temporarily or under conditions of emergency. But this choice would never be described as a lowering of qualifications. It would be described rather as a temporary condition under which unqualified persons are permitted to fill positions in the system until qualified persons apply in sufficient numbers. Thus, qualifications are likely to be lowered only when doing so can be described as leaving them unchanged and as filling positions temporarily by unqualified persons. Therefore, we may eliminate the possibility of lowering the qualifications from among the possible responses of the system to the conditions described in our second model case.

For similar reasons, but with somewhat less assurance, we may also eliminate the alternative of raising qualifications. When staff for the system are in short supply, raising the educational qualifications for positions in it remains a logical possibility. There may even be some reasons for raising

14. This judgment is not based upon the notion that incumbents seek status within the system. It is based, rather, upon the view that, all other things being equal, people will prefer larger opportunities to more limited ones.

them, but the existence of a shortage of staff could not be among those reasons. If it is done, it would be done in response to some other problems. For example, a shortage of qualified staff for the system may result in more people seeking positions in the system. This, in turn, might increase the likelihood that the educational prerequisites for employment in the system will be raised. But such a consequence is remote, both causally and temporally. Its occurrence as a short or medium range consequence of an undersupply of staff would remain unlikely. Thus, with these unlikely exceptions in mind we may conclude that, as a general rule, when there are more positions in the system than qualified persons, the practical argument of the system will not permit us to lower the qualifications for positions and is unlikely to permit us to raise them. They will tend to remain unchanged.

There remain then two possibilities for systemic response to the conditions described in our second model case. The first is to leave the qualifications for the vacant positions unchanged, and the positions unfilled. The second choice is to fill those positions temporarily with unqualified persons and encourage them or others to gain the necessary qualifications. The first of these choices can be declared unsatisfactory and unlikely on the grounds that in any successful organization the existence of any long-term vacancy will be taken as *prima facie* evidence that the position is unnecessary. The tendency within the system, as in any other organization, will be to fill as quickly as possible any position that is vacant. Under the conditions set in our second model case, this means that the positions will be filled by unqualified individuals.

Given even so cursory an examination of this second case, we are now in a position to extend the conclusions derived from our study of the first model case. We saw that when there are more qualified persons than positions, the main tendency of the system will be to either expand or to raise the qualifications for its positions or both. We see now that when there are more positions than qualified persons, the long term tendency of the system is to leave the qualifications unchanged, but to continue to expand nonetheless. Indeed, though Model Case #1 may be taken to describe the circumstances in which the system must contract, Model Case #2 expresses precisely those conditions that we would describe as growth. Any system with more positions than qualified persons to fill them is a system in process of expansion, whatever may be the causes of the shortage. Thus, no matter what alternatives are presented to the system, it is expanding under the terms of Model Case #2. Thus, we arrive once again at precisely the point that was to be explored. *Regardless of the supply of qualified persons, the system will tend to either expand or to raise the educational prerequisites for any position in the system or both.* I shall refer to this proposition as the Principle of Uniform Growth.

This principle covers all the plausible alternatives for the system presented by our two model cases. But it needs stressing that this principle is not a prediction that the system is always, *in fact,* expanding or that qualifications for positions within it are always, *in fact,* increasing.[15] We are searching for the practical argument of the system, not its causal principles. The result of a practical argument is a conclusion of the form "Do X." Such an argument is not invalidated if it turns out that one does Y instead of X. Doing Y rather than X implies only that there is another practical argument leading to the conclusion "Do Y" and still another leading to the conclusion "Do Y rather than X." In short, the principle enunciated here does not state that the system is always in expansion or that its prerequisites for employment are always rising. We have seen that other things may happen, but that the reasons for their happening will not be an undersupply or an oversupply of qualified persons for positions in the system. If there are other actions, there will be other reasons and other arguments.

Indeed there is a sense of "growth" and there are circumstances in which the system will not grow and may actually shrink. If there is a reduction in the size of the school-age generation, and, therefore, a reduction in the number of children needing education in the system, then we are inclined to think that the system will actually shrink. This inference, however, is one that we have already examined and found to be fallacious (Chapter I). A reduction in the size of the school-age generation will *automatically* produce a reduction in the size of the system only if all or nearly all of each generation are in the system. In the early 1940s, the actual size of the sixteen-year-old group in the United States was declining. But at the same time only slightly more than half of them reached the senior year of high school. And so, though the size of the school age generation was declining, the system could continue to grow in the proportion it served. In the same way, the system may shrink in the real numbers of persons that it serves and still grow in the proportion served in each generation. In real numbers the system may be shrinking and yet in a proportionate sense, it may be growing.

Currently, in the United States, these two senses of growth are often confused, and for good reason. All, or virtually all, children are in the system.[16] And so, for the first time in our history proportionate growth in

15. Constraints on the principle of uniform growth will include not only the demographic considerations mentioned, but also the political division between public and private goods (see Chapter VIII), the rate of general economic growth, and the strength of will and political influence possessed by the leadership of the system.

16. Actually, the rate of each generation of 17 year olds completing twelve grades in the American system leveled off in 1965 at about 76 percent.

the system from K through 12 is impossible. For the first time a decline in the size of the school-age cohort will produce a decline in the real size of the system.

But the principle of uniform growth, nonetheless, urges us to look, under these conditions, for continued expansion. And what do we find? We find proposals to extend the system downward and upward where proportionate growth remains possible and outward where the system has not yet reached.

The principle of uniform growth does not tell us what will *happen*, but elucidating, as it does, the practical argument of the system, it tells us what policy proposals to expect. It gives us the principles of the policy argument. The tendency of the system in the long run is to continually expand and to reach toward a point where it is staffed entirely by persons who have completed the highest level of the system. That is the proposition with which we began. We are now in a position to recognize that claim is a corollary of the principle of uniform growth.

But that principle itself requires more explication than we have been able to provide so far. The arguments offered in support of that principle constitute, as it were, a rank ordering of the choices available to the system under the conditions stated in our two model cases. Yet of any ordering of preferences one needs to ask "Whose preferences are permitted to govern?" What criteria of preferences have produced the ranking implicit in the principle of uniform growth?

The answer is straightforward. The principle of uniform growth reflects the interests of the incumbents of the system. Recall the principles developed in our discussion of the system of control. There it was pointed out that the interests of the incumbents of the system are more complex than those of the state, the society or parents. For that reason, they were not fully explored in that earlier account. They are sometimes the interests of employees, sometimes those of employers, sometimes those of professionals, and sometimes of technicians. In attempting to establish the principle of uniform growth and to let it rest upon a rank ordering of preferred solutions to certain systemic problems, we have in fact been delineating this set of interests left undefined in Chapter II. It is the incumbents of the system whose interests would be offended by any proposal to lower qualifications for positions in the system. Theirs are the interests violated in the suggestion that positions vacant might be left vacant.[17] The incumbents' interests are those advanced by raising qualifications for positions in the system, by increasing the number of positions and by extending the reach of the system outward to other institutions. But it is not simply the general

17. Is it some kind of metaphysical truth that when "the Dean" resigns, a position is vacated?

interests of the incumbents that I have been concerned to explore. It is rather their particular interests as employees and as employers.

I do not mean to suggest that no other interests can be enlisted to support the ranking of preferences implicit in the principle of uniform growth. Obviously, that would not be true. Nor do I mean to suggest that the interests of the incumbents are always voiced in the blunt and exposed way in which I have expressed them. Indeed, the interests of the incumbents of the system as embodied in the principle of uniform growth are often framed in arguments presented as advancing the interests of parents, the state, or the social good. Still, those arguments express the interests of the incumbents of the system. Consider, for example, the following juxtaposition of events. In 1975, at a major meeting of theological educators, it was asked why there was no limit imposed on admissions to theological seminaries, especially in view of the fact that there were fewer available parish positions than theological students preparing for them. The answer offered was that to impose any limit would be to contravene the will of God. He calls whomever He will call. And who are we to intervene? A few weeks later, at a meeting of the major graduate deans in the United States, the same question was asked and a remarkably similar answer was given. In the midst of a surfeit of Ph.D.s, why are no limits imposed upon the admission of students to Ph.D. programs? The answer is that the imposition of such limits neither advances the long-term good of the society nor the short-term interests of individuals. Who are we to place artificial barriers in the path of anyone of ability who wants to pursue advanced learning? These arguments, properly elaborated and clothed in their full meaning, clearly promote the interests of the incumbents of the system. They are, in fact, advanced *by* the incumbents of the system. But they are framed, unmistakably and authentically, in the guise of social interests, parental interests, and state interests.

Summary

Thus, we see that the vertical structure of the system is discoverable partly in what I have called the hierarchies of learning and in the self-regulating principles of the system as employer. They are found implicit in the hard intractable fact that learning takes time and that the system is staffed by persons who are themselves products of the system. There remain to be examined in equal detail those evidences of hierarchy that arise from the existence of something called status, a different kind of higher and lower ranking in the system.

·◦[V]◦··

THE EDUCATIONAL SYSTEM
Hierarchies of Status

STATUS AND THE ACADEMIC SYSTEM

The Reptilian Procession

DAVID RIESMAN observed long ago that the American college and university system can be viewed as a kind of reptilian procession in which the head is followed by the body and the tail so that any given point of the body at any given time will be found at a point previously occupied by the head.[1] Certain institutions will initiate reform — perhaps the introduction of a general education program, a revision of graduate education, interdisciplinary programs, or a series of small independent colleges within a larger university. Other institutions, seeing what has been done, will follow in the same path, reaching implementation usually at about the time that the original innovator has set off in a new direction.

Those institutions at the head of the procession, however, are not there by chance. They are first usually because they occupy a position of high status in a system of educational stratification. By a rough and intuitive application of a scaling procedure, it is possible to identify approximately where, in the status system and in the reptilian procession any given college or university may fall. The criteria are fairly well known: extent and type of library holdings, facilities, outstanding features of curriculum, number of Guggenheim Fellows, Nobel prizes, award-winning books, SAT scores of entering freshmen, number of National Merit Scholars, performance of students in graduate schools, and so forth. On these criteria and others like them, one can ask any institution to compare itself to others. If institution C aspires to be like B, and B to be like A, then the status system from top to bottom runs from A to C. Changes in the conduct of the

1. *Constraint and Variety in American Education* (Garden City, N.Y.:Anchor, 1958), Chapter I, pp. vi-1.

77

institutions are likely to take place so that C adopts B's latest ideas, and B adopts A's.

An institution, at any point in the reptilian procession, must keep moving to retain its place; but it may aspire to move rapidly enough to attain a position at the head. In order to do this, however, it must adopt the criteria of excellence, the institutional arrangements, and the image of leadership that is, or will be, characteristic of those at the head. Translated into more relevant but less pictorial language, the natural tendency, the natural sequence of change in the academic procession, to the extent that it is a procession, is to move away from diversity toward uniformity. Of course, this uniformity is never quite attained; but nonetheless, the tendency is to move in that direction. This principle suggests, for example, that unless there are explicit constraints or interventions to prevent it, junior colleges and community colleges will aspire more and more to become like four-year liberal arts colleges, and finally universities.

There are, however, other and more stringent criteria for identifying the status structure of the system. They arise from applying elements of the system, already familiar, to the problem of determining the rank order of institutions in the status structure of the system. First among these is our conception of the medium of exchange.

The common coinage of the system is found in its distribution of second-order educational goods (see Chapter III). These goods may be accepted at full value or they may be discounted, or they may be presented from one institution to another at higher than face value. Transferring from one high school to another with one year in French does not mean automatically that one will enter the second year of French. It could be "Ahead to the third!" or "Back to the first!" When such goods are reciprocally received among a set of institutions at face value, then we may say that those institutions have the same rank in the hierarchy of status. If the value of these second order goods, however, is discounted or inflated or if their receipt at face value is less than reciprocal, then we have institutions, still linked in the system, but of different status.

It bears special notice that though these transactional clues of status are formulated with an eye on the behavior of higher education, similar kinds of behavior are observable at every level of the system. And although their application will produce a kind of "higher" and "lower" ranking, the meaning of "higher" and "lower" here has nothing to do *directly* with "better" and "worse" in any educational sense. A school whose second-order goods are regularly devalued in such transactions, may, on other grounds, be regarded as educationally superior. High rank on criteria of status and high quality on educational criteria may be associated, but they are by no means the same thing. Thus, students who get "C's" in physics at

Harvard or MIT, and who therefore decide they are "no good at it" and give up, may have received "A's" at Northern Illinois and persevered to distinguished careers. The high-status institutions may, in this respect, do more damage educationally than those of low status. Here again, however, our concern is with the theory of the system, not the theory of education.

The Imperatives of the Academic System

The hierarchies of status are presupposed in the image of the reptilian procession, implying as it does, the idea of head, body, and tail. They are made more explicit in the systemic practices of exchange, and they become even more visible in the culture of the system, or in what I shall refer to as the imperatives of the academic system.

By "the academic system," I mean the tendency of colleges and universities to organize around an array of academic disciplines and to offer instructional programs consisting of units within those disciplinary divisions. It is useful to recognize that these divisions, typical of university and college organization, reflect neither the way knowledge is gained nor the way it is used. Learning does not come in departmental packages, nor is it utilized in that fashion. The usual "academic" system reflects, rather, the basic structure of the professional associations of scholars and the pattern of communication that scholars employ in transmitting their ideas to other scholars. Philosophers tend to write for philosophers, sociologists for sociologists, historians for other historians and so forth. The journals for the publication of research are similarly organized around such disciplinary lines. There is nothing new in such an observation, nor do I wish to suggest that such arrangements are without benefit. They do much to facilitate the advancement of learning in the various sciences and applied arts. I wish only to record the fact that such disciplinary divisions reflect the ways that knowledge is manufactured — if such a metaphor is permitted — and not the ways it is gained by students or used in the affairs of the world.[2]

The Principle of Distance

A somewhat more detailed view of the academic system will be useful because it results in a set of imperatives enormously influential in shaping the behavior of the higher components in the system. Many of those imperatives stem from what I shall call the principle of distance. The principle of distance is the formulation of a fundamental human trait, a trait

2. The popularity of the phrase "knowledge industry" suggests that the metaphor, though clearly unacceptable on other grounds, is, nevertheless, terribly *au courant*.

by no means found only in the system. The principle states simply that *the worth of any activity increases with the distance away from home at which it is conducted.* If a professor gives a lecture at his own institution, it will probably receive little attention. However, if he gives the same lecture to a distinguished audience at some remote esteemed university or on some well-publicized occasion a great distance away, it immediately increases in value [3] The esteemed university need not be a great one nor the audience as distinguished as its reputation. It will suffice that the university or the audience are both respected and remote. This formulation of the principle needs one addendum. The professor must manage to communicate news of his activities to those back home. He must either do this himself, or better yet, manage to get it done by some "disinterested" third party. The principle, of course, will operate also to enhance the value of activities other than lectures. Distance will add value to consulting, publishing, and any other act of public visibility. It may also add notoriety to an act of negative value. The principle of distance is of little interest in itself. But its consequences are important. It deserves special notice because it is a way of describing an enormous range of evaluational behavior. But when it is viewed as a guide for action rather than a mere descriptive role, then, like many other principles of wide application, it results in an interesting mixture of good and evil.

For example, the principle of distance is basic to the ways that academics are evaluated. It surely is a good — a rule of justice, in fact — that persons should be judged by those competent to be their judge. By applying the principle of distance, those within the academic system express their respect for the evidence that one's fame has spread, that one is known, respected and valued in other places than at home. That will surely strengthen one's value at home, because without such evidence, it often happens that those at hand do not know how to value one's activities. They need the testimony of people elsewhere. Familiarity may not breed contempt, but it certainly breeds indecision in evaluating people within the academic system. A prophet may not be without honor in his own land, but an academician is certainly more valued in his own land if his efforts are valued in some other land.

Thus, professional stature within the academic system tends not to be measured by the judgment of one's students or one's administrative superiors, but by one's professional peers and especially by those professional peers some distance away. They, after all, are the ones who

3. Does this principle operate also for teachers and administrators in the elementary and secondary part of the system? Probably to a lesser extent, but if not at all, then why not? Is there here another principle of the system?

can properly judge seriousness of thought and originality of conception. The fundamental dictum of the academic system is not "Publish or perish" but "Publicize at a distance or be overlooked!"

Corollaries of the Principle of Distance

Understood in this benign way, the principle of distance suggests immediately certain occasionally malignant corollaries. The first might be described as the rule of lateral authority. Thorstein Veblen observed years ago that the excellence of an academic institution varies directly with the decline of hierarchical authority within it. In a really good college or university, the loyalty of the faculty to the institution is fairly minimal. The allegiance of the academic runs not downward in the organization to his students nor upward in the university, but outward to his peers in the academic system. He offers his primary loyalty not to his students or to the organization, but to his field of study. This attitude is partly a consequence of what we mean by surpassingly good scholarship. The French historian, Fulstel de Coulange, is reported to have said, when speaking before the French Academy, "It is not I who speak, but history that speaks through me." That may seem a pompous and arrogant way of putting a point, but it goes to the heart of the matter. The concern of a really good scholar as scholar, is not with the welfare of his students nor with any kind of overriding allegiance to some other human institution. It is, above all, to the truth, or humanly speaking, to the search for truth. And in that activity, it is not to his students or to the organization of the university that the truly excellent scholar must look for competent assistance and criticism, but to those peers who are engaged in investigations similar to his. That is simply part of what we *mean* by a superior scholar and a true professional in the academic system. It follows that the community to which the really excellent academician appeals is nothing as limited as the local college or community. His is, at least, a national community, and, at best, an international one. Thus, the decline in the vertical allegiance of the faculty is a measure of the professionalization of the academic system and a symptom of the emergence of national colleges and universities.[4] It is the sign of a strengthened and increasingly excellent academic system. The decline of vertical authority is a sign of victory for the standards of the academic. But it is a sign of maturity likely to be followed soon by a general neglect of undergraduate teaching.

4. See Christopher Jencks and David Riesman, *The Academic Revolution* (Garden City: Doubleday, 1968), pp. 12–27. It is central to their thesis that the academic revolution consists of the professionalization of the academic system and the consequent emergence of "national" universities and colleges.

Thus, if one observes only the growth of enrollment, degrees, facilities and faculties in the expansion of higher education, then the more subtle and perhaps even more powerful forces of change may remain ignored. The more fundamental symptom of growth in higher education is not the mere increase or decline in students, but the numbers attending meetings of professional associations and the expansion in the numbers of such associations themselves. The increases have been enormous.

The associations of professionals exist in a symbiotic relation to the academic system. Such associations, whether of historians, philosophers, social workers, or landscape architects, have an inherent interest in both improving the quality of their membership and in expanding it. But they have interests in both under conditions of careful control. Thus, they must urge the expansion of the educational prerequisites for membership in their respective guilds together with more stringent standards of admission — an increase in prerequisites for admission to positions for educated persons together with a careful control upon the supply. One can witness these forces operating in the emergence of every new discipline in the academic system and in the organization of every new professional association. They are the constituent principles in the process I referred to elsewhere as professionalization.

There are other corollaries to the principle of distance, having to do less with the dynamics of growth, and more with strengthening the academic system and with the distribution of costs within it. For example, it is useful to keep in mind the general rule of lateral escalation. The operating principle is that an academic institution, partly as a consequence of the principle of distance, will allocate more funds to secure a teacher from another institution than it will to placate the economic appetite of people already on its staff. It is an extravagant practice, but almost universally followed. The consequence is that one is most likely to ascend the ladder of academic status by going elsewhere. It should be intuitively obvious that this practice, well understood in the academic system, is an essential factor in strengthening the academic system itself. Whenever it happens that the rule of lateral escalation is violated, it will also happen that the power of hierarchical authority will increase and the strength of professionalization will be hindered. Anyone bucking for promotion is easily intimidated by the hierarchy of the institution, and to that extent he will be less concerned with his relation to the community of scholars outside his own locale and more concerned with his relation to the local Dean or Provost.

The Dynamics of Advancing in Status

When the organization of status within the system is linked to the behavioral injunctions contained in the principle of distance, the result is a kind of dynamic resting upon the hierarchies of the system. The natural tendency is toward uniformity and toward the rather conventional standards of excellence represented by the colleges and universities at the head of the procession. To advance in status, there are in general, two competing objectives that any college or university must adopt. It must resolve the tension between the need to increase the demand for student places within the institution and simultaneously to restrict the number that graduate. In short, a college or university advances in status by producing graduates of high quality who will subsequently be distinguished alumni. It will accomplish this goal more rapidly if it grows in numbers of high quality graduates. We know also that the best way to accomplish this objective is to exercise stringent selection procedures in determining who is admitted, together with even more stringent measures to control who among those admitted will complete their studies. The best way to produce competent graduates, in other words, is to admit students who are already competent. And the best way to attain that goal quickly is to expand the demand for student places so as to provide a larger pool of talent from which to select, and to carefully control those who graduate. Thus, the twin tendencies to increase demand and to limit supply are supported once again by the academic status system.

Of course, there are apparent exceptions to this pattern, but they are apparent only. There are post-secondary institutions of low prestige, low status, and low selectivity that nonetheless retain a high morale among their faculty. There are many justifications that make this possible. "Consider how well we do with the less talented." "We are bringing to this community a better kind of education than they have had before." "These students make sensational efforts to overcome their deficiencies." Still, expressions such as "less talented," "better than they had," and "overcome their deficiencies" betray the underlying conviction that if things could be as they should be, then they would be the way they are at certain high-prestige institutions. It's all right to be where we are, but it's better to be on top. The natural direction of growth is toward uniformity, not diversity. And the drive for advancement in the status system will quickly bring into play the principle of distance, the resulting hierarchies of status, and the effort to increase demand together with the control on supply.

HIERARCHICAL PRINCIPLES AND THE SYSTEM IN MOTION

Sequence, Attainment, and Selectivity

At the risk of getting ahead of our story,[5] let us conclude this account of the vertical structure of the system by attending to what it would be reasonable to expect of a system whose practical arguments include as premises the hierarchical principles outlined. Let us imagine further, such a system operating under the following conditions: (1) it is sequential; (2) everyone completes the nth level of the system[6]; and (3) beyond the nth level, the system is selective.

The third of these conditions needs special comment. If the system is selective above the nth level, then it will follow that some go on beyond the nth level and some do not. But the mere fact that some go on and some do not is not what we mean when we say that the system is selective. Neither do we mean merely that some choose to go on and that some do not. We mean rather that some are chosen to go on and some are not. We mean that there are established social mechanisms whereby it is decided *from among those that choose* to go on, which will and which will not, It follows that such a system does not have "open enrollment" beyond the nth level. It is important to be clear as to precisely what this condition includes, because it is this assumption that will be the point of most severe initial tension in the morphology of the system.

Let us add one further condition to these three features of the system. Suppose that this educational system operates in a society where there is a widespread and deeply held belief that education is a powerful force in shaping the subsequent life-chances of any individual. It is believed, in other words, that education makes a significant contribution to securing a wide range of non-educational social goods. I have referred to this as the belief in educational efficacy. I do not include the principle of educational

---

5. A more complete and more general exposition of the system in motion is presented in Chapter VI. However, those dynamics relating most clearly to the hierarchy of the system are not fully developed there and can be profitably examined in the context where they belong, viz., in a study of the vertical structure of the system.

6. In Chapter VI, and thereafter, this condition will be described as the attainment of zero correlation in the system. The principle of zero correlation is merely the tautology that whenever everyone within a given age-cohort attains the nth level of the system, it no longer makes sense to speak of any correlation between attaining that level in the system and any subsequent social advantage or disadvantage. In short, zero correlation at the nth level of the system, describes a state of affairs in which the belief in the efficacy of education is no longer credible as associated with attainment of the nth level. In Chapter VII the relevant question is asked not about what happens at this point in the growth of the system, but what happens as it is approached.

efficacy as a feature of the educational system itself. It is rather a feature of the social and cultural environment.

Now, if we imagine an educational system satisfying the three conditions I have described, and a society, moreover, that accepts the belief in educational efficacy, then what would we expect to happen in the educational system? If the belief in educational efficacy is widely accepted in a society where everyone completes the nth level, we must clearly expect pressures for the system to expand at the level of $n + 1$. In other words, a strong and widely held belief in the efficacy of education, together with nearly universal attainment at the nth level, will be sufficient to produce pressures for expansion of the system at the next higher level. Why? Because under such conditions only at some point beyond the nth level can there exist any correlation between the level of education attained and any subsequent indicator of social standing or social mobility. So the principle of efficacy together with the condition of universal attainment at n will produce strong pressures for expansion of the system, *at that level where it becomes selective.*

Thus the condition of selectivity will come into play. What would it be reasonable to expect? We would expect not only pressures for growth at the level of $n + 1$, but also pressures for an intensification of the efforts in the system at the level of $n - 1$ and below. Why? We have reason to believe on empirical grounds that the system of higher education in the United States — that point in the system that is selective — will tend to maintain a constant ratio between those who enter the system for the B.A. degree and those who will actually complete the B.A., *no matter how many people are prepared to enter the system.*

There are two points that will help to make this fact more comprehensible. The first stems from features of institutional status within the system. The second is derived from the characteristics of the "academic system" itself. If we focus attention only on those paths through the presently existing American educational system that offer the Bachelor's Degree, then we can see that even through the period of most rapid growth in the American college and university system (1952–1975), there was a remarkably stable ratio between those who started the BA program and those who finished it. This fact in itself provides strong grounds for the presumption that it is one of the functions of the college and university system to hold constant the ratio between entries and completions at the B.A. level (see Table A-3).

What might account for that fact? We know that there are institutions within the American college and university system that graduate virtually everyone admitted. Thus, the maintenance of a constant ratio between entries and completions, though true of the system as a whole, is not true for some institutions within the system. Thus, such schools as Harvard College, Princeton, Yale, Columbia, Reed College, and so forth, graduate, sooner or later, virtually every student who gains entrance. If the ratio of completions to entries is approximately .56, it follows that there must be many institutions whose ratio is lower, because we know that there are some whose ratio is higher. But if we consider which institutions graduate virtually everyone, we find that they are almost entirely those of high status. One criterion of high status institutions is that they select and support their students so that virtually all of them complete the program at the Bachelor's level. But how does an institution reach the point at which that kind of behavior becomes possible and reasonable?

Let us imagine that at Alaric University there is a graduate department of X that is very much "on the make." How would we expect it to behave? It is likely to admit a great many students to its graduate programs according to standards of admission that are seldom stretched. It will probably admit a great many students in order to have a larger group from which to select the very best. The rest will, in some way, be encouraged, invited, or asked to drop out. It takes only a few years for the word to get around in the professional associations of X Department that there is no point in applying for entrance to Alaric University to work in the Department of X unless you are able to show an outlandishly high graduate record score. In a short time only those who have such outstanding credentials will apply. At that point the Department X and Alaric University can begin to behave as high-status institutions do. It will be so selective in whom it admits that it will not be able to fail anyone.

At the point where the American educational system becomes selective, it has acted in the past so as to maintain a constant ratio between those who received the B.A. degree and those who initially enter a program leading to that degree. This behavior is enormously important. Its importance will become evident in a moment, but the immediate point is to see that a possible explanation for this kind of behavior is to be found in the ways that the institutional status system of higher education operates in the United States.

There is another kind of explanation, however. It has to do less with the status structure of the college and university system and more to do with the features of the "academic system." The point is simple. If a professor gave the same course at University X in 1965 and at University Y in 1975, and if the students enrolled in his course in 1975 would all have received A's had they been enrolled ten years earlier, still it is not likely that the professor will give them all A's. Why not? Because it is one of the tasks of the professor to discriminate. He is supposed to distribute his grades. It seems, moreover, a reasonable expectation that if the quality of students in his course continues to improve, he is more likely to raise the standards of the course than to distribute his grades in the same categories. This process is defended within the academic system by a powerful and deeply entrenched ideology called "maintaining standards." It is in fact, an ideology that defends a constant fluctuation of standards. But that is not likely in the least to deter anyone from continuing to distribute his rewards as a teacher in approximately the same frequency year after year. This behavior results in maintaining a constant ratio for the system as a whole between those entering programs for the B.A. and those receiving such degrees, no matter how many may be prepared to enter such programs and no matter how well prepared they are to persevere to the end. Both the institutional status system and the culture of the academic system provide powerful justifications and pressures to maintain a stable relation between those seeking the B.A. and those receiving it.

In short, in any system where everyone completes the nth level, there will be powerful pressure to expand the system at the level of $n + 1$. But if the system at the level of $n + 1$ and beyond is selective, and if it operates to maintain a stable entering-leaving ratio at the next terminal point in the system, then what would we expect to happen? In the first place, we would expect strong pressures to raise the standards at the level of $n + 1$ and beyond. This, in turn is likely to bring about immensely powerful pressures to raise the standards at the level of $n - 1$ and below. And again, as persons completing the nth level are better prepared to compete for entrance at the level of $n + 1$, then we would expect the standards to be raised once again at the level of $n + 1$ and beyond. This is the cycle of growth that I described as intensification.

If we imagine a society in which the principle of educational efficacy is strongly accepted, and in which zero-correlation is satisfied at level n, then there will develop strong pressures to increase the demand for higher and higher levels of educational attainment. But if the system is selective beyond the nth level, then we would expect an equally growing pressure to upgrade the educational prerequisites needed for entrance into and passage through those higher levels of the system. The first tendency will create strong pressures for the growth of the system at the top. But it will also introduce a kind of growth down through the system in the form of more intensity of effort. Thus, under these conditions there is likely to occur an intensification of education throughout the system. What is it that drives that expansion? It is that the system is hierarchical in its structure, that it is selective beyond a certain point, and, finally, that everyone completes the level just preceding the point at which it is selective. In a more abstract or more general formulation, we say that a basic social function of such an educational system is to allocate human beings to subsequent social and economic chances. Since the system cannot serve this function at the nth level, if everyone attains at the nth level, it follows immediately that it must expand beyond that level, exercise selectivity, and thus intensify the system below.

Expansion, Itensification, and Differentiation

It is important to keep in mind the limits of the assumptions we have been discussing. They are the assumptions of an educational system in which there is a single ladder of success. It includes a sequential structure of grades extending from the elementary stages through secondary education into the mainline college and university system leading first to the bachelor's degree and finally through the master's and doctoral degrees. Such a system does not include degrees that may be offered beyond the secondary level and below the bachelor's level. It does not include Associate of Arts degrees, for example, or other kinds of institutions that may be post-secondary, but not within the limits of the college and university system.

It is important to keep in mind these limits, because one of the points in examining such a set of assumptions is to understand the emergence, the functions, and the importance of programs and institutions intervening between the secondary level and the usual college or university program. The point is that there is a second clear line of development that can follow from the set of assumptions we have been studying. The first is that when the conditions I have described are satisfied, we would expect intensification to occur in the lower reaches of the system. That seems clear enough. That is approximately what was happening in the American system from 1958 to 1968.

But there are other ways to respond to these conditions in a society strongly attached to the belief in educational efficacy. The system may respond not only by an intensification of the program at the levels below n, but also at the nth level by differentiating programs. That is to say, even though the completion of the nth *level* of education may not correlate with any later significant social distinctions, still, it may happen that educational programs *within* the nth level may correlate directly and strongly. Thus, under the conditions we have been describing *another* expectation within the system would be the strong pressure to bring about differentiation within the system at the nth level. This might take the form of vocationally oriented paths within the school system, job-work programs, or a variety of other options available to students. This kind of differentiation would constitute another form of expansion within the system.

We know, however, that it is impossible to expect any kind of useful differentiation to occur only *within* the nth level. Distinction in the curriculum must start at a point considerably below. There is a downward drift in specifying the curriculum. Thus, the pressures for differentiation can be expected to move progressively downward in the system creating a kind of growth as it goes.

In a system that is selective, sequential and has reached a point of universal attainment at a high level, we would expect more than one kind of differentiation to occur. We would expect pressures to open up fresh alternatives at the level of $n + 1$ and beyond. If post-secondary education is necessary in order to respond to the belief in educational efficacy, then we would expect the emergence of many kinds of institutions that intervene between the universally completed level of the system and the more selective paths toward advanced schooling. If the system is to be efficacious in the sense described, and if the system at the level of $n + 1$ and beyond is to retain its selective characteristics, then there must be developed essentially non-college institutions between the nth level and the level of $n + 4$ to provide such additional education.

The emergence of such institutions can be viewed then as the development of a kind of safety valve for the system and for the belief in the efficacy of education. It can be viewed as a means whereby the pressures to expand the system at the top can be satisfied without at the same time disturbing the essentially selective prerogatives in the distributive behavior of the system at its higher reaches. Without the development of such "intervening" programs, the system is on a collision course between the demands to expand accessibility to programs beyond the nth level and the equally strong demands to maintain their selectivity. The *initial* point of tension in this process will be the principle of selectivity, the third of the assumptions that I have been examining. But the ultimate points of tension must be the assumption that the system is sequential and the belief that it is efficacious. These two assumptions together with the belief in educational efficacy do much to define the dimensions of current change within the system. Whether they can be abandoned or modified will undoubtedly be central in evaluating any possible alternative constitution for the system.

THE SYSTEM IN MOTION

THE SYSTEM IS NOT A STATIC THING. It changes through time, but nevertheless, according to certain regularities established by the practical arguments of the system. It is not enough to describe its elements, its actors and the principles implicit in its primary and derivative properties. It is well enough to set out the principles of growth, distribution, hierarchical organization, and control. But these are merely discrete aspects of the system each with its own intrinsic interest. We must now attempt to put the different elements together and establish the principles of their interaction. In this, and the following two chapters, I shall attempt to set the system in motion.

THE SYSTEMIC RULES OF UNIFORM GROWTH

The Law of Zero Correlation

Let us imagine a society whose educational system has grown at a uniform rate over a period of one-hundred years. By this, I mean that there has been a uniform increase in the proportion of each successive age cohort attaining at the nth level of the system. Let us suppose, moreover, that that rate of increase is precisely 10 percent per decade over the one-hundred-year period. That pattern of growth will then be represented by the diagonal in Figure 6.1. I shall refer to that diagonal as the uniform growth line.

It will be true, without restriction, that if there is a level within the system that everyone completes, then completing that level can have no bearing whatever upon any social differences that may subsequently arise within the population. There may remain differences in opportunity, income, and so forth arising from the way that that level is completed, but, under such circumstances, there can be no social differences whose source

90

FIGURE 6.1
Hypothetical Uniform Growth Line

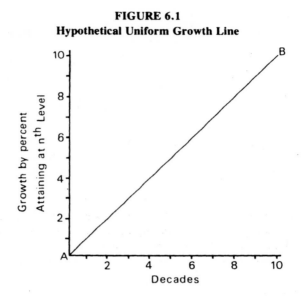

is traceable to completing that level. I shall refer to this proposition as the law of zero correlation. The law states simply that there is a point in the growth of the system at which there is no longer any correlation between educational attainment and either the distribution of educationally relevant attributes in the population or the distribution of non-educational social goods ordinarily associated with educational attainment.

The law of zero correlation is a tautology. Its truth arises from the fact that for there to be a correlation between any two variables, say, between educational attainment and lifetime earnings, both of the variables must be distributed in the population.[1] Neither can be uniformly distributed if its occurrence is to be used in explaining variations in the other variable. When the law of zero-correlation is understood in this way, no doubts can arise about its truth.

The name, "law of zero correlation," however, should not be misunderstood. It is not as though we set out to discover the correlation between educational attainment and other social differences and discovered that the correlation was zero. The point is rather that to even *try* to discover the correlation under such conditions is no longer an intelligible task. At point B on the hypothetical growth line the question "What is the correlation between completing the nth level and securing some subsequent social

1. It is vital to observe that this is a claim about educational attainment and not educational achievement.

benefit?'' is no longer an askable question. It would be like asking for the correlation between having a heart and having a particular social status. The question is nonsensical.

With this qualification in mind, we may return to Figure 6.1 and observe that point B in the hypothetical growth line is that point at which the growth of the system will reach zero correlation with respect to the nth level. Point B is the *point* of zero correlation. Let us now reinterpret the vertical axis in Figure 6.1 to represent a scale of the strength of correlation through time between attainment at the nth level and the acquisition of nondeducational social goods. We may then superimpose on the hypothetical growth line a curve representing this correlation at different points in the growth of the system.

We know by immediate inference from the tautological law of zero correlation that that curve will reach zero at a point on the horizontal axis opposite point B. Thus, we know the direction and terminus of a curve representing the declining strength of correlation between educational attainment at the nth level and whatever social goods are normally associated with education. We do not, however, know the full shape of that curve. We do not know its points of inflection nor the rate of its decline toward zero.

We may reason, however, that if Point B on the hypothetical growth line is a point of zero correlation, then so is point A, and for precisely the same reasons. When everyone attains the nth level of the system, there is no correlation between attainment at that level and subsequent possession of any particular social goods. But the same proposition will be true when *nobody* attains at the nth level.

We may now reason through a third step. Certified attainment at the nth level of the system is, of course, a second-order educational good distributed by the system. And so, at either A or B, it is impossible for the society to distribute non-educational social goods *on the basis of* the system's distribution of second-order educational goods. Yet, we know, as a matter of empirical fact and common knowledge, that the correlation between educational attainment, on the one hand, and the acquisition of non-educational social goods, on the other hand, rises at some point as the system grows from A to B. We know, therefore, that the direction of any line representing that correlation rises from A and descends ultimately to C on the horizontal axis.

We may summarize this set of inferences in a single observation. *The value of second-order educational benefits as a basis for allocating non-educational social goods is a curvilinear function of the proportion of each age-cohort that is successful in obtaining those goods.* We may represent this claim in Figure 6.2.

FIGURE 6.2
Utility of Second-Order Educational Goods

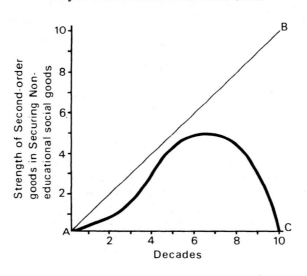

With the growth of the system, therefore, its distributive behavior changes. As increasing numbers of each generation are successful in obtaining higher and higher second-order goods from the system, the social value of those benefits at a specific level of the system will increase and then eventually decline. In a society where few have completed high school, high school completion is unlikely to be used as a screening prerequisite for job entry, job placement, or job security. The efficacy of such second-order benefits for the allocation of social goods will be fairly low. In a society where a great many of each generation have them, then their utility will be fairly high. In a society, however, where *every* youth receives such benefits of the system, the social value of having them will again decline and approach zero.

It can be doubted whether any society has reached a point of zero correlation at any level as high as, say, the twelfth level of the American system. There are societies that have not reached that point at a level as high as the third grade in the American system. The law of zero correlation, however, does not specify what will count as the nth level. It may be as high as college or as low as the first grade. But the important question is not whether or at what point it has been reached in this or that place, but *what, from a purely analytic point of view, can we expect to happen in any society as it approaches the point of zero correlation at some level of the system?*

Corollaries of Zero Correlation

The utility of educational attainment, and of the second-order educational benefits associated with it, is a curvilinear function of the proportion of each age cohort successful in securing such goods. That is the principle implicit in the tautological law of zero correlation. This principle, however, does not stand alone. It has its corollaries.

Transformation from Attainment to Achievement

The first of these is the *rule of transformation from educational attainment to educational achievement*. As we approach the point of zero correlation at the nth level of the system, then merely having a diploma or certificate at that level will no longer discriminate between individuals. It will become important to discriminate between diplomas, certificates, and programs. In a society where everyone earns a high school diploma, having one no longer bestows any particular advantages, but having one from this or that school or from this or that program may still represent a mark of distinction and may, therefore, bestow considerable advantages. Thus, attention will shift from the level of attainment to the quality of achievement.

But why should this shift occur? Are there no other choices? We have seen already that the system is unlikely to grow very large unless there is a strong, positive, relation between the acquisition of educational goods and the acquisition of non-educational social goods. We have seen, moreover, that that relation is implemented through second-order educational benefits and that it requires some principle of legitimation.

We know, already, however, that these second-order educational benefits — certificates, diplomas, transcripts, and the like — play multiple roles within the system. First of all, they provide the practical medium of exchange between the units of the system without which it would not be a system at all. Viewed in that role, they are tokens of attainment. But we noted, further, that they provide the practical social link needed between the distribution of educational benefits by the system and the distribution of non-educational social goods by the society. Viewed in this role, they are surrogates of educational goods and have a mixed function. They are indicators of attainment, but, to a limited extent, also they are indicators of achievement. But such goods enter the system in a third way. By providing a means of exchange between units of the system, they may be accepted at par value, at inflated value, or at discounted value. In this function they are explicit indicators of achievement, and they help to define the status rank of units in the system.

As zero correlation is approached, the society loses its capacity to allocate social goods to accord with attainment. Therefore, the function of second-order goods as indicators of attainment will decline and their function as indicators of achievement will become relatively more important. In short, the status differentials of the system will become more prominent and of more practical importance for the social distribution of opportunities, status, and the like.

If the distributive mores of the system are to be preserved when zero correlation approaches then something must change. There are only two choices, and functionally they are the same. The first is to allocate non-educational social goods on the basis of attainment at the level of n + 1 or beyond where, presumably, the approach of zero correlation is more remote. Thus, we would expect the educational prerequisites for jobs to be upgraded and the system to press for higher levels of universal attainment. And in this proposal the interests of the incumbents of the system as employees, professionals, and technicians will match the interests of parents. Both will have an interest in expanding the system for higher rates of attainment at higher levels. The dynamics of intensification will be set in motion (see Chapter V).

The second choice is to begin allocating social goods on the basis of different *ways* of attaining the nth level. This shift of attention from attainment to achievement is the functional equivalent of reducing the proportion of each age cohort securing a particular second-order educational good, and that is precisely, though not exclusively, what is accomplished, in another way, by the first of these choices. The tendency, in short, is to either press for levels of attainment beyond zero correlation or to find ways of replacing status differences associated with attainment by status differences associated with different kinds of schools and programs. This is the shift from attainment to achievement.

Transforming Utility

The second corollary of zero correlation is the *rule of transforming utility*. Let us recall that second-order educational goods appeared as the socially practical device permitting educational goods and non-educational social goods to be linked in their distribution. Their *justification or legitimation* in this function rests in their capacity to act as crude, but useful, surrogates of *educational* goods (see Chapter III). Their value, therefore, is purely instrumental. There are no normative principles governing their instrumental use except those requiring them to be rationally adequate surrogates for educational goods.

Under conditions of zero correlation, however, second-order educational benefits have no instrumental value for the allocation of social goods outside the system. But, as we have seen, these goods act also as indicators of achievement within the system. They are used for the allocation of social goods by the society, but they are also used by the system for the allocation of access to the system, and this latter function is unaffected by the conditions of zero correlation. Thus, as we approach the point of zero correlation at the nth level, we must expect that the instrumental value of second-order benefits, as the tool for allocating social goods, will become more and more problematic. Their remaining, and still secure, value will be their instrumental worth in securing access to subsequent levels of the system. In short, the chief instrumental worth of education is then merely to secure access to more education.[2] The chief value of a high school education is then that it permits access to the next level of the system. This is the meaning of the principle of transforming utility.

Shifting Benefits and Liabilities

The third corollary of zero correlation may be expressed as the principle of shifting benefits and liabilities. As the social utility of second-order benefits declines for those who receive them, then the social liabilities suffered by any individual as a consequence of *not* securing them will increase. I state this principle as a corollary of zero correlation. It is of such importance, however, and its implications are so far-reaching that it might be viewed as a second and distinct law of systemic behavior. To secure anything approaching its full exposition we shall need to give this principle central attention for the remainder of this chapter and beyond.

To more fully grasp its significance, however, we need to return to Figures 6.1 and 6.2. The diagonal in Figure 6.1 was presented as a purely hypothetical account. In fact, however, it corresponds roughly to the experience in the United States from about 1900 to the present (see Table A-1). In 1910 about 7 percent of the 17-year-old cohort completed high school. By 1940 it approached 50 percent and in 1965 it reached 76 percent. This means that in the United States we have been approaching the point of zero correlation at the 12th level of the system. It would be reasonable to expect this growth to level off. No matter what system we may choose to consider, its natural limit will fall short of its mathematical limit. In the

---

2. One may note the similarity of this formulation of the rule of transforming utility to the remark of Dewey's that the only goal of education is more education. Dewey, however, had in mind an important point about the nature of *education,* how it contributes to the reconstruction of experience. The rule of transforming utility, however, says something about the nature of the educational *system.* It should not be confused with Dewey's point.

United States, this growth curve levelled off at about 76 percent where it has remained since 1965. That this has happened at the 12th level in the American system is a fact of enormous significance, and especially so in view of the further fact that the period since 1965 has witnessed the most monumental effort in the history of American educational policy to continue its increase.

With these considerations in mind, let us re-examine the schema presented in Figure 6.2. There, on purely conceptual grounds, I sketched the shape of a curvilinear function representing the social utility of second-order educational benefits corresponding to different points on a hypothetical path of uniform growth. If we examine that schema carefully, we shall see that the American system has reached a point in its expansion at the 12th level corresponding to an inflection point in the declining value of second-order educational benefits. In short, if the system expands further, the value of attainment, for those who secure it, will decline at that level *with increasing speed*. Can this conjecture be supported?

It presents a pair of puzzling questions. First of all, it is becoming more and more widely recognized that, *to those who possess it,* a high school diploma is less and less decisive in the scrap to secure the social goods of life. A higher level of attainment is required. Yet, if its efficacy is so slight, then why is there no apparent decline in the desire and effort to secure it? The immediate answer is that it is required for access to the next level of the system. The principle of transforming utility operates. Secondly, we would anticipate that in approaching the mathematical limit in the growth of the system at this level, each marginal gain will prove to be more difficult for the society to reach. And there seems to be no abatement in the continuing effort of the system to reach such a goal. Why then does the system appear to many as increasingly unsuccessful?

The answers to these questions are discoverable in the principle of shifting benefits and liabilities. That principle is that *as the social value of second-order benefits declines for those who receive them, the social liabilities suffered by any individual as a consequence of not securing them will increase.* As a first step in rendering this principle precise, we may begin with its schematic formulation in Figure 6.3.

This schema extends beyond what is contained in the principle itself. The principle deals only with the dynamics of the system at the upper end of the uniform growth line. It refers explicitly only to that point where the social utility (not the systemic utility) of second-order benefits declines *for those who receive them.* The representation in Figure 6.3 *suggests* that this point is not reached until the growth of the system at the nth level passes 60

FIGURE 6.3
Shifting Benefits and Liabilities

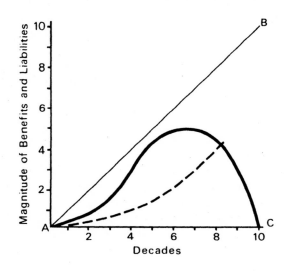

percent and that the downward slope of utility is not steep until slightly beyond that point.[3]

Such precision is more than we are warranted in concluding from the mere formulation of the principles so far set down. The principle of shifting benefits and liabilities explicitly warrants conjecture only about the *direction* of the liability curve at the upper end of the uniform growth line. The schematic shape of the lower end in Figure 6.3 is based, however, upon the following considerations that are plausible enough on other grounds.

It seems, on the surface, unlikely that any society, in its allocation of social goods, will seriously limit the future of those who fail to secure a high school diploma when only 20 percent to 40 percent secure one. Surely in a society where less than 10 percent of each generation secures a high school diploma, nobody is likely to be either greatly advantaged in getting one or greatly disadvantaged by not getting one. Tenacity, guts, inventiveness, perhaps miserliness, and certainly long life, and just plain luck are likely to

3. Note carefully: We have been considering what, from a purely analytic point of view is likely to happen as we *approach* the point of zero correlation. Zero correlation is a *terminus* in the growth of the system at a certain level. It is identified in recognizing that the law of zero correlation is a tautology. The point at which we begin to *approach* zero correlation on the utility curve must be determined empirically. Its meaning, however, is not determined empirically. These schema are intended to present the *meaning* of the systemic principles of behavior.

be much more significant than educational attainment. Thus, both the utility curve and the liability curve are schematically represented as fairly flat at the lower reaches of the uniform growth line, and this characterization seems justified even though it cannot be substantiated as a direct inference either from the law of zero correlation or from the principle of shifting benefits and liabilities.

There may seem to be a counter-argument. There have been societies where only a few are educated and where those few are greatly advantaged. However, if we think seriously about such examples, we shall recognize that such societies are usually characterized either by a caste system, a feudal system, or a strongly aristocratic tradition. In such cases, the educated few are greatly advantaged. But they are not advantaged *by* their education. They are advantaged *by* their birth. Is birth a matter of luck? It seems odd to say so, although in common parlance, people do speak of it as a matter of "good (or ill) fortune." In any case, the counter-argument cannot be sustained as a serious objection to the conjecture upon which we base the *schematic* shape of the utility and liability curves at the lower end of the uniform growth line.

Implications of Shifting Benefits and Liabilities

The import of these conjectures can be gathered from two further observations on problems that have emerged on the American scene over the past two decades. To the best of my knowledge, the so-called drop-out problem was never viewed as a *social* problem in the United States until the mid-50s. By that time, curiously enough, the attainment rate at the 12th level of the American system had passed 60 percent. The drop-out problem in short comes into existence and intensifies as the number of drop-outs declines. It is now less talked about than it was in the mid-50s, but it is more intense as a problem. This peculiarity — that as we have fewer drop-outs the "drop-out problem" becomes more serious — is accounted for by the principle of shifting benefits and liabilities. Being a drop-out is nothing new, but the seriousness of being one is new. It began to be apparent in the United States when the growth of the system at the 12th level passed the 60 percent point on the uniform growth curve. When there are lots of drop-outs, being one is no problem. When there are few, being one can be a disaster. The reason that we have a drop-out *problem* is not that we have too many drop-outs, but that we have too few. This is an uncharitable formulation, but, nonetheless, it expresses the point vividly.

Similar observations may be offered on the so-called problem of credentialism. Where only a few have finished high school, the society cannot use the completion of high school as a screen for either job entrance, advancement, or security. Credentialism can arise only in a society where lots of people have credentials. It becomes a problem, if it is a problem at all, as a consequence of the growth of the system. It is easy to see then that as any society approaches the point of zero correlation, as in the United States at the 12th level of the system, having a high school diploma is no big deal for those who have them, but not having one can be an unqualified disaster for those who do not. These points add weight to the conjectured shape of the liability curve in Figure 6.3, both in its upper and lower sectors. They lend credibility to that schematic portrayal of the principle of shifting benefits and liabilities. These problems in the American system arise not because of the failure of the system, but because of its unparalleled success.

It might be countered, nonetheless, that the principle of shifting benefits and liabilities is something of a fraud. After all, avoiding a disaster is a kind of good in itself. Nobody would doubt that. So it is misleading to suggest that attainment at the nth level may have declining worth, when, in fact, the principle of shifting benefits and liabilities suggests that it is increasingly valuable. This view we may also chart schematically. In doing so, we shall have to redirect the utility curve in Figure 6.4 to follow the path of the liability curve in Figure 6.3. The utility of attainment at the nth level is understood to rise at an increasing rate as the system grows toward its natural limit.

FIGURE 6.4
Utility of Attainment as the Converse of Liability

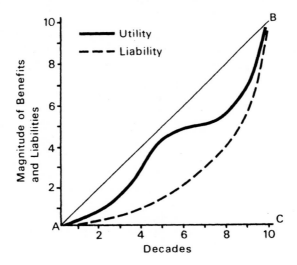

Thus we can schematically represent the idea that the degree of benefit secured by attaining at the nth level is proportional to the magnitude of the disaster incurred by *not* gaining that level. This is the idea central to the counter-argument. It rests on the undoubted truth that avoiding evils and calamities is a good thing, and the greater the evils and calamities, the greater good it is to avoid them. Figure 6.4, no doubt, is the expression of a certain truth, but what truth is it? That is the important question.

When we suggest that the social utility of attainment at the nth level rises sharply at the upper end of the uniform growth line, what we are really saying is that *the value of educational attainment changes.* It changes when attaining at the nth level of the system is no longer viewed as something worth doing for the sake of some good, and is viewed instead as something necessary to endure in order to avoid certain evils. Schooling becomes defensive for the individual.[4] It becomes compulsory in ways that it was n⬛⬛⬛⬛⬛⬛⬛⬛⬛⬛⬛ is a case where supply creates demand. ⬛⬛⬛⬛⬛⬛⬛ ool graduates creates the social compuls⬛⬛⬛⬛

That schooling becomes defensive and compulsory in new ways is the insight providing answers to the two puzzling questions with which we began. As the social utility of second-order benefits declines *for those who receive them,* they become of intense and even overriding necessity *to those who do not receive them.* And this is precisely what is needed to account for the fact that as the social utility of attaining at the nth level declines, there is nonetheless, no decline in the demand to attain that level and no apparent slack in the effort of the system to achieve the next marginal gain toward the natural limit of growth. *It is the interaction between the two principles of zero correlation and shifting benefits and liabilities that is expressed in Figure 6.4.*

Indeed, if we understand Figure 6.4 in this way — as portraying not the continuing value, but the *transforming* value of benefits and liabilities under conditions of approac⬛⬛⬛⬛⬛⬛⬛⬛⬛⬛⬛⬛⬛ are led immediately to two additional ⬛⬛⬛⬛⬛⬛⬛⬛⬛ first is the possibility that at the upper ⬛⬛⬛⬛⬛⬛⬛⬛⬛⬛⬛, instead of anticipating a decline in the an⬛⬛⬛⬛⬛⬛⬛⬛⬛⬛⬛⬛nt at the nth level, we would anticipate either a stable or increasing rate of marginal gain. The reason for this suggestion should be obvious. When the system reaches that state of its growth then any additional increase in attainment is also an increase in the magnitude of potential disaster to be suffered by those who do not complete the nth level. Assuming that there are no counter

4. See Lester C. Thurow, "Education and Economic Equality," *Public Interest* (Summer 1972):66–81.

forces at work, we would anticipate the rate of marginal gain in achievement to press on with *increasing* magnitude because of the desire of people to avoid an increasingly large and personal disaster. But this is not what has happened. Why not?

There are counter forces. There always are. Consider the following illustrative tale. In the mid-60s in the School District of Syracuse, New York, there was a great deal of vigorous discussion centered on the failure of the schools to educate the black population of the district so that they graduated from the high schools in proportion to their numbers among youth of the district. Ten years later, after substantial effort and considerable success in increasing the graduation rate of the district, it was discovered that many students were graduating from the high schools of the city even though they had not achieved skills in reading and mathematics at a level as high as eighth grade norms. Thus, in the mid-70s, the School Board established a qualitative standard of eighth grade achievement in reading and mathematics as a requirement for graduation from the high school.[5] Here we can observe the transformation from attainment to achievement in operation. But that transformation, expressed in the policy of the School Board, probably constitutes a movement in opposition to increasing marginal gains in attainment. As the achievement standards are raised for attainment at the 12th level, the attainment rates are likely to decline — at least for a period of time. Thus, in the interplay between the desire for increased attainment and the desire for established levels of achievement, we find grounds for expecting the size of marginal gains in attainment at the upper end of the uniform growth line to stabilize or vanish rather than increase. Indeed, beyond a certain point in the growth of the system at the nth level, we could construe the size of *any* marginal increase in attainment to constitute a *measure* of the *perceived* magnitude of the disaster to be avoided (on the part of individuals) acting jointly with the transformation from attainment to achievement.

5. The probability is high that there always were students graduating from the 12th level without achieving in these areas at the eighth level; but it was not a problem. It became a problem. Why? Because as the system approaches the limit of its growth at the nth level, the certificate of attainment at that level discriminates for employers less and less. In New York State, however, the high school equivalency test places those who pass it at about the 33rd percentile among eighteen year olds. This is somewhat higher than the eighth grade level. Thus, we know that students passing the high school equivalency test achieve in these areas of the curriculum *at least* at the eighth level of the system. We know nothing of the kind, however, for those who hold the high school diploma. Thus, the "equivalency test" is more informative for employers than the high school diploma secured in the normal way by school attendance. What is needed then is some policy to reestablish the claim that the high school diploma is *at least* equivalent to the equivalency test. Though this need was, in all likelihood, present all the time, it was not recognized as a need until the value of *mere* attainment was threatened by the approach of zero correlation.

But there is a second point to observe in this pattern of interacting forces. Let us suppose that there is no decline in the size of the marginal increase toward attainment as the system approaches zero correlation at the nth level. In that case, we should surely anticipate a rise in the amount of frustration and even rebellion against the school on the part of youth who see school as not particularly worthwhile, but nonetheless necessary. I suppose that nobody who is vibrantly alive likes being compelled to do anything. The distaste of the compulsion might be ameliorated if one can see a clear immediate or a long-term worth in complying. But in the absence of such a vision, the distasteful qualities of the compulsion must become all the more distasteful. And this is precisely the condition described by the principle of shifting benefits and liabilities. Having the diploma is no big deal, but not having it is a disaster.

There is, of course, a problem, not peculiar to this suggestion, but especially evident in it. And that problem is the difficulty in determining the time lag between one development and another in the system. It is one thing to advance the principle of shifting benefits and liabilities as a logical consequence of system growth. It is another thing to suggest that its social consequences will become immediately evident. There is likely to be a delay. It is unreasonable, of course, to suppose that youth are aware of the changing balance of benefits and liabilities *at the time that it begins.* The more reasonable view would be that there is a delay of some years — possibly a decade — in realizing the significance of such changes. In fact, and especially in view of our rudimentary or even non-existent knowledge of how the system works, even on the part of practiced experts, it would not be surprising to discover that *nobody* is aware of these changes *as they occur.*

If we can better understand the system, however, we may become aware of such changes and even learn to anticipate them. If there is increasing disenchantment, frustration, and even rebellion against the school on the part of teen-age youth *of certain groups,* then its presence may be documented by survey data, but its sources are likely to be found in systemic movements of a decade earlier. They are unlikely to be discovered even by the accumulation of survey data at several points in time unless those investigations are embedded in some theory about the system and especially about the nature of systemic time lag.

But there is this further problem in the case of education, namely that the memories of youth are necessarily short. In any *literal* sense of *memory* nobody's memory is longer than his life. Within the educational system, the time lag between developments may be so extensive that if we are to understand the behavior of youth partly in the light of systemic changes, we must recognize that we are trying to understand their behavior in the light of developments for which they have no memory and their elders possibly no awareness.

Thus, we have a second reason for believing that as the system approaches zero correlation, marginal gains in its growth will lessen and perhaps vanish altogether. The first is that the transformation from attainment to achievement will slow the marginal growth of attainment. The second is that as the incentives for attainment shift from the pursuit of a good to the avoidance of a disaster, then the quality of the perceived reasons for attainment will also change and marginal gains in attainment will further decline. And these points are important because the principle of shifting benefits and liabilities, taken by itself, would suggest that the magnitude of marginal increases in attainment in the system might increase, when in fact they have not. But now we see that the theory of the system, taken as a whole, can account for this result. If we consider the phenomena of shifting benefits and liabilities, together with transforming attainment to achievement, the rule of transforming utility, and the possibility of rising frustration from a good changing to a mere necessity, then the actual data become intelligible.

THE SYSTEMIC RULES OF GROWTH ILLUSTRATED

We must persist, however, in our study of these dynamics. Their full meaning is not yet clear. It would be a severe test of the theory of the system if we could establish that it constitutes a different, and in some definable way, a better way of viewing problems of educational policy than more familiar views embedded in the "conventional wisdom." For this test we may turn to an important policy study on the costs and benefits of investment in high school completion. I refer to the reports of the *United States Senate Select Committee on Equal Educational Opportunity* — the Mondale Committee. Consider the following passage.

> Although the census reports the income level associated with each level of schooling, how do we know that these relative income differences are stable over time? More specifically, let us consider the income differentials between persons who have attained various levels of schooling below high school completion and those with high school diplomas. Can we use these differentials to assess the national income foregone as a result of not investing in a minimum of high school completion? Economic theory would suggest that as we increase the supply of high school graduates *vis á vis* ones with less than high school, the relative incomes of the former will decline. If this is true, then

by applying the present observed differences in incomes between the two levels of schooling we would be overstating the returns to the higher level.

In this case, however, the evidence suggests exactly the opposite trend. That is, as the supply of high school graduates has increased, the incomes of high school graduates relative to elementary graduates or high school drop-outs has also increased. [What are the reasons] for this *paradox...?*

The point is that concomitant with the increased supply of high school graduates and persons with college training is an increase in quality or such a large increase in the demand for more highly educated persons that *their incomes have risen relative to persons with less schooling.* In 1949 male high school graduates were receiving about 134 percent of the income of male elementary school graduates. By 1966 the differential had risen to 156 percent *despite* massive increases in numbers of persons with high school diplomas.[6]

We have here a rather familiar approach to the study of educational efficacy from the vantage point of economic theory. If we wish to go beyond the mere conceptual level and actually determine the magnitude of economic benefits to be obtained as a consequence of attainment at a particular level of the system, say, high school, then we might think that there is but a single figure to be obtained. It is a properly discounted figure describing the difference between the mean income of those who complete high school and those who fail to complete it. Now this is a perfectly rational and reasonable procedure to adopt. It is the procedure adopted in the report cited here. It is a procedure that I wish to reject.[7]

Suppose that we divide the uniform growth curve into three equal sectors. If we then calculate the relative advantage to be gained by completing high school in a society where only 10 percent complete it, we might find that there is no mean difference at all. The procedure is impeccable, but in that case, it would yield no policy. On the other hand, if we apply the same procedure in the middle sector of that curve, we are likely to find that there is a difference in the mean earnings of the two groups. And this fact, together with arguments of justice, tells us what to do. The relative advantage gained by greater educational attainment should be extended to all persons. It would be unjust to withhold that opportunity from anyone. The procedure used to determine the magnitude of the benefits of attainment remains as good as it was, but now it produces a policy argument about what to do. The difficulty is that *that argument has application only within that middle sector of the uniform growth curve.* As we extend that oppor-

6. *The Costs to the Nation of Inadequate Education, A Report Prepared for the Select Committee on Equal Educational Opportunity of the U.S. Senate,* Henry M. Levin *et al.* (January 1972), p. 20. The age cohort studied in this report is 25–34. Emphasis added.

7. Appendix C, Benefit and Liability: Further Investigations, contains an extended and detailed defense of this rejection.

tunity to everyone and as increasing numbers avail themselves of it, then the system expands. What then?

The reasoning contained in the passage cited is as follows. As attainment levels increase, we would expect a decline in the relative earnings differences between those who attain a high school diploma and those who do not because as the supply of graduates increases, the market needs to pay less for their services. Confronted with more and more people at a certain level of the system, the market can afford to pay them less and less. And so we would expect the mean difference in earning between those who attain and those who do not will decline. But, as the report notes, this is not what has been happening. What has been happening is portrayed there as a paradox.

But what has happened will seem paradoxical only if we do not consider the converse to the economist's perspective. The point is that as the number of high school graduates increases, the market will pay less to secure their services, but by the same token the employer can begin using that level of attainment as a screening device below which he need pay others even less. In short, as the expansion of the system continues, we produce circumstances that are new. We no longer have a manpower market that fluctuates between scarcity and a glut on the supply side. Especially at the lower levels of the system, we produce a market that is always on the glut side. It is perpetually an employer's market.

What we should expect, therefore, is that, for a time, expansion of the attainment levels in the system will produce a narrowing in the mean difference of earnings between those who drop out and those who do not. But, at another stage, we should expect once again, a widening in that gap between the earnings of the one group and the earnings of the other. And this means that though we may continue using the same measures of the benefit of higher attainment, *we are no longer measuring the same thing*. The widening gap of earnings between attainers and non-attainers, *had* been construed as a measure of the benefit of higher attainment. Now it must be construed as a measure of the increasing liabilities suffered by non-attainers — the increasing liabilities that are produced, moreover, by the mere expansion of the system, and not by the behavior of the labor market. This is a partial declaration of independence of the educational system from the economy.

The three sectors of the uniform growth curve then represent drastically different sets of circumstances. The same measures do not apply equally well at all points on that line. They do not measure the same thing in the higher end of the growth line, *nor are the policy arguments in any degree the same in the three sectors*. Instead of focusing single-mindedly upon the justice of extending the benefits of higher attainment, we must now focus on the magnitude of the liabilities that we create in the very effort to extend those benefits.

The manpower economist will argue that in calculating the individual marginal utility of higher attainment in the system, we must take into account the value of work experience, as against the worth of greater long-term opportunities afforded by continuing one's education. And from these factors we must subtract the work experience and earnings that are lost when one decides to defer entry into the labor market. When these two values are in balance, then one is confronted with a genuine educational choice. But it should be clear, by now, that as the system expands into the third sector of the uniform growth curve this choice is never presented. The costs of not going on increase constantly at the same time that the benefits of going on, relative to all others who go on, are reduced. This, in effect, is the operation of the principle of shifting benefits and liabilities. *It requires a fresh perspective on the data, and a different approach to policy for the system.*

In short, what is regarded by the familiar theory of the Mondale report as something paradoxical is viewed by the theory of the system as something expected, and what has happened in the relation between benefits and liabilities, as the report says, *"despite* massive increases in numbers of persons with high school diplomas" is regarded by the theory of the system as something that happened largely *as a consequence* of the rise in attainment.[8] These are important observations, for they are significant signs that the theory of the system, as outlined so far, leads to different interpretations of the empirical data and an improved capacity to account for the known facts when contrasted with more familiar and conventional views of how the system works.

These observations on the behavior of the system — the relation among attainment, benefits, and their distribution — arise from our study of the law of zero correlation and its effects superimposed upon a uniform growth rate. The changing utility of attainment, the shifting balance of benefits and liabilities, the transforming social meaning of attainment in the system — all of these are derived from considering the consequences of increasing attainment in the system. They might, therefore, be collectively referred to as "the systemic rules of uniform growth in attainment." These

8. It is also worth noting that though the report to the Mondale Committee places great importance on the "massive increases in numbers of persons with high school diplomas," that fact received much less weight within the theory of the system. We can have "massive increases in the numbers of people with high school diplomas" purely as a consequence of a massive increase in a certain age cohort. The vastly more significant growth is the increase in the *proportion* of each age cohort securing such a diploma. This difference, however, may only reflect loose language used in the report rather than a genuine difference of approach.

principles are concerned, for the most part, with the connection between the distribution of second-order educational benefits and non-educational social goods. It follows that in these observations we have been concerned to make specific some of the ways that the system is related to the society. Furthermore, we should observe that one of the major consequences of attending to these features of systemic behavior is that, taken together, they begin to establish the fact that the relation of the system to its society will not be the same, and therefore, the internal behavior of the system itself will change, as it passes from one sector of the uniform growth line to another.

THE LAW OF LAST ENTRY

The systemic rules of uniform growth, however, do not exhaust the principles of the system. They are derived from the elaboration of a single principle that is itself tautological. We must consider, however, another general law that is neither tautological nor *a priori* in any sense. It is, however, a sound empirical generalization.

The Group of Last Entry

It appears to be true that no society has been able to expand its total educational enterprise to include lower status groups *in proportion to their numbers in the population* until the system is "saturated" by the upper and middle status groups. I shall refer to this principle as the law of last entry. It states that there is a definable law describing which groups, in which sequence, and in what magnitude will benefit from any given expansion of the educational system. In other words, as we approach the point of universal attainment at any level of the system, the last group to enter and complete that level will be drawn from lower socioeconomic groups.[9] The

9. See *Social Objectives in Educational Planning* (Paris:OECD, 1967). This is a report of the OECD Study Group in the Economics of Education. In her "Summary Review by the Rapporteur," Leila Sussmann, of Tufts University, reports: "expansion of higher education in the United States since 1947 *has* been associated with some equalisation of participation as between the manual and non-manual classes. However, this equalisation has set in at a point when the participation of the top occupational strata is approaching 100 per cent. ... Thus the American case is no exception to the rule that substantial room in selective schools is made for the manual strata only after the demand of the non-manual

law of last entry contains the dual assertion that (1) there will be a group of last entry, and (2) that group will be defined by lower socioeconomic criteria.

What is the logical status of this joint claim? The first part of the law of last entry might be construed as an analytic claim. In any finite series, there is a last element. That is part of what we *mean* by saying that it is finite. Thus, the claim that there *will be* a group of last entry can be construed as analytic provided we understand that group to be defined *by its being last*. But when we speak of there being a *group* of last entry, that is not what we mean. We are implying instead that the group is to be defined on independent criteria, and not merely by its being last.

Imagine a society in which the attainment rate in year Y for the age cohort x at the nth level is zero, and that the next year the attainment rate for the same cohort is 100 percent. There would be no group of last entry. But no educational system behaves in that way, and it is doubtful that any could, except possibly at the very first level of the system. When we say that there will be a group of last entry we are implying that increases of attainment may be regular, but they are also gradual.

Imagine a society in which attainment, over an extended period of time, has grown from 10 percent to 80 percent at the nth level of the system. Let us suppose further that there are no discoverable marks of ascribed status (like family income or parents' social status) by which we could define the last 20 percent, and that further there are no indicators of native ability or cultural characteristics that will define that group. The last 20 percent is in every way exactly like every other 20 percent in the movement of the system from 10 percent to 80 percent attainment. In that case, we could not say that there is a *group* of last entry either. The concept of a *group* of last entry implies that there are criteria for identifying that group

groups has been satisfied" (p. 18). She reports also on data collected on the social composition of freshmen at the University of Puerto Rico in 1944, 1952, and 1960, and remarks that "the equalisation . . . was confined within the middle class. In effect the new middle class (and the agricultural operators) was catching up with the old" (p. 19). She says that "It is plausible to suppose that when the near-monopoly of the upper middle classes is broken, it is the lower middle classes who first grasp a disproportionate share of the new places available. After their demand is met, the attendance rate of the manual strata may begin to 'level up.' . . . social class differentials do not necessarily decline as selective schools expand their intake. Much depends on how great an expansion takes place. If growth is limited, as in the case of the English grammar schools, it is mathematically impossible for the numerous offspring of the white collar and manual classes to attain an attendance rate even nearly equal to the existing rate of the sparse upper and professional classes. Usually there is a process of class succession with the upper classes reaching near-saturation of their demand before the occupational categories just below them in the class structure begin to raise their rates of attendance. Even the United States has followed this class-succession pattern" (pp. 19–20).

independently of their being simply last. These observations are sufficient to *demonstrate* that the law of last entry, unlike the law of zero correlation, is a purely contingent claim.

As far as I can determine, there are no formal or *a priori* reasons to suppose either that there must be a group of last entry or that that group will be defined by criteria of lower socioeconomic status. Under most conceptions of distributive justice we would assume that membership in the group of last entry *should be* defined only by educationally relevant criteria (see Chapter III). But that is not how the system behaves wherever it appears.

A little reflection will suffice to show that the specific *form* that issues of equal educational opportunity assume will be defined for the system by the interaction of the law of zero correlation and the law of last entry. Issues of equal educational opportunity are always defined as issues of distribution. They always arise from perceived inequities in the distribution of resources, access, or benefits. And their resolution is always construed to be the restoration of equity in resources, access, or benefits. But which issues of distribution turn out to be politically crucial for educational policy will depend substantially upon the size of the educational enterprise. The issues will be shaped by the position of the system on the uniform growth line.

In the early stages, there may be many children having no school to attend at all. That can be viewed as a problem of unequal opportunity. It is resolved by providing some school for every child. But then it may be discovered that though there is *some* school for *every* child, they are not equal in their resources, facilities, or curricula. That, in turn, may be viewed as a problem — though a different problem — of equal opportunity. It is resolved by providing equal facilities, resources, and curricula. But having resolved that problem, we may discover that though every child has access to some school, and though that school has resources, facilities and curricula equal to all others, still those attending some schools do not achieve at the same levels as those in other schools, nor do they go on to successive levels of the system at the same rate. Thus, the successively different definitions given to equal opportunity correspond to the different sectors of the uniform growth line. And those issues progress roughly from (1) the attainment of equal access to *some* school, to (2) securing equal resources and curricula, to (3) securing equal educational and second-order benefits. The apparently arbitrary division of the uniform growth line into three different sectors turns out to have its justification partly in the claim that in each sector education in the system is valued differently and the political issues of policy for the system are transformed.

Corollaries of the Law of Last Entry

Clearly, the law of last entry, like the law of zero correlation, is rich in associated principles. Primary among these is the *principle of the moving target. As the group of last entry reaches its target of attainment at the nth level, the target will shift.* By this I mean simply that the individual motivation of members of the group of last entry to attain at the nth level in a system approaching zero correlation is to secure the *relative* benefits that the system has afforded other groups. But in this aspiration, the group of last entry will be disappointed, because as they attain their target, the law of zero correlation will set in and there will be no *relative* benefits to be secured by attainment at that level. They will not gain the relative benefits that others have secured. They will only have avoided a disaster that is uniquely their own. As they attain their target, the target will shift to a higher level of the system, and the dynamics of intensification sketched in Chapter V will again be set in motion.

Even though the system will not operate for the group of last entry as it does for others, still there are aggregate benefits for the society in seeing that the group of last entry attains its target. The trouble is that the aggregate good for the society will never suffice as a motive for any individual to advance in the system. No youngster trying to master the French verb or simultaneous equations is likely to be much encouraged by the knowledge that society will be improved if he succeeds. The group of last entry then, is faced with a dilemma. As the system approaches its limit of attainment at the nth level, the group of last entry may persevere either in order to merely avoid a disaster or in order to benefit from the system as others have. The first reason to persist constitutes an unsatisfactory kind of compulsion, and the second is destined not to be satisfied. Perhaps the most rational strategy for members of the group of last entry is to promote whatever public policies would offer the best chance of avoiding membership in the group of last entry at the level of $n + 1$ and beyond. Hence, we can appreciate the meaning of strategies for promoting racial quotas and patterns of educational assistance favoring the lower socioeconomic groups. Their purpose is to escape membership in the group of last entry.

We must ask, however, why these systemic principles are presently important on the American scene? We have experienced the consequences of a system reaching zero correlation at the fifth and eighth levels. What is so different about approaching that point at the twelfth level? The answer is that these general principles will be especially important in any system where zero correlation is being approached at the last level intended to be inclusive and where the next higher level of the system is intended to be selective. Such is the case in the American system. The comprehensive secondary school is intended to be, as its name implies, comprehensive and universal. Its very *raison d'être* is to include everyone. But it is a basic feature of the traditional higher educational system that it is intended to be selective. There is an admission process in the system of higher education, and there is not, typically, for the secondary system.

Under these conditions, the phenomenon of the moving target will turn out to be one of the most significant, perhaps even decisive, factors in leading to expansion beyond the secondary system. For unless the belief in the efficacy of education is abandoned altogether, we would expect two simultaneous pressures for expansion — the one aimed at easing access to the next higher level of the system, and the other aimed at maintaining the selectivity of that access by intensifying the educational process below the nth level. These are the modes of expansion whose dynamics have already been explored in our first attempt to set the system in motion in Chapter V.

Conclusion: The Independence of the System?

By setting the system in motion, we begin to discern the principles of its internal behavior. Whether we attend to the systemic rules of uniform growth or to the law of last entry, it becomes more plausible to suggest that the system has its own life. The principles so far stated have to do primarily with the operation of second-order educational benefits, those transcripts, certificates, diplomas, and other evidences of attainment, whose functions are so ubiquitous in the structure of the system. But those second-order benefits are, in one of their forms, the tokens of exchange that link not only the units of the system to one another but also the system itself to its surrounding society. When we begin to grasp the internal laws of the system, then we can begin to ask from a fresh perspective whether its behavior is controlled or guided by its relation to the surrounding society or whether it is in fact the other way — that the relation of the system to its society is determined by its own internal necessities.

These alternatives, of course, are framed too simplistically. There is, no doubt, some dialectic in the matter. But the point I have wished to stress is that there *are* two sides to that dialectic. There *is* a system, and it *does* have its own laws of behavior. The point of the matter may be approached in another way. It is a common claim nowadays to suggest that we can change the dynamics of the educational system, especially in relation to the law of last entry, if we will only change the character of our society. It does not seem to me uncharitable to suggest that such a claim is highly problematic. Indeed, it seems to me doubtful. By setting the system in motion, that is, by identifying its own independent laws of behavior, we have reason to conjecture that *that* system is unlikely to change even in the midst of drastic social alterations surrounding it. We know of no society, for example, in which the system exists and in which the law of last entry has been successfully repealed.

These are the larger implications toward which this effort to set the system in motion has been pointing. They remain in the realm of conjecture. That is to say, though some systemic laws have been stated and have been provided rational defense, still they stand without the careful definition and formulation that empirical confirmation or strict deductive demonstration would require. And surely, they stand at this point even without historical illustration. To thoroughly test the principle of shifting benefits and liabilities, for example, is a task quite beyond the limits of this exploration. However, as an illustration of what, in the hands of more able persons, such a test might look like, I have included an extended illustrative inquiry in Appendix C. There, for the principle of shifting benefits and liabilities, I have attempted to provide the definitional precision that empirical test requires. I shall leave it for the reader to decide whether the results of that effort strengthen or weaken the central claim that the educational system has a dynamic of its own not to be explained by the economic and social events surrounding it.

It bears repeating that in this entire effort to set the system in motion I have been concerned primarily with the value of second-order educational benefits. It is time, however, to reach beyond this preoccupation with second-order goods and consider other dynamics describing how the system seeks to deal with the value of educational benefits themselves.

·◦[VII]◦·

THE DIALECTIC OF TWO PRINCIPLES
Best and Equal

Oᴜʀ ᴀᴄᴄᴏᴜɴᴛ ᴏꜰ ᴛʜᴇ sʏsᴛᴇᴍ is seriously incomplete. In this chapter I propose a partial remedy by exploring the dialectic between two principles especially fruitful in their implications. I shall refer to them as "the best principle" and "the equal principle." By "the best principle" I mean the principle that each person is entitled to that education that is best for him; and by "the equal principle" I mean the claim that each is entitled to receive an education at least as good as (equal to) that provided for others.

These principles are appealed to in an enormous number of practical arguments of the system. The dialectic between the "best" and "equal" principles underlies all arguments seeking to establish the boundaries between what education must be common to all and what education can be specialized and, therefore, peculiar to some. But the tension between them underwrites also all arguments for and against such practices as tracking, special education in all its forms, and the distinctions between groups within the system that produce such things as bilingual education and full service legislation for the handicapped. Arguments appealing to the "best" and "equal" principles constitute an extensive domain.

But there are additional and serious reasons for attending to these principles. There is a common view, though much disputed in recent scholarship, that the educational system, at least in America, became universal because it was made compulsory. Our study of the system to this point, however, would suggest a counter view. The system becomes compulsory because it is made universal. The thesis emerging from our study of the system in motion is that the system can expand to the point where going to school for children and youth — and in prospect for adults as well — may become compulsory in the same sense as going to the hospital is probably compulsory for anyone who suffers serious injury in an accident on the expressway. The point is not that there is any law requiring it, only that not doing it is the path to certain disaster.

114

But if it is true that the system becomes compulsory, in this sense, because it is made universal, then we need an independent account of the practical arguments that contribute to its being universal. By asking how the system becomes universal, I mean to ask how it comes to be open to all and, in fact, how it comes to include all persons within some expanding range of ages. Becoming universal, in this sense, is a process by which the system develops from involving some to involving all. Thus, if the expansion of the system is to be described by a range of practical arguments, it will be described by a range of arguments that reason from "some" to "all." By fortunate coincidence, these happen also to be the arguments within which the "best" and "equal" principles most clearly operate. Thus, it is by examining such arguments that we shall best understand not only the dynamics of these two principles, but also uncover the needed independent account of the practical arguments contributing to the system becoming universal.

RESTRICTED AND UNRESTRICTED ARGUMENTS

Let us, therefore, examine the interaction of the "best" and "equal" principles as displayed in the employment of "some-to-all-arguments."[1] There are two forms of the relevant some-to-all-argument. I shall refer to them as the restricted version and the unrestricted version. Consider the following argument that we are disposed to use in almost endless variety.

> If there is a particular student, A, who has a specific liability, L, by virtue of which he is less likely than others to succeed in the educational system,
> And if there is some educational program, E, that promises to overcome that liability, then that program (or pedagogy), E, is the best one for A, and for everyone else with the property L.
> And since each is entitled to receive the program that is best for him (the best principle).

> Therefore, everyone with the characteristic, L, is entitled to receive E.

1. I refer to these as some-to-all arguments not because they are, in any sense inductive, but because they appear to reason from a particular case to a universal conclusion. Any strict formalization of such arguments will show that they are deductive in the conventional sense. They reason through the employment of either the best or the equal principle, either of which suitably formulated will require the universal quantifier.

I shall refer to this argument as the restricted version of the some-to-all argument, because the class generated by the property L is restricted.

We may, however, modify this argument so that, instead of concluding with the claim that certain persons are entitled to a certain program by virtue of their special characteristics, we conclude that all persons are entitled to the *same* program. This inference is permitted by the addition of a single premise concerning the distribution of the property, L. We may add to the restricted argument, the claim that

The property, L, is possessed by everyone.

Therefore, everyone is entitled to receive the program E.

E is therefore the best program to which everyone is entitled by "the equal principle." This is the unrestricted version of the some-to-all argument. It states that if A is entitled to receive a particular education by virtue of having the property L, and if everyone has that property, then everyone is entitled to receive E. The class generated by the property, L, is unrestricted. It is important to note, however, that in the unrestricted version of the argument, the property, L, changes from a liability to some common characteristic like having intelligence, being a citizen, or the like.

Restricted Argument Examined

In setting forth such an argument as belonging to the theory of the system, we must be able to state when the argument applies and when it does not. Consider the restricted version. Will the restricted argument work for any property, L, for example? Will it work for any program E? In short, is the domain of the argument limited? To what kinds of fallacies is it subject?

It seems *prima facie* true that the restricted argument will work for any value of L, provided that L is a property having some causative and deleterious effect upon educational success. The argument will not work, however, to support the claim that all children are entitled to the kind of educational program received by those who are successful in the system. For that inference we need the "equal principle" or the unrestricted argument. Suppose there is a group of children who do very well in the system. They are successful; they have no apparent liabilities or difficulties. We are not permitted by the restricted argument to reason that every child is entitled to the program that *they* receive.

Why not? Because we do not ordinarily believe that the program they receive is a causative factor in their success. Their success is due to the fact that they have no liabilities. Presumably they would be successful in any program and not *because* of any particular educational program. L and E, apparently, have limited domains in the restricted argument. They refer only to properties construed to constitute liabilities and programs deemed effective in overcoming those liabilities.

The "best principle," that each is entitled to that education best for him, is often construed to imply the necessity of "individualized instruction." But this is another kind of fallacy. Seeing why such a conclusion is unwarranted, however, will permit us to identify other, more serious constraints on the restricted argument.

It is true that no two human beings are exactly alike. There is always some property or set of properties unique to each. *In short, there are individual variations.* We cannot, however, reason from this truism to the claim that individual educational programs would be best for each. To derive that conclusion, we need to meet two further constraints on the argument. The first is to show that the variations in question meet certain *standards of relevance.* These standards are required, because not every variation among persons matters, and among those that do matter for certain aspects of life, not all will matter to success in the system. So some variabilities will be relevant, and some will not. The variability in question, however, must also exist in a *certain magnitude.* Small variations, even though relevant, will not count. For example, no one, I suppose, would argue that stable differences of two points on an IQ scale would warrant distinct educational programs. Variations of ten times that size, however, might. In short the restricted argument may be successfully used only if it meets certain standards of relevance and magnitude in the variabilities that it refers to.

Though there are differences between persons, there are also similarities. In attempting to understand the constraints on the restricted argument, we need to know which of these realities — variability or similarity — we are to count as more important and when. How do we determine what is to count as a relevant difference and what is to count as a significant magnitude of that difference? How does the system make this determination?

Standards of Magnitude

I believe that a direct answer can be given. In the use of the restricted argument, the standards of magnitude will be determined by scale, and standards of relevance will be determined by the operation of the principle of fair benefit distribution (see Chapter III). But this point needs explanation. Let us consider standards of magnitude first.

It is tautological that each individual has his own birthdate, and in a randomly selected population of, say, 10, it is unlikely that any two will have the *same* birthdate. However, in a randomly selected population of 300, it is practically certain that some will have the same birthdate. We may reason by extension. It is tautological that each child learns at his own rate, and that seems, on the surface, to be an educationally significant variability. But the claim that each learns at a rate different from all others is not a tautology. It is, in fact, unlikely to be true at all. It is likely to be true only as long as we have in mind a very small population randomly selected. The probability that each child learns at a rate different from all others, like the probability that each has a different birthdate, will be reduced with every increment in the size of the population we have in mind. It is possibly true in the family; it is unlikely to be true in the school.[2]

Children learn at different rates. And those differences are relevant for certain purposes. Granted. But how large must those differences be if we are to say that they *must* be considered. In a small group, say two or three children, quite minute differences in the rates of learning might be counted as significant. But in a very large group, say one hundred children, we are unlikely to permit such differences to count heavily unless they are also quite substantial. And if they are very substantial, *and* if such variabilities occur with a high degree of frequency, then, for reasons of educational effectiveness, we are likely to turn to some kind of grouping that will have the effect of reducing the magnitude of the variability in each group. Here clearly, the best principle is operating in a formulation of the restricted version of the some-to-all argument.

We may conclude that standards of magnitude are likely to be established by the scale of the setting within which the restricted version of the some-to-all argument is applied.

Standards of Relevance

But what of the standards of relevance? We see how the system determines what *magnitude* of a variability is to be counted as important.

2. In these observations I do not wish to suggest that the only difference between school and family is a difference in scale. I wish only to emphasize the ways that differences in scale affect standards of relevance and magnitude in the variabilities that count in the some-to-all argument. Nonetheless, these observations may help us to understand what sociologists have meant in claiming that one difference between the family and the school is that the social norms applied in the family are more often particularistic and those in the school are more often universalistic. See Robert Dreeben, *On What is Learned in School* (Reading, Mass.: Addison-Wesley, 1968).

But how does the system determine which variability is to be counted as *relevant* to the restricted argument?

The answer again, is readily at hand. You will recall the claim in Chapter III that there are only three sets of educationally relevant attributes entering into the operation of the principle of fair benefit distribution. They are choice, tenacity, and ability. Whatever variability is selected, whatever property is identified, in using the some-to-all argument, that characteristic must be subsumable under one of the "educationally relevant attributes" entering into the operation of the principle of fair benefit distribution. That is to say, in order for the some-to-all argument to work, it must be shown that the individual property referred to in the argument is a property affecting the exercise of choice, tenacity, or ability.

Suppose, for example, that we wish to enlist the some-to-all argument in establishing the claim that those with defective sight are entitled to special educational programs. Then we must establish the claim that defective sight is a causative factor limiting the exercise of ability, or choice. We do not ordinarily take the pains to do so because the connection is so obvious. The need to establish it escapes our notice.

The need for that connection is more apparent where it is less easily provided. Suppose that we wish to use ascribed characteristics, like social class, or personal characteristics, like ethnicity, in establishing the claim of certain groups to special treatment in the system. It is not immediately obvious that differences of social class and ethnicity would constitute "relevant" variabilities in meeting the standards required for the some-to-all argument. However, if we can establish a strong claim that the possession of these attributes impairs the exercise of choice, ability, or the power to persevere in the system, then we shall have demonstrated that they are suitable attributes to employ in using the some-to-all argument. The demonstration of this connection is, in fact, a premise in virtually all arguments commending the adoption of culture-free tests of ability or achievement, the need for bilingual programs of education, and for special services related to all forms of learning disability and physical or medical handicaps. In short, the standards of magnitude implicit in the some-to-all argument are established by the *scale* of the educational setting, but the standards of relevance are established for the system by appealing to those attributes that are relevant to a just distribution of its benefits. Relevance, in other words, is established by appealing to the principle of fair benefit distribution.

Unrestricted Argument Examined

So much for the logic of the restricted version of the some-to-all argument. How does the unrestricted argument operate in the practical arguments of the system? Instead of being employed to establish the claim of certain groups for a distinctive education, the unrestricted argument establishes the claim of everyone to the *same* education. We arrive at this conclusion by a premise stating that the property L, no longer interpreted as a liability, is a property that is universally distributed. Therefore, the class generated by that property, whatever it is, is unrestricted.

But what specific property and what specific program are referred to in the unrestricted argument? We are not yet in a position to offer even the crudest definition of these two variables. Yet, they must be defined, and their definition will be specified, in any successful application of the unrestricted argument. Which of these two variables will carry the heavier burden of inference in any instance of the argument will depend on which of its two forms is employed. The unrestricted argument has two versions. There is what I shall call "the systemic formulation" and "the educational formulation."

The difference between them arises from the different order in which the relevant variables of the argument are defined. The systemic formulation gains whatever credibility it has from its place within the theory of the system. It begins by providing an *operational* definition of the educational *program* referred to in the argument and ends by identifying the relevant property. The educational formulation, on the other hand, belongs primarily, though not exclusively, to the theory of education rather than the theory of the system. It begins by identifying the relevant human attributes referred to in the argument and ends by providing an operational definition of the program.

The Systemic Formulation

What kind of education is the best program to which everyone is entitled by the equal principle? We may answer directly: It is the education that the rich provide for their sons, *whatever that education may be*. It is not merely that education that the rich *can* provide, but the kind that they *do* provide, and not for their daughters, but for their sons.[3]

---

3. I am assuming, perhaps erroneously, that many, though certainly not all, of the *educational* goals of the feminist movement would be secured if women received the same education as men with approximately the same results in employment and in social roles.

Now it must seem outrageous to suggest that the education the rich provide for their sons is a suitable definition of the education that everyone is entitled to by the equal principle. But recall that I am offering an *operational* definition of one of the terms required in the unrestricted version of the some-to-all argument as it appears in the practical rationality of the system. A full defense of the adequacy of this definition is difficult, but some observations can be provided that tend to support the claim that it is the operational definition that we, in fact, employ.

Consider the following. The most significant thing that distinguishes the rich and the poor is wealth. That is the only difference between the two that permits the one and prevents the other from buying the best education there is. If it be asked how we can operationally identify the best education that can be secured, we could look at that kind of education that is purchased by those in a position to purchase any kind there is. That would operationally identify the education that all are entitled to as the education that the rich buy for their sons.

Secondly, we should note that the education provided by the system *includes* the education that the rich — either rich school districts or rich parents — provide for their sons. By "the system" I have not meant to refer simply to publicly supported education, but to the system as described in the first six chapters of this study. Private schools, of the sort often supported by the wealthy in America, are nonetheless schools, and they are linked to all other schools by media of exchange and by the mechanisms of status established by the media of exchange. The education provided by the system includes the education provided by such schools. In short, the education to which everyone is entitled, if that be the education that the rich buy for their sons, is an education provided by the system.

But it is more important to note that this education that the system provides — that the rich buy for their sons — is usually taken to be the example of the best to which everyone is entitled. If we did not believe this, then why, in our concern to equalize fiscal resources, do we never seek equality by levelling *down?* The reason we try to equalize educational resources is to make available to all the education to which they are entitled, and the reason we never seek to equalize down is that we believe the system is supposed to bring into everybody's reach the education that is bought by the rich. Equality is not really our interest in equalization. Our interest is rather to make accessible to everyone the education that the rich buy for their sons. That is the operational standard that the system uses in identifying the education to which everybody is entitled.

Finally, we should note that the effort to make available to everyone that education that the rich buy for their sons is so fundamental a theme in the story of American education that it must be regarded not as a mere ideological tenet to be occasionally honored, but as a principle of basic policy or fundamental purpose. It is a fundamental premise of the system. The argument has often been that among the chief and highest benefits of American institutions has been their capacity to level those massive, evident and intractable distinctions of rank and privilege that were so marked a feature of European institutions. They were intended, as it was argued in the Kalamazoo case, to make the paths of honor and office open to all.[4] And so when it was argued, as it was in that case, that the general public could not be taxed to support schools that taught foreign and classical languages and other subjects of no practical necessity to American youth, the court argued in reply that it had always been the most central and persistent purpose of policy to make such opportunities available to all that desired them, and all the more so since they were precisely those topics of study that marked the education of those of high rank and of high birth. I cite the opinion of the court in this context not because it is so unusual, but precisely because it is not. In short, we cannot lightly cast aside the claim that central in the expansion of the system has been the effort to make available to all that education that had been available only to the rich, and to do so on the grounds that that is the education that everyone is entitled to. If we ask what kind of education is best for all, what kind it is that all are entitled to receive and that must, therefore, be provided to all by the system, we shall find it operationally defined as the education that the rich buy for their sons.

The Unrestricted Argument Extended

For the moment, let us grant that the proposed operational definition of the education to which all are entitled by "the equal principle" has been established as the definition that actually prevails in the behavior of the system. The education each is entitled to is the education that the rich provide for their sons. Even so, an additional step would be required if we are to discover in the unrestricted argument the practical reasons for the system becoming universal. Note the following, however. *If it could be established* that the educational program referred to in the unrestricted argument is one and the same as the educational program provided by the system, then it would follow as an immediate inference from the equal principle that the education provided by the system — whatever it is — *is* the education that everyone is entitled to. In short, the system must become universal. It takes a moment of pondering, but a moment should suffice to

4. 30 Michigan Reports (1874–75):70–85. Excerpted in Daniel Calhoun, *The Educating of Americans: A Documentary History* (Boston: Houghton Mifflin, 1969), pp. 298–304.

show that this extension of the unrestricted argument would provide the practical reasons for the system becoming universal.

I grant, however, that the necessary premise for this inference cannot be established. Not even by the most sophisticated — or sophistical — trickery could one claim that the education provided by the system — whatever it is — is the education to which each is entitled by the equal principle. To advance such a claim would be equivalent to advancing the claim that the education provided by the system is always as good as the education the rich buy for their sons. Such a claim is patently false.

Nonetheless, in order to better explore the dynamics of the unrestricted argument and its relation to the universality of the system, I wish to exercise a peculiar kind of suspension of reality. Let us momentarily accept as true the claim that *the education provided by the system —whatever it is — is the best education that can be provided for all*. This is somewhat different from the claim that the education provided by the system is always as good as the education that the rich buy for their sons. It may be no more true, but that remains to be determined. Nevertheless, it is a different claim. It has a different meaning.

The claim that E is the best education that can be provided *for all* is quite compatible with the proposition that it is not the best education that can be provided, or the best that can be provided for each, or the best that can be secured by some. Consider an analogy. It might be argued that a very good, large-scale cafeteria provides the best cuisine that can be provided *for all*, but no one would argue that it can provide the best that can be secured by some individuals considered separately. It will probably lack the delicacy of bouquet and the nuances of flavor that can be secured in a truly good gourmet restaurant where each portion is prepared individually. It can be very good indeed, and still not be the best that can be secured by some persons individually. However, if such a cafeteria is supposed to provide the best food that can be provided for all, and if it is discovered that some can get better food than it provides, then it would have to attempt incorporating *that* cuisine into its offerings.

In short, the claim that the education provided by the system, *whatever it is*, is the best education that can be provided for all — this claim does not imply that the education provided by the system cannot be improved. I do not mean to suggest that it is the best education that there can ever be. On the contrary, I mean only that *the education provided by the system stands in a dynamic and constantly changing relation to a standard of the best that is available at any particular time, when "the best" is defined operationally as that education that the rich buy for their sons*.

In effect, there is a standard, operationally defined by the system, as to what constitutes the best education. The *claim* of the system, whether justified or not, is that it takes that standard of the best that can be provided and makes it available to all. In this effort, the system, like a large-scale cafeteria, always falls short. But the claim remains nonetheless, that what the system aims to do, and *must* aim to do, is to apply that standard of what is best, making it available to all. But, of course, the meaning of "the best that can be provided for all" is constantly hedged about with limitations of time, resources and other constraints. It comes to mean "the best that is feasible within X or Y limitations."

We may put the dynamics implicit in this tortuous pattern of thought in yet another way. By the equal principle each is entitled to an education at least as good as that provided for others. In the unrestricted form of the some-to-all argument the education they are entitled to is operationally defined as the education that the rich buy for their sons. But how can that be provided for all? Why, through the educational system, of course. The system is precisely that set of arrangements through which there is provided the best education that can be provided for all. That is the very heart of what the system is about. *Insofar as it makes good on the claim to provide for everyone that education that the rich buy for their sons, and insofar as it can be claimed that no other means of education does better, then justifiably, the system must be universal.* It provides what everybody is entitled to, and by "the equal principle" everybody is entitled to what it provides. And insofar as the system fails in these claims — which is always, in some degree — we are justified in calling for reform. Indeed, it seems to me highly probable that if there were some means of securing such a standard of education outside the system, then that other set of institutional arrangements would become part of the system connected to the rest by a medium of exchange and adopting the same operational standards of what constitutes "the best."

The Educational Formulation

This is the systemic formulation of the unrestricted argument. That argument, however, may receive another formulation. Instead of beginning with an operational definition of the educational program referred to in the argument, we can begin by attending to certain properties of individuals, universally distributed, but differently defined. Everyone shares in the capacity for a developed sense of craft, the exercise of intelligence, and a sense of style. Everyone has a desire for self-autonomy and a sense of individual integrity. These are distinctive human capacities and, no doubt, they are universally distributed. If these capacities are used to define the relevant property in the some-to-all argument, then the kind of education that everyone is entitled to is that education — whatever it is — that cultivates these capacities.

We would not identify this kind of education as the education that the rich buy for their sons. Indeed, to discover this kind of education, we may have to look totally outside the system, or at specific things that may occur from time to time within it. But, in any case, this kind of education — whatever it is — would have to be identified on grounds independent of what the system itself does. This is the *educational formulation* of the unrestricted version of the some-to-all argument. It is an argument that belongs to the theory of education, not to the theory of the system. It includes the opening premises of a theory of education; it does not elucidate the practical arguments of the system. For that reason, I shall not expand on the educational formulation of the some-to-all argument. It is important, but it leads to the theory of education and away from the theory of the system.

However, between these two versions of the argument — the systemic and the educational — there clearly exists a relationship, although, equally clearly there exists a certain tension. They have the same structure. They are formally the same argument. Yet, by filling in the blanks of the arguments — by introducing different values for the variables — we produce, on the one hand, a description of the practical arguments for the universality of the system, and, on the other hand, the beginnings of an approach to educational theory. And the conclusions derived in these two ways may not be altogether consistent. What the system defines operationally as the best education may not be what, on other grounds, we would recognize as a good education at all. Between the systemic and the educational versions of the expanded argument, we clearly encounter the tension, perhaps even conflict, between competing conceptions of what constitutes a good education.

THE DIALECTIC OF RESTRICTED AND UNRESTRICTED ARGUMENTS

We have then a restricted and an unrestricted formulation of the some-to-all argument, and within the latter, a further division between the systemic and the educational versions. Just as there is a tension or dialectic between the educational and systemic versions of the unrestricted argument, so we should also expect to find a dialectic between the restricted and unrestricted versions and, therefore, a dialectic between the best principle and the equal principle.

These principles express independent claims in the sense that either can be satisfied under conditions leaving the other unattained. It is quite conceivable that a society providing each person an education equal to that received by all others, may not, at the same time, provide anyone that education that is best for him. And conversely, it is quite conceivable that a society providing the best education for each individual will not provide to anyone an education that is equal to all others. Neither of these principles is ever fully satisfied in practice, of course. But that is not the point that I wish to note. The vital point is rather, that these are independent principles in the sense that either *may* be satisfied without the other.

But can they be satisfied *jointly?* Or are they competing principles, inversely related, so that in maximizing the one we necessarily pay a price in the effort to maximize the other? The unrestricted version of the some-to-all argument provides the principles underlying the universality of the system, but the restricted version provides the practical arguments for its specialization. Both principles belong to the system and can be appealed to at any time. But we should not expect them to have equal weight at all times. There will probably be some kind of dialectic established by the presence of these two claims. But what is that dialectic?

The Shift from Unrestricted to Restricted Arguments

Let us begin with the hypothesis that the expanded version of the some-to-all argument will predominate in the system until it approaches the group of last entry. Then the restricted version of the some-to-all argument will assume a more weighty role in directing the behavior of the system. The unrestricted version provides the practical arguments for the initial expansion of the system. That argument urges maximization of the equal principle that all are entitled to the *same* education. But, at some point, the continued expansion of the system will demand substantial attention to the special needs of special populations so that they can succeed in the system. And that means that the restricted version of the some-to-all argument will take on fresh importance and greater weight. Attention will then shift to maximizing the best principle. In short, up to a certain point in its expansion, the system can treat the population as homogeneous, but at another point it shall have to either approach the population as heterogeneous or probably cease its expansion. And ceasing its expansion would mean ceasing in the attempt to maximize the equal principle. The system cannot give up either principle at any time. But neither will it give them equal weight at every time.

This then is the systemic shift of attention from similarities to variabilities in the population.[5] This is the shift from the unrestricted to the

5. Correspondingly, in that transformation of attention we should anticipate a shift of emphasis in policy analysis away from the modal tendencies of the system to the variability of effects. Policy, after all, is policy for the system.

restricted formulation of the some-to-all argument. When this shift of emphasis occurs, we should expect that formulating standards of relevance and standards of magnitude in the application of the some-to-all argument will become a more pressing problem. Clarity on such matters is no problem as long as we are applying the unrestricted version of the some-to-all argument because that argument places no emphasis upon variabilities in the population. Standards of relevance and of magnitude become essential concerns only when we begin to apply the restricted some-to-all argument. But let us recall that standards of magnitude are established by the scale of the setting where the argument is applied, and that standards of relevance are established by the definition of "educationally relevant attributes." The first step in the dialectic of the system is, therefore, to move from the maximization of the equal principle to the maximization of the best principle. Whether there is a pendulum effect to this transition, a shift returning to the maximization of the equal principle, and whether these two principles can be jointly satisfied are matters that must be deferred for the moment.

Every application of the some-to-all argument makes implicit reference to some standards of relevance and some standards of magnitude. Furthermore, it has been argued that standards of magnitude are established by the scale of the setting in which the argument is applied, and that standards of relevance are established by reference to the educationally relevant attributes of choice, tenacity, and ability. At no point, however, have we examined the interaction of these two sets of standards considered independently of scale and independently of those attributes.

Furthermore, I have suggested by hypothesis that between the "equal" principle and the "best" principle, there exists an important kind of dialectic. We are maximizing the "equal" principle under conditions where the relevant variabilities between individuals are few and when the magnitude required of them is large. This is the combination that will produce the smallest number of distinct groups and the smallest number of distinct programs in the system. On the other hand, we are maximizing the "best" principle under those conditions when the relevant variabilities between individuals in the system are numerous and when the required magnitude of them is small. This is the combination that will produce the largest number of distinct groups and will require the largest number of distinct programs in the system. According to this reasoning, the cells occupied in Figure 7.1 represent the difference between the maximization of these two principles. We can detect in that representation the basis for the claim that these two principles are inversely related. It seems that as

FIGURE 7.1
Interaction of Standards of Relevance
and Magnitude

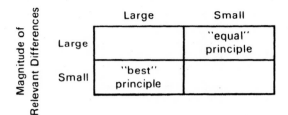

one is maximized, the other is not. Indeed, it suggests that either principle is maximized at the sacrifice of the other.[6]

This conclusion, however, must be precisely understood. These two principles are most fully realized in *circumstances* that are inversely related. Nonetheless, it remains true that standards of magnitude and relevance are *logically* independent. Consider. Let us imagine an educational system that employs a single variability in determining appropriate differences of treatment between groups. Let us suppose, further, that the single difference permitted is variability in intelligence. Under these conditions, we may still imagine the educational system taking into account differences of extremely small magnitude in this single variability. There is nothing in the *logic* of the some-to-all argument that forbids attention to small magnitudes of difference on a single dimension of variability. Neither is there any *logical* difficulty in an educational system taking into account a large number of relevant variabilities occurring in large magnitudes. In short, when the number of relevant differences are few, the system may, nonetheless, attend to either large or small magnitudes in those differences. And conversely, when the number of relevant differences is large, the system

6. This relation between the "best" and "equal" principles is important because it makes explicit the claim that the interaction between them is a prototypical policy problem. The two principles represent rather complex sets of goods in conflict. The problem of policy for the system is to adjust that conflict, to balance it, to find the course of action that will optimize the two sets of goods taken together instead of maximizing either taken separately. But this point properly elaborated would carry our discussion beyond the limits of this study and into a discussion of values and the nature of policy, i.e., the *educational* content of policy for the system.

may attend either to large or to small magnitudes of variability. This appears to be the *logic* of the interaction between these different standards implicitly referred to in the some-to-all argument. It is the logic of independence.

But our hypothesis concerning the dialectic between the restricted and the unrestricted arguments states precisely that these standards are unlikely to be independent of the scale of the system. Whether the relevant variabilities are many or few and whether their required magnitude is large or small is something that will be strongly related to the scale of the system itself.

Human Scale and System Scale

To grasp this point properly, however, we need to discriminate carefully between system scale and human scale, between the scale of the system itself and the scale of human settings within it. By human scale I mean to refer to the number of persons engaged in a relatively stable setting of human interaction. A family is a setting of small human scale. Those witnessing an athletic event in a stadium are in a human setting of large scale. By a large-scale educational system, in contrast, I mean to refer to one with relatively high rates of attainment at increasingly higher levels in the hierarchy of the system. Now it is true that in a very small society or in a society within a sparsely settled territory, the system may be large according to this definition, and still involve very few persons in low concentrations. But in referring to a system of large scale, I mean to refer to one in which it is a contingent fact that concentrations of persons within the system are fairly dense. These are the circumstances that occur within most societies where the system is highly developed and where "modernization" has progressed to a high degree. Thus, by a "large scale system" I am referring to one with high rates of attainment at relatively higher levels, within a society at an advanced stage of economic development. It seems intuitively obvious that a system of large scale in such circumstances may contain human settings that are either large or small, and that similarly, a system of small scale may contain human settings that are either large or small in scale. Human scale and system scale are independent of one another. We may ask how standards of relevance and magnitude are influenced by variations, first in human scale, and secondly, in system scale.

Now, I have already pointed out that the transition from a small human setting, like the family, to the setting of the school is the transition from a setting in which attention is paid to individuals to a setting in which

FIGURE 7.2
Interaction of Human Scale and
Standards of Magnitude and Relevance

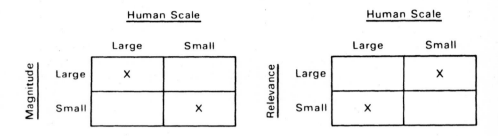

important differences are those between *groups* of individuals. When the human scale is small, as it typically is in a family, then relevant differences between persons can be numerous and the magnitude of those differences can be quite small. But in a setting of larger human scale, a setting like the school, the relevant differences that can be attended to will be relatively fewer and the magnitude of those that are attended to will have to be relatively larger. These relations are schematically represented in Figure 7.2.

We shall get very different results, however, if we examine the relation of *system* scale to standards of relevance and magnitude. When the system scale is small, powerful practical limits are imposed upon the number of variabilities that can be taken into account. Whatever the system scale, it will probably be unable to take account of as many variations among individuals as it is possible to consider within a family. Furthermore, we must recall that the relevant property referred to in the some-to-all argument always defines a class, never an individual.

Let us suppose that at some particular time or place, and for purely contingent reasons, it turns out that the relevant property referred to in the some-to-all argument, defines a class that has only one nember. In that case, the system will have to find enough others with such a property to constitute a group. In short, the system will probably either refuse to count that particular property as relevant in determining the kinds of educational programs that must be provided, or else it will broaden the definition of the relevant difference so as to generate a class of more than one member. If, for example, there is only one genius in the population or only one person with a particular handicap, then the system is unlikely to provide a special program for that particular gifted or that particular handicapped person. On the other hand, if there are *lots* of geniuses or *many* persons with a particular handicap, then those differences are more likely to be counted as relevant. Thus, the relevant difference will be counted as relevant only if it occurs fairly frequently. If it does not occur with enough frequency, then the relevant property will be redefined to generate a class of sufficient size to warrant a special program. Thus, *any* property used in the restricted version of the some-to-all argument is more likely to generate a class of sufficient size in a system of large scale than in a system of small scale. The restricted version of the some-to-all argument recognizes differences *between* groups, but not between individuals *within* groups. However, as the system scale increases, the relevant groups already included in the system will grow in size and differences between individuals *within* groups may then occur with enough frequency to permit the creation of still more sub-groups defined either by new variabilities or by the application of more refined criteria to old variabilities.

Now, these considerations argue strongly for the view that standards of relevance and magnitude are affected by system scale in a way precisely contrary to the way they are affected by changes in human scale. Where the *system* scale is small, relevant variabilities will be few and the magnitude required for them will be large. And when the *system* scale is large, then the relevant variabilities can be more numerous and they can be defined with more discrimination. These conclusions are represented schematically in Figure 7.3.

The relationships represented in the figure are precisely the converse of those in Figure 7.2. They are, moreover, precisely those relationships that were advanced as conjecture in our hypothesis about the dialectic of the restricted and unrestricted versions of the some-to-all argument. As long as the scale of the system is small, it will follow the practical argument in its unrestricted version. The system will behave as though to maximize the equal principle. But as the scale of the system becomes greater, it will

FIGURE 7.3
Interaction of System Scale and Standards
of Relevance and Magnitude

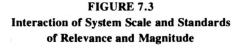

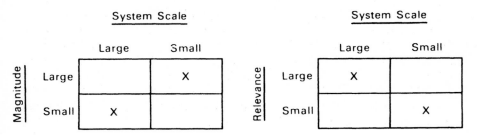

give more weight to the restricted version. It will behave as though to maximize the best principle. Indeed, we can see now that as the system increases in scale, its capacity to maximize the best principle should also increase.

Maximizing Best and Equal Principles

We are, at long last, in a position to confront the question that I have steadfastly deferred throughout this extended analysis. There appears to be one possibility of jointly satisfying the best and equal principles. It might seem that were we to succeed in maximizing the best principle then we could claim also to have succeeded in maximizing the equal principle; for, in that case, since each would be getting that education that is best for him, it could also be said that each is getting an education as good as that received by all others.

It bears repeating that the systemic function of the equal principle is to impose upon the system the need to acknowledge the claim of each to receive an education at least as good as that received by everyone else. But if the best principle is maximized, that is, if each receives that education that is best for him, then it can be claimed also that each is receiving an education at least as good as that received by all others. Hence, the two principles are jointly satisfied under precisely those conditions that constitute the realization of the best principle.

This suggestion, however, is spurious. Why? Because whatever credibility it has rests not upon a realization of the equal principle, but upon its redefinition. If, in providing for each that education that is best for him, we must, in fact, provide an education that is *unique* to each, then we might indeed claim that we have provided for each an education that is as good as that provided for all others. But the reason we can make such a claim is that we have redefined the equal principle. If the education that A receives is the best *for A*, and if we do not claim that it is also best for B; and if, further, the education that B receives is the best *for B*, but not the best for A, then we might indeed claim that the education one receives is as good as that received by the other. But the meaning of this claim has now changed. "Equally good" is no longer the "equal" in "What A gets is equally as good as what B gets." It is now the "equal" in "What A gets is equally as good *for A* as what B gets is good *for B*." The latter sense of "equal" can be made to *sound* like the former in the following way: If A and B get that education that is best for each, it follows that there is no education for either that is better. That is the meaning of *best*. But it also follows that neither gets an education less good than the best *for him*. *It follows that the education A gets is equally as good as what B gets.* And this conclusion is syntactically and grammatically the same as the equal principle. Nonetheless, the equivocation remains.

In the first sense of "equally good" we are assuming that the value of the education that A and B get is assessed by some standards *independent of either A or B.* In the second sense of "equally good" we are assuming that the value of the education received by A and B is its position in a rank order *relative to A and B,* and *not* independently of either. These are quite different meanings of "equal." The former is the sense of equal that is implicit in the "equal" principle. It is the sense of equal implied in the unrestricted version of the some-to-all argument. But the latter sense of equal is the sense that we adopt when we assume that maximization of the "best" principle is simultaneously the realization of the equal principle. This is an equivocation. Changing the meaning of the equal principle in this way is the same as abandoning it.

By assuming that each person, in receiving an education best for him, receives also an education unique to him, we have rendered the education each receives incomparable to that received by anyone else. If nobody receives an education that is the *same* as anyone else, and if each receives what is best for him alone, then indeed, it follows that nobody receives an education that is significantly better than anyone else's. But this conclusion is, in fact, a redefinition or an abandonment of the "equal" principle and not its realization. The unrestricted formulation of the some-to-all argument results from the claim that the defining property in the argument is universally distributed. But the line of reasoning leading to the joint maximization of the two principles through the full realization of the best principle is clearly the declaration that there is *no* property universally distributed such that everyone is entitled to receive the *same* education. It represents the abandonment of the claim that any two individuals are entitled to the *same* education. Therefore, instead of jointly satisfying the best and equal principles, we end up with the satisfaction of one and the total abandonment of the other.

Clearly, what we seek in the system is some balance between these two principles without the sacrifice of either. What is sought is (1) the provision of the best education for each, so that (2) what is provided for some is not significantly different from what is provided to all others. The equal principle expresses the demand for an education for each that is the *same* as that provided for all others.

Thus, the system clearly progresses then, from an initial stage in which the prevailing practical argument is the unrestricted version of the some-to-all argument. But, as the system expands, the dominance of this argument will yield before the need to apply the restricted version of the some-to-all argument. And indeed, the increased scale of the system, which is what produces this shift, will increase also the capacity of the system to pursue the new argument in practice. So we learn to discriminate, for example, between different racial groups distinguished from the majority. Then later we learn that there are relevant differences between language groups within those minorities, and so we further extend the application of the restricted argument. At each step in this process we identify a new variability connected with the educationally relevant attributes that enter into the just distribution of benefits of the system. But if this process is extended to anything approaching its natural limit, it will clearly produce the complaint: "The system is not providing for us what it is providing for others." The insistence, in short, for the *same* education will reemerge. The equal principle will again prevail in the policy agenda.

We may offer a conjecture. It is that as the system reaches maturity, it will pass from the unrestricted version to the restricted version and back to the unrestricted version *in its educational formulation* rather than in its systemic formulation. The issue that will become vital, in short, is the question as to whether the education that the rich buy for their sons is, indeed, the *operational* standard of the education to which everyone is entitled. And this explicit reference to the *operational* standard is meant to convey the claim that what will emerge as the most intractable and vital question *for the system* is the question as to what constitutes a good education. The juncture between the theory of the system and the theory of education will, thus, become the most important and vital question to be discussed, and to be discussed not merely as an element in the academic training of educators, but as a vital matter of public policy.

Summary

The system is not universal because it is made compulsory. Rather, it is compulsory because it becomes universal. This thesis requires that we give an account, on independent grounds, as to why the system becomes universal. It begins with fairly high rates of enrollment and attendance. But we have seen in the preceding chapter that as each level of the system becomes more universal in scope, it becomes more necessary for each successive generation to complete that level and to go beyond. Attainment at that level becomes compulsory because it becomes universal. But now we see in the unrestricted version of the some-to-all argument the logic that underwrites that expansion. The advantages that some secure must not be withheld from others. The system must be made available to all because what it provides is what everyone is entitled to.

The unrestricted version of the some-to-all argument provides the grounds for its becoming universal. The restricted version of that argument, on the other hand, provides the grounds for its becoming specialized and differentiated. It provides the grounds for such practices as tracking, bilingual education, special programs for racial groups, special education in all of its forms, and full service legislation for the handicapped. If we were to provide a rank ordering of all those groups in society that might appeal to "the best principle" in order to secure their educational interests, and if we were to regard that rank order as a sequence, then I suspect that the last groups to advance such an argument would be the handicapped and the so-called retarded. I base this judgment on the claim that if we were to actually identify the *social meaning* attached to the categories defining the populations of special education, we would identify them as the ugly, the strange, the useless, and the dying. The blind are treated often as though they were dying, the handicapped as though they were ugly, the retarded as strange or useless. Surely these groups, like the elderly, are likely to be the last to claim a kind of special treatment as their due. Yet just as those voices urging special programs for blacks are somewhat more muted and are replaced by those insisting on blacks getting the same education as others, so also the movement is on for the deinstitutionalization of the handicapped and retarded. Institutionalization can be construed as stemming from the application of the best principle. Mainstreaming is the shift to the equal principle. I suspect that we have witnessed the most strident applications of the best principle, and are now entering a period in which the equal principle in its educational version will become more forcefully voiced.

·◦[VIII]◦·

ARGUMENTS OF PUBLIC AND
PRIVATE BENEFITS
Political Support for the System

THE DYNAMICS OF THE SYSTEM's second-order benefits, as well as the role of parental interests and incumbent interests have been abundantly considered. But no one would suppose that either the worth of education itself or the behavior of the system has been exhausted by such considerations. Our account of the system remains, then, more incomplete than it has to be. We must give some detailed attention to the value of educational benefits themselves — the knowledge, skill, and the expansion of human sensibilities that, in common parlance, constitute the substance of what makes the system an *educational* system. But neither have we examined in any detail the role of social interests or social goods in the behavior of the system. Though the system has been described independently of the polity, we cannot sustain the fiction that it will survive without political support.

To meet these problems, it will be helpful to take two additional steps. In order to grasp the value of educational goods (in contrast to the second-order benefits of the system) it will be helpful to identify what kind of mixed goods these are by constructing a general taxonomy within which different kinds of goods are identified according to their different distributive properties. Being in possession of such an account, we shall then be in a position to identify the array of political arguments that can be used in support of the system and the different systemic circumstances in which they will have greater or less political weight. The assumption here is that political arguments have to do always with the distribution of human goods; that is, they are arguments concerned with how the society should allocate its resources, benefits, rights, opportunities, and so forth. By examining first the distributive properties of various goods, we shall be able to locate the value of educational benefits, establish the rank order of their corresponding political arguments and thus discern still another way in which the system is set in motion.

THE DISTRIBUTIVE PROPERTIES OF EDUCATIONAL GOODS

What kinds of worth do educational benefits have? What kinds of goods are they? In order to answer this question, let us construct a simple classification of human goods in general. There are four kinds to consider: (1) divisible and indivisible goods; (2) relative and absolute goods; (3) primary and secondary goods; and (4) escalating and de-escalating goods.

Divisible and Indivisible Goods

Indivisible goods are those that cannot be secured for anyone unless they are secured for everyone. National defense and security cannot be divided. Therefore, they cannot be distributed in parts or in varying degrees to different individuals. They can be obtained for each only if they are obtained for all. Divisible goods, by contrast, are those that can be divided and, therefore, can be distributed. Divisible goods, like money, land, and securities, can be obtained by individuals for themselves and in varying degrees or quantities. The conventional wisdom is that divisible goods can be distributed, therefore, by a market mechanism. They are subject to consumer rivalry. Indivisible goods, on the other hand, are not subject to consumer rivalry, and therefore, cannot be distributed by a market mechanism. This is another way of expressing the idea that divisible goods are private goods, and indivisible goods are public goods. The second-order benefits of the system are divisible goods. They are distributed by the system, but they are appropriable by individuals.

Relative and Absolute Goods

Relative goods are those that cannot be possessed by anyone if they are possessed by everyone. Their *value* is derived entirely from the fact that some people possess such goods and others do not. That is why, by distributing such goods to everyone, they have no value to anyone. It is easy to see then, that the second-order benefits of the system are also relative goods, especially when we understand their value to lie in their efficacy for the social distribution of non-educational goods.

Suppose, for example, that high status is regarded as a good (it is in fact included in the list of non-educational social goods set forth in Chapter III). That there are positions of high status presupposes that there are positions of lower status. The notion that everyone can have high status is self-contradictory. It is impossible in principle. The notion that everyone has high status means nothing unless it means that differences of status do not exist. In that case, however, the good that we are speaking of is no longer high status, but equality. Recall the form of address so popular during the French Revolution — "Citizen X" or "Citizen Y." This was a form of address devised to recognize everyone's claim to the same lofty status of citizen. The entire point was to substitute the values of equality and fraternity for the value of rank. The value of high status was supposedly destroyed by granting everyone the same high rank and by granting no one any rank higher. High status, thus, is a relative good. It cannot be enjoyed by everyone. We may generalize. Indivisible goods cannot be secured for anyone unless they are secured for everyone; but relative goods have no value for anyone if they are secured for everyone.

Relative goods cannot be universally distributed and retain their value. There is no such impossibility, however, in the distribution of absolute goods. Unlike indivisible goods, absolute goods do not *need* to be universally distributed; unlike relative goods, however, they *can* be universally distributed, even though in the actual world, they usually are not. Their value, in short, does not rest upon the fact that some enjoy such goods and some do not. Health, for example, is a good. It is extremely unlikely that at any time or in any society, everyone will be in good health or in equally good health. Such a state of affairs is unlikely; nonetheless, it is not impossible in principle. It is doubtful in the extreme that everyone in a society can be described as wise; yet, there is nothing, in principle, that prevents it. Health and wisdom are absolute goods; high status is a relative good.

Primary and Secondary Goods

By primary goods I mean to refer to such things as land, money and status that can be distributed by the society in varying amounts to different individuals, as well as such goods as virtue that can be possessed by individuals in varying degrees. By secondary goods, however, I mean to refer to such goods as equality that consist simply in a definable distribution of other goods. In short, there are certain goods in the world that I shall describe as secondary because they consist simply in a particular distribution of other goods that are then defined as primary. Liberty, for example, is a good. Civil liberties, however, are secondary goods. They consist of a distribution of those liberties that must be distributed to all persons by virtue of their being citizens. Civil liberties, therefore, are certain goods defined by a required distribution of other goods. Equality, in most of its forms, is also a secondary good. It consists in a certain distribution of rights, money, legal powers, land, and other primary goods. Equality of opportunity is a particular distribution of opportunities. Equal educational opportunity is, therefore, a secondary good because it is a particular distribution of educational opportunities.

Escalating and De-escalating Goods

By "escalating goods," I mean to refer to those goods that are subject to increasing marginal utility; and by "de-escalating goods," I mean to refer to those that are subject to decreasing marginal utility either to an individual or to the society. But in this formulation, the notion of marginal utility receives an extremely broad meaning. I mean it to refer to the value of virtue, and to the value of such things as skill and knowledge, as well as such goods as food and housing.

The point is that there are some goods in the world that can be possessed by individuals. Therefore, they appear to be divisible. Yet, they also are goods whose worth to the society or to the individual possessing them increases the more widely they are possessed by others or the more they are possessed by the individual. They have increasing value on the margin to the individual or to the society. These are escalating goods. And within this class, there will fall most of the goods that we have described as educational benefits in Chapter III.

Imagine a society in which there is extensive regulation of the normal affairs of life and, therefore, a practical need, almost daily, to be able to read in order to stay out of trouble. Let us suppose, further, that, although some can read, many, even the vast majority, cannot. Under these conditions being able to read is likely to be a marketable skill in a quite specific sense. Those who cannot read will probably have to pay those who can, to do their reading for them. Thus, the skill of reading is likely to have economic value. The circumstances imagined are like those that exist in the modern world and that make it possible for lawyers to charge a fee for their services.

In such a society, those who can read will have a certain relative economic advantage over those who cannot. But, on the other hand, in such a society, publishers and book stores are likely to be few and published materials scarce. Reading is unlikely to be a common activity of leisure. As the skills of reading become more and more widespread, however, the society can rely more and more upon the ability of its citizens to read. Thus, the need for such skills is likely to increase even further, and publishing, as an important enterprise, can come into existence. At the same time, however, with the spread of such skills, the relative economic value of possessing them will decline and their inherent value is likely to become more apparent. The skills of reading will cease being relative economic goods and will become escalating goods. Reading, then, is one of those goods whose value, both to the individual and to the society, will increase the better one is able to read and the more widespread in the society the skill is distributed. Being able to read thus becomes an escalating good of a certain kind.

But there are escalating goods of other kinds. The virtues, in general, are goods of increasing marginal value to individuals. But they do not behave in the same way as the increasing value of reading. *Sophrosyne*, the Greek virtue of moderation, is likely to have more worth in a society in proportion as it is more of a problem, and therefore, rare. *Sophrosyne* was perhaps as high a virtue as it was among the Greeks because immoderation was so characteristic of them and therefore so much of a problem. Thus, it seems that the worth of a particular virtue will be greater within a society in proportion as it is rare and needed. The view would, therefore, be that the *social* value of a particular virtue, in this case *sophrosyne*, is related inversely to the range of its distribution, and directly to its need.

On the other hand, and from a somewhat different point of view, it may be argued that precisely the opposite is what happens. The more of a particular virtue an *individual* has, the more that individual is likely to value the next increment. The more courage one has, the more one is likely to value the next increment of courage. The more one knows, the more one is likely to value any increase in knowledge. Why, for example, does any extension of the system seem always to benefit most those who need it the least? Because those who need it the least are those who have gained the most in the way of educational benefits. They are, therefore, those who most value the next increment in such goods.[1] Such goods have increasing value, on the margin, not merely in proportion to their distribution in the society, but in proportion to the amount that an individual already possesses. Their value to any individual is likely to be an increasing function of the amount already possessed by that individual.

This classification is not intended to exhaustively characterize all the kinds of goods there are. It is meant only to capture certain of their distributive properties. Each type, except for the last, is distinguished by the kinds of distribution that it can receive. And, even in the case of the last group, we can see that whether particular goods are escalating or de-

1. Such a view invoking the idea that educational benefits have increasing marginal value to individuals is seldom, perhaps never, used to explain the different participation of populations in such developments as the open university in Britain and life-long learning in America. Why?

escalating is often influenced by the nature of their social distribution. Neither does this classification correspond exactly to the more familiar distinction between goods of intrinsic and instrumental value. Nonetheless, a little reflection will suggest that escalating goods *tend* to be those with intrinsic value. They tend to be those goods that are worth securing in their own right, for their own sake, and not merely for the sake of any good beyond them. Escalating goods *tend* to be of inherent or intrinsic worth. I follows neither that intrinsic goods are always escalating nor that escalating goods are always without instrumental value. Knowledge is an escalating good. It *can* be pursued for its own sake. But it is also useful. It ha instrumental value, as well. That knowledge is an escalating good is a claim that is more unequivocal and more certain than the claim that it is an intrinsic good.

We may now state, by way of summary, that the goods I have described as educational benefits are (1) divisible, (2) absolute, (3) primary and (4) escalating. This identification of their value leaves it an open question whether they are goods of inherent or only instrumental value Educational benefits, however, have at least two additional features of importance. First, they are limitless, and, secondly, they do not behave as scarce goods.

Exchange and Educational Resources

By saying that educational benefits are limitless, I mean merely that, in principle, no matter what anybody has learned, no matter how much somebody knows, no matter how great one's skill, it is always possible to learn more, to know more, and to extend one's skills. It is this limitless feature of educational benefits that underlies the illusion that there cannot, in principle, be a desirable limit to the size of the system. Because there is no limit to the expansion of educational goods, therefore, we are inclined to think, there can be no desirable limit to the expansion of the educational system. However large it is, things would be improved if it got larger because things would be improved if educational goods were more widely enjoyed.

In saying that educational benefits do not behave as scarce commodities, I mean to suggest an altogether different point about their distributive character. Nobody is deprived of knowledge because somebody else has more. Nor is anyone deprived of gaining some increment of skill simply because someone else has gained it. In short, we do not take from anyone his knowledge, skill, or sense of taste when we place such goods within the grasp of others. We cannot increase educational benefits among some by taking them away from others in the way that we can and do increase the wealth of some by taking away from others. The "ethics of *re*distribution" simply do not apply to educational goods.

The extension of educational benefits is, in this respect, less like an exchange and more like plain and open bestowal. Consider any simple and rudimentary example of exchange between two persons. If you and I enter into an exchange, our act ends by me giving up something that was mine and gaining something that was yours, and conversely, by you giving up something that was yours and gaining something that was mine. Exchange, no doubt, is reciprocal in this way. That each of us, in balance, counts the gain and loss as benefit, should not obscure for us these elementary facts. But the important point is that I end by having less of whatever it was that I gave up, and you end by having less of whatever it was that I gained. The extension of educational goods is not like that. In their increase, although somebody *gives* something, nobody gives *up* anything. When I teach you to tie a bowline, you gain a skill that I have and your gaining it leaves me still in possession of it.

If I have given up anything in this encounter, it is merely the time it takes to teach you. And if you give up anything, it is the time it takes to learn. Nonetheless, I give it up. So there is cost, after all. What I give up, however, is a part of my time, not a part of my skill. Time *is* a scarce commodity. But it is not an educational *benefit*. Instead, it is an educational *resource*, something that we spend in spreading educational goods. We may increase the share of others in educational goods without anyone giving up what he had of them to begin with.[2] What we give up, both individually and collectively, is the time needed to spread such goods about.

This observation is deceptively simple, but extraordinarily important for two reasons. First, it is the close *association* of educational goods with scarce commodities, like time, that makes it appear as though educational goods themselves have the accustomed features of economic goods. Secondly, this proposition is also the rudimentary truth that, as we shall see, underlies the necessity for a social decision or political argument in the effort to spread educational benefits.

Given such an analysis, it follows that the concept of Pareto optimality has no application to the distribution of educational goods. We may describe the distribution of a set of goods as Pareto-optimal when there can be no redistribution of those goods to make some persons better off without

2. Actually, in the case of educational goods, it makes no sense to speak of "having one's share" since such goods are distributed — or, rather, spread around — without ever being divided.

at the same time making some others worse off in their enjoyment of those goods. It should now be obvious, however, that educational benefits are the kinds of goods that can be indefinitely extended in the society without ever depriving anyone of the educational goods that they already enjoy. Thus, we are perpetually in the position of being able to make certain persons better off in their enjoyment of educational goods without ever making anyone worse off. The point of Pareto optimality, in the case of such goods, can never be reached. The claim is not that it *will* never be reached, but that it, in principle, *cannot* be reached because there is no such point.[3]

In the world of ordinary human affairs, however — and this is our second point — we are almost never in a position to consider the expansion of educational benefits totally independently of the distribution of other goods. Learning, we have observed, takes time.[4] And time is a scarce commodity. Furthermore, learning often, though not always, requires access to a teacher, books, newspapers, or conversation. It always requires access to resources of some kind, and those resources often include a person willing to give up the necessary time — a father, mother, neighbor, or teacher. Access to educational resources, like access to the system itself, is not an educational benefit.[5] Nonetheless, it is a *means* to the acquisition of educational benefits — a necessary means — and we cannot will the expansion of educational goods without willing the means. Thus, even though the concept of Pareto optimality has no application to the distribution of educational benefits, nevertheless, it can be applied to the distribution of such resource goods as access and time. These goods *can* be distributed so that certain persons might be made worse off in the effort to make others better off.[6]

3. In the lexicon of economics, the movement of any system *toward* a point of Pareto optimality, even though never reached, is called a Pareto movement. The term cannot be applied, however, to the expansion of educational goods because in the case of such benefits, there is no point of Pareto optimality, and, therefore, no movement toward such a point.

4. See Chapter IV, pp. 54, 57, where this simple point is shown to figure prominently in accounting for the downward drift of learning as well as the functional imperatives of the technological market.

5. See Chapter III, p. 46, where it is argued that access to the system appears to be an educational benefit because it is a good that is clearly distributed *by* the system. On the other hand, it is typically distributed by the system on the basis of the possession of second-order educational benefits, and thus *functions* as a non-educational social good.

6. Note the striking similarity between this formulation of a violation of Pareto optimality and the dynamics described by the law of shifting benefits and liabilities. The argument has been that, in the United States, we have consistently pursued policies that have benefited some through extending the possession of second-order goods, and that, in doing so, we have made others progressively worse off in their ability to appropriate non-educational social goods like income.

The essential point may be grasped as follows. If I am to teach you to tie a bowline, then I must take the time to teach, and you must take the time to learn. And if I am to teach this skill to many others or if many others are to do it, then I must be able and the society must be able to devote a great deal of time in spreading this skill. If I am to spend all my time in this missionary work, then I must be freed from the burdensome task of gaining a living either by relying on the charitable impulses of others or by selling my services or by being granted a salary. The cost to the society is not only whatever it takes so that I can spend the time, but also the sacrifice of what I might have done instead.

Thus, we begin with a concern to spread the acquisition of educational goods, but we end with a problem in the allocation of resources.[7] As long as the scale is modest, and the resource required is "my own time" — whatever that means — then no serious problem is posed for the allocational policies of the society. But when the scale is large and the amount of time spent in acquiring educational benefits is correspondingly large, then we have a problem for the society. Time must be liberated, and therefore sacrificed, for many persons to engage in the mission of spreading educational benefits and for many others to acquire them. Many must be paid, in short. And that, in all probability means that the society will be confronted with a social choice. The system must be expanded.[8] In short, an expansion in the acquisition of educational benefits requires an expansion of the system, and, therefore, it requires a public choice.

This conclusion, however, is likely to be most secure in societies where the system is very large and in those where it is very small. It will be more secure where the system is large because the cost in time and money for the spread of educational benefits, and especially for any expansion in their spread, will be very large and, therefore, more subject to public scrutiny. Besides, since educational benefits are escalating goods, demand for them is likely to grow at a more rapid rate where the system is already large. But there is a third reason. In any society where the system is large,

7. See Chapter III, pp. 37–40. We are now in a position to grasp the more subtle implications of several statements presented in these pages. It is argued there that (1) the allocation of resources may be the most important problem in the politics of the system, but it is much less important in the logic of the system; (2) the allocation of resources *to* the system is important because it is vital in determining the proportion of the public budget that is devoted to public goods; (3) any distribution of resources *in* the system must rest upon some view concerning the desirable distribution of educational benefits; and, finally (4) such a problem is politically sensitive because it is believed that the distribution of resources within the system affects the distribution of educational benefits.

8. Remember that the system includes proprietary (for profit) schools and private schools. See Chapter I, pp. 5–7. Also, Table 1.1, mode of growth #8. See also Chapter VII, p. 121.

and where the concern is to spread the possession of educational goods as broadly as possible, then in order to liberate the necessary time, it will not do to rely on charity, nor will it suffice to rely on the mere sale of services. The first will not suffice because human beings are not sufficiently charitable; and the second will not suffice because the capacity to free the time needed to *use* such services is unevenly distributed. Thus, those who can buy the time will be served and those who cannot will not, even if they want to. In short, the equal principle will have to be applied, and the system, as we have seen, simply is the set of arrangements through which that principle is applied in the spread of educational benefits.[9] The system will expand, and its expansion will require a political argument.

In a society where the system is small, however, it is also probable that any large expansion in the spread of educational goods will benefit the system. For in those circumstances, it is more likely that the cost will be larger in proportion to the total resources available to the society than it would be in a society where the system is only moderately developed. Thus, in such circumstances, the expansion of educational benefits will be a serious social decision drawing people away from productive activities into other activities that, for the moment at least, are unproductive.[10]

9. See Chapter VII, pp. 123–24. The argument here is not that the system has been *successful* in applying the equal principle. The argument is only that the system is that set of arrangements whose function it is to do so in the distribution of educational benefits.

10. I am suggesting that the social costs incurred by the extension of educational benefits will be highest at opposite ends of the uniform growth line. Can we discover in this observation the idea of a curvilinear function describing the social costs in the distribution of educational benefits that is precisely the contrary of the curvilinear function describing the social value of second-order benefits? Consider the following schematic representation (see Chapter VI, p. 92).

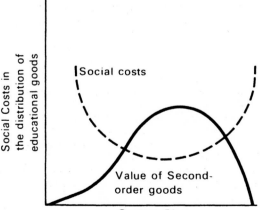

Let us return to that universal knot, the bowline. There may be some society, perhaps a seafaring one, whose people are willing to tolerate the social dependency, the parasitic life of one whose sole preoccupation is to pass on that skill and associated others to all who come and ask. Their decision to do so, however, cannot be the expression of a mere willingness to bear the presence of an odd one in their midst. Neither can it be construed as the aggregate of everyone's desire to learn the bowline. It must be viewed not as a decision to exchange time and other goods for the receipt of an individual good, but rather as a social decision to secure a social good. It is a decision that stems from the realization that, for some reason, it is good to have lots of people who can tie a bowline and that when there comes an emergency at sea or a storm in port, that is not the moment to take the time to teach it. Thus, the members of that society may regard a widespread knowledge of the bowline as a social good of sufficient value to warrant the sacrifice of private goods that might have been secured instead. Educational benefits, in short, are divisible and absolute primary goods of escalating worth. Yet, their large scale propagation, requiring, as it does, a large expenditure of time, requires also a social decision. The determination of that choice is a political act and a policy decision. Though it is always an individual who learns to tie the bowline, nonetheless, a social decision is required to make that learning widespread.

We are apt to forget that this is also the way that the system behaves. A decision to raise school taxes is a social decision to purchase more social goods instead of more private goods; and conversely, a decision to lower school taxes is a social decision to purchase more private goods rather than social goods. In either case, a political decision is required. Which decision it will be depends upon the political appeal that can be enlisted for the advancement of the social goods that are sought through the spread of educational benefits. Thus, educational benefits are private goods, by nature, insofar as they are divisible and primary. Yet, their advancement in the society may be a social good requiring a political decision. How can the political support for the system be made to emerge from the harmony of these individual and social goods?

SOCIAL GOODS, SOCIAL INTERESTS, AND THE
ARRAY OF POLITICAL ARGUMENTS

Social Goods and Social Interests

By social goods I mean simply those goods whose pursuit is justified to any *individual,* on the grounds that the advancement of such goods is a benefit to *everyone,* and therefore, a benefit to each. Thus, social goods are defined by the kind of appeal that is made in seeking the support of individuals in their advancement. If that appeal consists in pointing out that the good is a benefit to everyone or to a certain large class of persons — like all children, all veterans, or all who are sick or injured — a class in which one is presumed to have an interest, then the good whose advancement we are asked to support is a social good. Social goods then are those goods promoted by a social argument, that is, by an argument appealing to what is good for all. Given such a conception of social goods, we may then define "social interests" as those interests that are required if such an appeal is to be successful. They are those interests that lead each of us to express a concern not simply for our own welfare, but for the welfare of many others.

An illustration may help to clarify the point. The claim may be urged upon any individual that he ought to support the education of a few to be competent plumbers not simply because in doing so he is providing for his own convenience, but on the quite different grounds that he is contributing to the well being and health of everyone. Such an appeal to any individual to support the education of some or of all is an appeal to a social good. And similarly, as we have seen, in some seafaring society, one may be persuaded, on grounds of mutual safety, to support the effort to make the skill of tying bowlines universal. Mutual safety and general health are not equally indivisible goods, but they are equally social goods. Appeals to such goods as grounds for the support of education are, no doubt, sometimes unsuccessful. But no doubt also, when they do succeed, they do so only if individuals are able to see that their own good is implicated in the good of others. A social argument succeeds in the promotion of a social good only because there is already such a social interest.

Externalities and Appropriable Goods

To this account of social goods and social interests, we must add, however, two further features of human goods generally, both being drawn once again from the lexicon of economics. The first arises from the need to attend to the concept of externalities or spillovers, and the second from the need to recognize the existence of appropriable goods. By "externalities" we mean to refer to the costs — or benefits — that accrue to society as an incidental consequence of the mere process of producing and consuming goods. But these costs or benefits, if they are true externalities, are not normally included in the costs of production or among the benefits of consumption.

Suppose, for example, that in the manufacture of automobiles or cement, the factory lays a heavy layer of smoke and soot over a wide area, increasing cleaning bills, speeding the deterioration of buildings, and in general reducing the value of the surrounding property and destroying the amenities of the region. These are costs incurred in the process of production, but they are not usually included in the price of an automobile. They are costs, but they are not costs to the manufacturer. And suppose further that the resulting low cost of an automobile produces a growing need for traffic lights, larger traffic arteries, and expensive expressways, making more distant land accessible for settlement, more desirable and more expensive. These are both costs and benefits that stem indirectly from the process of manufacture and consumption, but they are excluded from the costs of cars and cement. They are externalities. Similarly, we may picture the construction of a new school that greatly increases the value of land in its locale. That would be a benign externality, an external good. We might think that such a gain should then be counted against the cost of building the school, but it is not.

The *private costs* of such externalities to the manufacturer may be less than the social costs to the rest of us who pay for highways and for traffic and smog control through either higher taxes or higher prices. But consider the other side. Externalities may be either malignant or benignant. Picture a person who, in anticipation of a new school or a new road, holds on to land as its value increases. Then he sells. He is the beneficiary of an externality. The benefit he gains is called an appropriable good. By "appropriable goods" then we refer to those beneficent externalities whose good is appropriated by individuals or by classes of individuals, like land holders and real estate brokers.

The Political Arguments in Rank Order

The advancement of educational goods produces both externalities and appropriable benefits. Apart from a grasp of this fact, we cannot hope to understand the political arguments offered in support of the system and how they are likely to change. Indeed, with these concepts in mind, together with our brief taxonomy of goods, we are at last in a position to establish the rank order of the political arguments that can be mustered for the support of the system.

That rank order is roughly as follows: (1) the political support for the system is secure when it rests solidly and evidently upon the fundamental or compelling interests of the state; (2) it is also strong when it rests upon the aggregate of individual or parental interests; (3) it is less strong when it rests entirely upon social interests; and (4) it is weakest when it must rely upon the quest for educational goods for their own sake.

How can this rank order be justified? We may begin with the claim that whenever the distribution of educational benefits or second-order benefits can be directly related to satisfying a compelling interest of the state, then the political argument for the system is very strong. Whenever the spread of educational goods can be linked as means to the preservation of national defense or national security, for example — as in the passage of the National Defense Education Act — the political argument for the spread of such benefits is very strong indeed. Similarly, the political argument is strong whenever the spread of such goods can be persuasively linked to the maintenance of civic order or to the enhancement of individual economic independence. To subsume the advancement of education under any of these fundamental or compelling state interests is sufficient to produce political support for teaching everything from religion, ethics, languages and history to race relations, the practical skills of the trades, ordinary business practices, and even cooking.

Indeed, such an argument is strong enough to enlist political support for almost any effort — regardless of its cost — even if it has nothing to do with the spread of educational goods. The enormous expense of constructing the Interstate Highway System in the United States, for example, was made politically palatable, in part, by its conception as essential to national defense. The original construction of the railroads, at vastly greater costs than necessary, was made possible largely on similar grounds, and nobody can doubt that the development of the space program was solidly grounded in what were construed to be the compelling interests of the state. That kind of political argument, persuasively advanced, could be used, but less persuasively, for the support of symphony orchestras and art galleries as well as for schools and research laboratories.

But political arguments for the system need not be rooted in the compelling interests of the state. They may rest in an appeal to social goods instead. Educational benefits can be construed as public or social benefits. We do not ordinarily support education simply because we believe it is necessary for society itself. We may support it rather because we believe it is necessary for a good society, a free society or a humane society. But there is a problem in this perspective. Even though we may acknowledge that education is a public good, still, nobody ever has sought to get an education for that reason. We can admit readily enough that society will be better off it it has enough plumbers and enough people who know the calculus. Yet, I doubt that anyone has ever struggled to master the jute and the lead or differential equations because of the belief that in doing so he is improving society.

From one point of view, the advancement of educational benefits is a social good. But nobody seeks to secure such goods for that reason. For example, nobody pays and perseveres through four years at Colgate University because doing so is good for Colgate even though it is good for Colgate that some do so. And if we can be sure of that, then we may be equally sure that nobody does it because doing it is good for American society even though it is good for American society that some do so. Rather, in seeking education we seek something in it that is good for us, and good for us as quite specific individuals. We seek education because it is a private good. It increases our opportunities. It is just plain fun. It increases our enjoyment. Through it, we gain first access and then advancement in a profession. In short, the spread of educational benefits is a public good, but we seek to secure such goods for ourselves because they are private, individual and escalating goods.

There is, in this arrangement, a peculiar and quite old-fashioned harmony. By the pursuit of our own individual interests, we advance a public good; and by promoting a public good, we increase the opportunities of individuals to pursue their private interests. Thus, in a society where everyone seeks his own advantage through the acquisition of educational benefits, a substantial constituency is created. The aggregate of such individual, private or parental interests will add up to political support for the system. In pursuit of their own good, for example, youth attend college. In doing so, they support the system, and help to make it possible for those who follow to pursue their own good. Colgate University continues to exist only because there are those who, seeking their own good, support it.

But that is not all. Externalities and appropriable goods are also created by the resulting spread of educational benefits. In a society where everyone can read, there is more to read and the quality of what is printed may rise. That is a long-term externality, a social good produced by the spread of educational benefits. There is thus created also a set of appropriable goods. Merchants of the printed page, of all varieties, are likely to then have a private, individual, though admittedly long-term interest in the further spread of educational benefits. Children learn music, and the externalities of enlarged, if not elevated, sensibilities benefit everyone, presumably. But those who gain the appropriable benefits of such externalities are the manufacturers and marketers of records, guitars, recorders and stereo sets. They then have at least an incipient interest in supporting the system. Therefore, to those who will support the system out of parental interests — that is, because it advances their own or their childrens' good — we may add those who see the system as creating appropriable goods. The two groups together constitute a large constituency, of uneven fidelity, ready to support the system on grounds of largely private interests.

Thus, through the externalities of the system, the creation of appropriable goods, and the encouragement of individuals to pursue their own private advantage through the system, strong private incentives are created for the advancement of undoubted social goods. The political support for the system is assured by the harmony and mutuality of these interests. But now what happens if the pursuit of education is no longer seen as the avenue to the purely private, relative, and individual advantages that it was believed to be? Suppose, in other words, that this benign connection between social benefit and private incentive is fractured? In that break there will occur a quiet, but decisive, revolution. The political support for the system must be transformed.

The view that education pays — that it pays in advancing the quite specific self-interest of individuals, and that it pays at the work place — this view remains at the heart of the American valuation of education itself. It is furthermore, the view that lies at the heart of our capacity to enlist political support for educational institutions. Yet, it is becoming clearer and clearer that attaining a high school diploma is no big thing to those who have them, and neither is a bachelor's degree for many who have them. Yet, such goods remain a desperate necessity for those who do not have them. The expansion of the system itself creates a different valuation of education, and it requires an entirely different kind of political argument. If there is a strong reduction in that demonstrable, touching, and occasionally confirmed belief that more and more education positively advantages individuals, then it becomes increasingly difficult to see how the aggregate of individual interests can continue to be translated into political support for educational institutions. The fidelity of that group who support the system out of essentially parental interests will be weakened.

There remains, of course, the possibility of building a political argument on an appeal to education as a social good. Yet, such an argument, whatever its details, can be no stronger than the social interests on which it rests, and the human disposition to pursue the interests of remote others is notoriously weaker, however more noble, than their devotion to their own. Furthermore, though the pursuit of individual advantages through education is always a long term venture, the social benefits are even more remote. In such matters one speaks of decades and generations, a length of time unlikely to possess much political appeal. The social argument for the support of the system, however sound, is likely to have political strength only if it can be supplemented by other arguments appealing to individual interests or to the fundamental interests of the state.

Finally, there is the prospect of developing a political argument based solely upon the acquisition of educational benefits for their own sake. It is hard to imagine, however, what that argument might be. It might constitute an argument in support of the freedom of all persons to learn, read, study, and practice new skills in much the same way that we preserve their freedom to go to the movies or to attend public worship. Such an argument is less likely to endorse the public support of the system and more likely to simply aim at removing barriers to its existence within whatever limits are permitted by the compelling and derived interests of the state.

These then are the considerations leading to the rank order that we have given to the political arguments for the support of the system. The strongest is an argument lodged in the interests of the state. The next strongest is one lodged in the aggregate of private, individual or parental interests. Third strongest is one that makes an appeal to social goods and social interests,[11] and the weakest is an argument that appeals to those interests, whatever they are, that lead to the pursuit of educational goods for their own sake.

These arguments, of course, never appear in total independence of one another. Arguments for the preservation of state interests are never totally quiescent, even though they are more dominant when those interests seem threatened.[12] There are always those who will be persuaded by a political appeal to social goods. There are probably more, however, who will be persuaded by an argument that seeks advancement of their own private and individual interests. There are always also those who will support the system simply because it advances our knowledge and spreads the acquisition of educational goods. The strongest argument is one that makes all of these appeals, and in every real-life situation, each is likely to be present in some degree. Nonetheless, any reduction in our capacity to advance one of these arguments is a reduction in our capacity to gain the political support of some constituency.

11. It is interesting to note that social arguments for the support of the United States space program focusing on the spillover benefits of that effort were not seriously advanced until NASA was faced with budgetary cuts, and that arrangements for the continued support of space exploration, appealing to our interests in simply knowing more, have been unsuccessful except when associated with techniques for surveillance (state interests) or techniques for weather forecasting, mapping, the search for natural resources, and for monitoring crop diseases (social benefits). These observations also tend to confirm the rank order of the political arguments set down here.

12. See Chapter II on the social logic of general educational goals, pp. 35–36.

Educational benefits, admittedly, must be distinguished from the second-order goods of the system. But they are also related. The system remains a major instrument for the social spread of such goods.[13] Any decline in our capacity to advance a persuasive political argument for its support is a decline in the social capacity to spread the enjoyment of educational benefits. We should anticipate then, that as the purely relative and individual value of second-order benefits declines, as they do at any level where the system approaches zero correlation, the political argument for the support of the system will be weakened, and will have to rest more strongly on an appeal to social goods and state interests or upon those interests, whatever they are, that lead to the pursuit of educational goods for their own sake. Thus, the approach of zero correlation constitutes not only a transformation in the utility of attainment, and a shift in the balance of benefits and liabilities, but also a transformation in the grounds of the political argument for the system.

The Rank Order Illustrated

These dynamics can be vividly illustrated from the remarks of Alan Pifer, formerly President of the Carnegie Corporation of New York, in "Higher Education in the Nation's Consciousness." It is worth quoting at length:

> It stands to reason that indefinite expansion of the number of degrees awarded throughout the nation would sooner or later bring about a decline in their monetary value to the recipients. . . .
>
> The researchers themselves conclude that the apparent decline in economic value of a degree represents a serious threat to the financial viability of colleges and universities in the years ahead since it will lead to sharply falling enrollments. In fact, they say it already has. . . .
>
> But this conclusion does not take into account other factors that may explain the falling enrollment rate for young males. . . . There is the point (for example) that, whatever the cost of going to college today, the cost of not going, if one wants a white collar job, is prohibitive as long as college is virtually the only route to such employment.
>
> Far more disturbing, . . . however, is the mischievous implication . . . that the declining economic value of a degree is somehow indicative of failure on the part of higher education and is yet another reason for losing confidence in it. Such a verdict rests on three utterly fallacious assumptions.

13. See Chapter IV on the imperatives of the technological market, pp. 55–56.

The first of these assumptions is that because the relative economic value of a degree to the individual is declining, the general economic value of higher education to society at large is also declining. A moment's thought will show how erroneous this assumption is. The economic value of higher education to the nation lies, of course, in its research and service capabilities and in the trained manpower it produces.... Only if the earnings of the former in certain fields essential to the economy, such as engineering, fell to a point where there was little incentive for anyone to enroll would there be a connection between individual and societal returns. And it would not be long before the unsatisfied demand for engineers forced the relative earnings of graduates in this field up again, thereby stimulating increased enrollments. In short, market forces would quickly take over.

The second assumption is equally dubious, namely that the value of going to college is to be measured principally in economic terms. One cannot blame young people for thinking this since college has often been sold to them on the basis of such a tawdry and selfish rationale. The appeal to them should, of course, have been made on the much more legitimate grounds that higher education helps individuals develop intellectual abilities, humanistic understandings, and aesthetic sensitivities that will enable them to enjoy life more fully and contribute more effectively to the general welfare of mankind.

The third false assumption is that the decline in the relative economic returns of higher education to the individual is necessarily a bad thing. It stands to reason that there should be some monetary reward for personal investment in higher education in addition to the many non-pecuniary rewards, but this need not be as great as it has been in the past to provide adequate incentive for attending college — provided the true value of the experience is explained to young people. In fact, if the economic rewards do prove to be smaller, higher education is likely to be less a determinant of class status and less socially divisive than it has been in the past. This is good both intrinsically and for the welfare of higher education, since the latter's continued viability must depend on the support of the entire populace, not just those citizens who have reaped its benefits in their own personal lives.

In sum, while it may be true that a degree, in relative terms, is worth less money now than it used to be, it is utterly wrong to conclude from this that higher education is of less value to the nation and therefore deserves less support, or that its future is necessarily in jeopardy, or that it is a poor way for the individual to spend his money. Conclusions such as these are totally unwarranted.[14]

Indeed, such conclusions are totally unwarranted. They rest upon the failure to distinguish between the value of the second-order benefits of the system and the value of educational benefits themselves, a distinction that

14. *The Report of the President, Annual Report of The Carnegie Corporation of New York*, 1975, 437 Madison Avenue, New York.

Pifer, in his rebuttal, is careful to observe.[15] What he does not observe, however, are the transformations in the political arguments for the system that are represented by the reasoning in his own rejection of these fallacious inferences.[16]

His own account, for example, rests upon a shift from arguments lodged in the aggregate of individual interests to those that appeal to the social goods of education for the nation and to the personal value of educational benefits to the individual. Faced with declining political power in an appeal to the aggregate of individual interests, he turns instead to an argument that relates the social and external benefits of education to the interests of the state. This is precisely the move that one would expect given the rank order of the political arguments that we have sketched. Nonetheless, Pifer clearly believes that the appeal to individual interests is the politically strongest argument for the support of the system even though it is educationally and logically weak and represents a "tawdry and selfish rationale" for the pursuit of education. He argues, for example, that there must be pecuniary rewards for the individual derived from the pursuit of higher education, even though the "adequate incentive" need not be as large as it has been.[17] And furthermore, he believes that "market forces" will "take over" at least in those fields of study essential to the economy. He claims, moreover, that if we are to rest the political support of education on its "true" value to the individual, namely on the worth of educational goods themselves, then that "true" value will need to be explained to young people. But he nowhere suggests that the individual and economic value of education will need to be explained.

This passage, coming from an acknowledged leader in American education, clearly illustrates the dynamics of and endorses the rank order given to the political arguments for the support of the system. They reinforce that rank order, not only directly, as we have seen, but also by inference as we may now show in two further observations.

There is danger for the system as well as virtue in Pifer's appeal to the "true" value of educational goods, namely the development of "intellec-

---

15. One should note also that in these remarks Pifer appeals to several principles of the system. In the initial paragraph quoted, for example, he *appeals to* the law of zero correlation. In the third, he *applies* both the rule of transforming utility and the rule of shifting benefits and liabilities.

16. This failure is not serious since Pifer is concerned in these remarks to *advance* a political argument, not to *analyze* it.

17. In this remark Pifer endorses the normative principle that we argued in Chapter III underlies the legitimacy of the system and that establishes the link between the distribution of educational goods and the distribution of non-educational social goods. He again appeals to a principle of the system. See Chapter III, p. 43.

tual abilities, humanistic understanding and aesthetic sensibilities." If the political support for the system were to rest *entirely* upon the value of these educational benefits, then, if we take the matter seriously at all, the political support for the system would rest upon the capacity of the system to deliver these goods. Such a position, however worthy as aspiration, would be a politically dangerous one for any institution to be in. Making someone more humane, let alone more fully human, is a task that is vastly more difficult even than making them more wise. The degree of difficulty increases even more rapidly when we compare it with making someone more knowledgeable in a certain field or more competent either in professional practice or in ordinary life. When one grasps this point, one grasps both the *political* wisdom in reaching for modest goals and the folk wisdom of the system in seeking the development of little "competencies" rather than large vision when it can no longer bestow on individuals any clear and marked *relative* economic benefits.

Thus, in this stress on educational benefits in the political argument of the system, some will see the risks of almost certain failure and, consequently, a politically weakened system. Others however, will see the promise of great improvements. "Finally," they may say, "we can attend solely to the propagation of those benefits that are *truly* educational." Both views are probably correct. Such a path is likely to be educationally appealing, and, at the same time, politically dangerous.

The System and the Role of Educational Statesmen

But Pifer's remarks suggest a further point of considerable importance. It is the function of "educational statesmen" to voice those arguments for the support of the system that it is not in the interest of anyone else to advance or that nobody else is in a position to advance. The system needs educational statesmen. They are those sufficiently attached to the system to be credible to the incumbents as leaders and as friends and yet sufficiently independent of the system to be credible to the rest of the population as not merely the voice of the incumbents. They are thus, virtually the only persons who are in a position to voice, *in politically effective ways*, those arguments for the support of the system that are framed entirely on grounds of social benefit.

To say this, however, is not to suggest that the Alan Pifers and Horace Manns of the world, *as educational statesmen*, are insincere or do not believe what they say. Nor is it to suggest that such arguments of social good are fallacious. The promotion of education *is* a social good. Advancing the system benefits everyone in many ways. I am suggesting only that such arguments of social benefit, however true and compelling intellectually, are likely to be without strong political appeal *except* when they are advanced by educational statesmen and leaders. It is their peculiar function and their special office to remind us of such truths so that they can receive their proper political weight. Such leaders, however, do not have to lend their voice in a similar way to arguments for the system that rest upon the aggregation of individual interests. Such arguments, even though they may represent a tawdry and selfish rationale for the support of the system, are nonetheless *politically* stronger than those based entirely on the advancement of social goods. Special advocates are needed only to enlist support for the system on grounds of social interests. It is the function of educational statesmen to be such advocates.

Expansion of the System and the Changi

There is, however, a counter-argument and a counter-movement. There is, on the one hand, that dynamic telling us that the system can expand to the point where the aggregate of individual interests in attainment no longer provides a basis for the political support of the system. On the other hand, there is that dynamic telling us that as the goals of the system are reached, they become transformed into functions, and that when the functions of the system are unsatisfied, that is a problem more serious than if the goals are not met. It invites the attention of the state, and, therefore, the extension of state's interests into areas previously untouched by such authority (see Chapter III for the full argument). Thus, as the system expands to the point where the aggregate of individual interests no longer offers adequate political support, then instead of anticipating a weaker political argument appealing to the social benefits of education, we might anticipate a stronger political argument appealing to somewhat enlarged state interests. Indeed, this is part of the move that Pifer makes. Yet, the point I have in mind is not that. Pifer's remarks are focused primarily on the social arguments for the support of higher education. Yet, the capacity to find political support for the system in the aggregate of individual economic returns has long declined at the eighth level — at least in the American system. Nonetheless, the political support for the system at that level does not seem correspondingly threatened. The more likely claim, in fact, is that it has been strengthened. Why?

The answer lies not merely in the operation of the rule of transforming utility — by which the principal value of attaining at eighth level becomes the chance to attain the ninth. The answer is rather than having already reached a goal of virtually universal attainment at the eighth level, support for the system at that level is regarded as supporting a *function* of the system rather than supporting the achievement of a goal. The political argument for the system at that level can now be advanced by appealing to ate interests, and that is a stronger, not a weaker, argument than one pealing to the aggregate of individual interests.

The dynamic that we seek to understand, therefore, appears to take e following form. As the system expands, political arguments appealing the aggregate of individuals seeking their own self interests tend to ecline in strength at the upper reaches of the system and to be replaced by ocial arguments appealing to the external benefits of spreading the acquisition of educational goods. Yet, at the same time that these changes occur at he higher levels of the system, stronger arguments appealing to state nterests are expanded upward through each successive level in the lower reaches of the system.

in itself: a living reminder of his own potency. He remembers Vannozza's first pregnancy when she was carrying Cesare: the way her breasts swelled, how the line of dark fuzz thickened from her navel to the pubic bone, how he would rest his head on her stomach to try to feel the push. Except even in the womb Cesare had been sly, always a flip or a kick when you didn't expect it. How he had come out fighting, fists knotted, a pent-up energy already on his squashed little face. Not like Lucrezia. Aah, she has been a tiny goddess from the start, so small, so perfect that he could hold her in the palm of one of his hands. Never had there been a baby more beautiful.

His fingers idle down from under Giulia's belly to the neat moist pleat beneath, and this time she stirs.

"Are you awake?"

"Mmmm."

Her voice delights him. "It is almost dawn." He pushes aside the great net of hair and kisses the nape of her neck. "I must leave soon."

Though he never says a word, the omnipresent, ever-reliable Burchard, Master of Ceremonies, knows when the Pope does not wake in his own bed. The censorious German thinks that he keeps his feelings to himself. Alexander smiles. He must be a man who never looks in a mirror, for if he did he would find disapproval etching itself ever deeper into the lines on his face.

She shifts over onto her back, dislodging his hand and curling herself into him. He draws himself up on one elbow and looks down at her face, the perfect skin, pearly, like moonlight in the dark.

"Did you sleep well, my lord?" she says, her voice husky with sleep.

"I sleep with a goddess. How could I not?" He traces a few strands of hair that have come loose.

She gives a small laugh and a sigh. "Before you go . . ."

"Before I go?"

"I . . . I have a favor to ask."

"What could you possibly desire that you don't already have, Giulia Farnese?" he says indulgently. She receives so prettily that he gets even more pleasure from the giving.

"Oh . . . it is a nothing. A silly thing. Not for me really."

"Then it is granted already."

"After the baby . . . I mean, when things are settled here . . . I would . . . I would like to visit Orsino."

The pause tells her what she already knows. That this is not a nothing after all.

"It would not be for long. He has been in the country for almost a year now. And he will hear about the baby. However secret it is kept, I think it would be right if I was the one to tell him."

Whatever some people may say to the contrary, Alexander is not a man without a conscience. Of course, he has given some thought to his unfortunate young cousin with his crossed eyes and cuckold's horns pressing hard out from his forehead. Unlike some men he knows, he takes no great pleasure in other people's pain. On the contrary, he would like Orsino to be content, has tried to make him so, with gifts of lands and benefices. But when faced with a direct challenge between their two opposing states of happiness, he finds it remarkably easy to ignore the discrepancy and for that reason does not like to be reminded of it.

"His mother will tell him all that he needs to know when it is right. He understands the situation well enough. He is a Borgia and respects his family."

"But he is also a man, Rodrigo. And not a happy one."

"Man is not born to be happy," he says portentously, his voice booming now. "Does he press his distress upon you through letters?"

"No. No. But it is not something I need to be told." She smiles winningly. "I love *you,* my lord. Not him. You know that. And I would not go for long. But he is my husband."

"And I am your Pope." He surprises himself by the ferocity inside him. "I will give you anything, but not him." As he says it, he knows how fully he means it. No, he will not give her him. And she is not for the giving either. Not to her husband or to anyone else ever. It is as if, without her by his side, warming his bed and his thoughts, he risks no longer being the man he is, the force that he needs to be in the world.

"Ask me something else instead," he says, pulling himself back onto dry land. "And it shall be given."

·◦[IX]◦·

RECONSIDERATIONS AND DEPARTURES

W E HAVE REACHED A POINT where it may be fruitful to turn attention away from any further constructive account and instead review and evaluate what has been accomplished. A thorough recapitulation is perhaps unnecessary. But there are two points in particular that merit reconsideration. First of all, it would be useful to ask whether it was a wise decision to avoid any simple, restrictive, and explicit definition of the system. But secondly, if it is indeed true that educational policy is essentially policy for the system, and that a knowledge of the system would be useful, then, provided the account given so far is successful, it should lead us to some fresh perspectives in thinking about educational policy. Can it?

RECONSIDERATIONS

On Defining the System

Instead of defining the system with all of its elements, parameters, and relations at the beginning, I have tried to show how a systematic and dynamic account of the system can be made to emerge from examining what is implicit in our common discourse about the system. Thus, I began by identifying three primary or primitive properties — and only three — that we do in fact seem always to include in one way or another when in common parlance we speak of the educational system. Those primitive features are that the system is (1) a system of schools and colleges, (2) related by a medium of exchange, and (3) arranged according to a principle of sequence. Because the system has these properties, however, it has also certain derivative features. It has (1) some size, (2) some means of control, and (3) some principles that describe its distributive behavior. It will expand according to certain principles, and because of the distributive

159

properties of its benefits it will produce an array of political arguments in its support.

We need not have begun with these simple elements. We might have started instead with as exhaustive a list as possible of all those institutions and forces that enter into shaping the style and the content of the education of individuals. They would include the family, church, vocation, mass media, the institutions of the arts — like museums, theaters, symphony orchestras, and the recording industry — as well as libraries, the public press, and the institutions of travel. Schools then would come to be viewed as those institutions that attend most directly to mediating some configuration of learning in the lives of people, some way of orchestrating or harmonizing, or bringing together the learning that takes place through the influence of these other institutions of life. This might be an appropriate approach were we concerned to develop the theory of the system in closer relation to the theory of education.[1] We did not begin in this way, however. We began instead by distinguishing between the way any society goes about educating its members, on the one hand — its system of educating — and the educational system, on the other hand.

This decision, however, can be evaluated. It need not stand without justification. Its adequacy rests upon (1) whether it is sufficient to satisfy the interests of our inquiry, and (2) whether it is sufficiently powerful to encompass the salient features of the system that are given prominence by alternative approaches. Consider, for example, that most useful and yet neglected functional definition of the system provided by James McClellan, who defines "the system" as "that part of the total educational enterprise of the society which automatically receives more students, or better students, or longer control over students, or some combination of the above, whenever a decision is made to upgrade educational requirements anywhere in the nation's economy."[2]

In the approach followed in this study, every essential feature of this definition is included, but in a somewhat refined and elaborated form. Let us note to begin with that the educational system itself is a part of the "nation's economy" as those words are understood in this definition. The system is an employer. And from our study of the hierarchies of the system

1. For an exposition of such an approach, both brilliant in its detail and clear in its outlines, see Lawrence A. Cremin, *Public Education* (New York: Basic Books, 1976), the Fifteenth John Dewey Society Lectures. In this set of lectures, Cremin sets forth what he calls "an ecological view of education." His aim is to provide an approach to the theory of *education* that would surmount the dichotomy between school and society that both captured Dewey and was resisted by him.

2. McClellan, *Toward a More Effective Critique of American Education* (Philadelphia: Lippincott, 1968), p. 20.

as employer we learn that the levels of the system — only hinted at in the principle of sequence — are strongly related by the fact that there are educational prerequisites for anyone to assume a position in the system. Whenever those requirements are increased, the system will expand. It will receive either more students or better students or longer control over students. We can now see, however, what is not included in McClellan's definition, namely that the long-run tendency of the system is to "upgrade educational requirements" for positions in the system to a natural limit in which each position is filled by a person who has completed the highest level of the system.

Secondly, we should observe that, according to this definition, there may be schools or educational institutions that are not part of the educational system. Thus, the definition suggests that the system is only a part of the total educational enterprise of the society. It is that part that automatically receives more students, or better students or longer control over students whenever there is an upgrading of the *educational* requirements for positions anywhere in the economy. By "educational requirements" McClellan means what I have called second-order educational goods, i.e., diplomas, certificates, transcripts, and the like. And what he means by "upgrading" is either raising the levels of mastery in the hierarchies of learning that are reflected in such second-order goods or requiring a higher level of such goods themselves.

Consider the following illustration. Suppose that General Electric upgrades the educational requirements for certain positions within the corporation. Let us suppose further that those raised educational requirements can be satisfied only through attendance at some program of instruction provided exclusively by General Electric Company for its own employees. In that case, the educational programs operated by General Electric would automatically expand in the ways suggested by McClellan, but they would not automatically expand as a consequence of such a decision *anywhere* in the nation's economy. For example, the educational programs provided by General Electric would not expand if a decision were made in Westinghouse Corporation to upgrade the educational requirements for positions in that company. Nor would such educational programs expand automatically if a decision were made to upgrade educational requirements for positions in the cosmetic industry. We have here an educational program, but it is not a part of the educational system.

On the other hand, let us suppose that the educational requirements for positions in General Electric can be satisfied by attendance at instruction in any similar program at any other institution offering instruction. In that case, the decision to upgrade educational requirements for positions in General Electric would automatically result in an expansion of the kind

McClellan describes in other institutions. But then General Electric would have to find some way of assuring that the instruction offered is as good as or better than that offered by themselves for their own employees. They would need assurance that certificates secured elsewhere are equivalent to their own. We would have the beginning of a system of exchange. General Electric might accept as valid, certificates received for instruction elsewhere, but would institutions elsewhere accept certificates secured through instruction provided by General Electric? If they would, then programs in General Electric would behave as part of the system. The process of exchange would be reciprocal.

The point is to see that the system as we have described it, behaves in a way corresponding to the insights contained in McClellan's functional definition, but what makes it behave that way is the existence of a medium of exchange, together with an extension of the hierarchical principles of the system as employer to include positions in the entire economy. The system, in short, relates to other positions in the economy in the same way it relates to positions within the system. It behaves as a consumer of what it produces. We depend on the educational system, in other words, to develop the array of skills and abilities needed in the economy including the skills and talents needed within the system itself.

McClellan's definition is derived from focusing upon the interaction between the educational system and the institutions of employment. There remains, however, a second complementary definitional approach. We could conceive of the system as describable by a set of concentric circles distinguishing between those aspects of the total educational enterprise that are central and those that are, as it were, more peripheral. Let us consider what might be called the system of post-secondary education as a means of illustrating the principles involved in this approach.

At the heart of the post-secondary system we will find a range of institutions usually associated with formal higher education. They are the universities and colleges with related graduate programs. Next, moving outward from the core, we shall find a variety of undergraduate institutions; then the public junior colleges, private business colleges, two-year community colleges; and, finally, the university connected centers of adult or continuing education. Outside these institutions, but still tenuously connected to them, are other educational institutions such as museums and art centers; and even more remotely, but still related to the university graduate centers are the technical institutes; and, finally, programs in business and industry, basically in-service, and related primarily to the manpower requirements of the sponsoring business enterprises, together with other institutions for youth including camping programs, scouting, and youth centers of all kinds.

Such a portrait of core and periphery has this apparent advantage over the approach applied within this study. It permits us to incorporate into the system all manner of educational agencies that lie outside the domain of the formal school system in the usual sense, but which nonetheless are undoubtedly educational in their purpose and their primary effect. It makes it possible once again to see the system as the system of educating. But this advantage is apparent only.

We must ask what it is that permits this picture of the system to be described as a system? What is it that permits us to distinguish between core and periphery in such an image? The systemic features of this approach are derived chiefly from two features, both of which are prominent in the exposition developed in these pages. The first derives from the systemic principles of hierarchy and more especially from the principles governing the ways that the system is staffed. The second feature stems from that ever-present and inescapable system of exchange.

Passage through the core university and college with their associated graduate schools is virtually the only way in which persons currently may gain access to positions of leadership within the educational system itself. This function, as we have seen, is one of the central systemic features of the system. As things stand now, the leadership, and to a large extent, the faculties of junior colleges, community colleges, adult education centers, and university related centers of continuing education receive their training and, more importantly, their credentials in the regular, formally instituted centers of university and graduate education. This is increasingly true, even of those taking leadership positions within the educational programs of labor unions and business.

The result is that increasingly the system of post-secondary education tends to behave in a fashion very like a closed economic system in which an expansion of demand in any part of it will be felt as an expansion of demand in other parts. This is the principle that led to our discussion of the hierarchies of the system as employer. On the other hand, it is not true that leadership in the core college, university and graduate centers is drawn from graduates of those peripheral institutions. That is why they can be regarded as peripheral. They draw their leadership from the core institutions, but the core institutions do not typically draw their leadership from them. Thus, expansion in the core institutions will not necessarily be felt as an expansion in the peripheral institutions, but expansion in the peripheral institutions will tend to produce expansion in the core.

The distinction between core and peripheral institutions rests, therefore, upon principles already explicated in our more limited account of the system. But there is a second source of the tendency to distinguish core and peripheral institutions. Not only does there tend to be a one-way path in the practices of staffing the system, but there is a correspondingly limited exchange in the uses of second-order educational goods. That is to say, certificates, credits, transcripts and the like for activities satisfactorily performed within the core institutions tend to be received as valid tokens for exchange of activities that could have been performed in the peripheral institutions. But the converse tends not to be the case. Credits and certificates earned in the peripheral institutions tend not to have *prima facie* validity in the core institutions. Similarly, as a student, one may move from an "accredited institution" to a non-accredited one more easily than the other way around. But this phenomenon also is incorporated into our account of the system.

In short, I have not viewed the system as consisting of a set of core and peripheral institutions standing in some systemic relationships. Yet there is nothing in principle advantageous in such a view that is not also incorporated in the approach that I have pursued. By extending our study of the hierarchies of the system as employer, and by examining in more detail the dynamics of the system of exchange within the system, the portrait of a set of core and peripheral institutions can be made to emerge. Precisely similar remarks can be made extending the image of core and peripheral institutions to the elementary and secondary system. What produces the conception of the system as core and periphery is the joint effect of the employment system and the mutuality or lack of mutuality in the exchange value of second-order educational goods.

On this note, I am content to let the matter of definition rest. There are, as far as I know, no advantages to any alternative view of the system that are not either subsumable under the exposition I have given or that do not severely abridge the common-sense distinction between a theory of the system and a theory of education.

But what of the second point of reconsideration, the claim that if educational policy is policy for the system, then a knowledge of how the system works should open up new vistas for thinking about educational policy?

An Immodest Proposal to Reduce the System

Let us accept as given (1) that the high school attainment rate has stabilized and will remain at its present level, and (2) that the effects of the principle of shifting benefits and liabilities are genuine (see Appendix C for an illustrative study of this claim). It follows that about 25 percent of each generation are disadvantaged not by any lack of native ability, but simply by not attaining at a certain level in the system. This is a socially unacceptable result.

Question: What might be a remedy? *Answer:* By a variety of measures, reach a point where (1) possessing the high school *diploma* can no longer be used by the system for awarding access to post-secondary education, and (2) 12th grade attainment is stabilized at 55 to 60 percent of each successive 17-year-old cohort. The first of these conditions has the effect of abandoning the high school diploma as a second-order benefit of the system, which is the same as changing the operation of the principle of sequence at a particular point in the hierarchy of the system. The second of these conditions is the equivalent of returning the 12th grade attainment rate to its level between 1945 and 1955.

What might be the advantages? Let us consider three contrasting sets of conditions, holding constant, for the first two, the *total* number of employment positions open in the private and public sectors of the economy. Consider an 18–24 age cohort of 1,000 persons in an employment system with 850 positions and a twelfth level attainment rate of 75 percent. Suppose further that employers rigorously apply attainment at the 12th level of the system as a screen for job placement, a practice that, together with job-related tests, is followed by many industrial firms. It follows that 750 jobs will be allocated to high school graduates and 100 to the remaining 250 non-high school graduates.

Consider the same assumptions under conditions where the high school attainment rate is 55 percent. In that case, 550 positions would be allocated to high school graduates and the remaining 300 to non-high school graduates. Under these circumstances, employers will either leave positions unfilled or else they will have to develop stronger devices for screening applicants *on other grounds than high school attainment.* The high school diploma then becomes an increasingly less useful device in allocating employment opportunities. Furthermore, it is likely to become increasingly apparent under these conditions that using the high school diploma as a first or even second step in allocating jobs is a practice that, with increasing probability, will eliminate persons of high ability. More non-attainers will secure positions; and among those who do, there are likely to be many who would not have had opportunities at all under a higher attainment rate. In short, the 300 non-graduates who are employed are more likely to include some of the 250 who would not get opportunities when the attainment rate is as high as 75 percent.

Consider a third set of conditions, one in which there are only 600 positions available for the 18–24 cohort. That is, let us suppose that unemployment in that cohort remains at about 40 percent and that high school attainment remains at 75 percent. In that case, on the assumptions I have laid out, there will be *no* jobs for non-high school graduates. Indeed, some high school *graduates* will be without jobs, and so the employment sector will have to develop devices for screening among *graduates* in the 18–24 age group. That screen is likely to take the form of required attainment at the 14th level. The demand for higher levels of education is not created by the demand for higher levels of skill in employment. Rather, the demand for higher levels of education is created by the *supply* of those who have education *matched against* the aggregate number of opportunities for *all* persons.

On the other hand, with an attainment rate below 60 percent, then even at a level of 40 percent unemployment in the age group, it follows, on these assumptions, that some among the non-attaining group will have opportunities for jobs.

The point of these remarks is to seek a useful conceptualization of the claim that, *expressed in terms of attainment rates,* there is an optimal size for the system, especially at the 12th level.[3] We are unaccustomed to such a view because we are disposed to discuss the benefits of the system not in relation to second-order goods, but in relation to educational goods themselves. But in the distribution of educational goods there is nothing like Pareto optimality nor anything resembling a Pareto movement. The world can always stand to have a little more wisdom, and nobody is worse off for it. But the underlying problem I have been pointing to is different. There may not be an optimal spread of knowledge, but there can be such a thing as an excessive power of the system to determine the life chances of individuals. My suspicion is that there is an optimal size of the system when viewed in this way, and that we have passed it at the twelfth level. Under conditions of a lower high school attainment rate, the capacity of the system to shape the destiny of youth is reduced, the non-attaining group is better off and the society *necessarily* will provide more opportunities for people *independently* of their attainment level in the system. What we need

---

3. Consider this set of assumptions: (1) Earnings opportunities for the entire 18–24 group are normally distributed. (2) The population is divided into those who have attained level n and those who have attained below n. (3) The society allocates earnings opportunities so that those attaining level n monopolize the opportunities at the upper end of the distribution. From these assumptions, the following propositions are derivable by straight deduction: (1) As the attainment rate rises, the mean income of the higher attaining group declines toward the mean for the entire group, and the mean income of the lower attaining group declines toward zero. (2) The means for the two groups will be most nearly equal when the attainment rate is 50 percent. (3) The distance between the means for the two groups will increase with increasing speed as the attainment level passes 60 percent. Is 50 percent a point of optimal size? Probably not.

is not so much a system that is more equitable (although we need that too), but a system that is less powerful, less fateful in determining the futures of individuals.

These are by no means small advantages. Yet, there are two conditions without which such a social movement should not be encouraged. The first is that if there is any reduction in the high school attainment rate, say, to the level of 1950, that reduction can only be given a decent political argument if it is accompanied by a distribution of the non-attaining group on criteria of class, race, and ethnicity more equitable than existed in 1950. But the force of "the equal principle" coming into play in the next ten years may make such an accomplishment possible. Certainly as a consequence of recent emphasis upon "the best principle," we are now in an improved position to achieve an equitable social distribution with a lower high school attainment rate than we would have been had the attainment rate never risen above its 1950 level.

Secondly, although it may be desirable to have a somewhat lower high school attainment level than we have, it would be undesirable to do so without providing increased opportunities for *all* to continue learning. We should not seek a lower rate of attainment if that means cutting off for anyone the opportunity to continue the search for educational benefits. In meeting this requirement, it would be helpful to introduce measures preventing the educational system itself from using criteria of attainment for the allocation of places in the post-secondary sector of the system.

But such a proposal means more. It amounts, in effect, to abandoning the cherished American ideal that the comprehensive secondary school should be universal. It amounts to a workable revision of the system, one in which the eleventh and twelfth levels of the system are permitted to atrophy and the high school is seen as an effective transitional school whose main purpose is to empty itself as rapidly as possible and in as many ways as is feasible.

Under these conditions it may again become possible to speak of the decision to continue one's education not as a response required to avoid personal disaster, but as a genuine *educational* decision to improve the quality of one's life.

The optimal size of the system should be represented by a rate of attainment that fluctuates with the level of employment *for the 18–24 age group*. That rate of attainment should always be low enough so that attainment in the system cannot be used decisively as a screen for employment. This sets an upper limit on the size of the system. Thus, under conditions of sustained high employment for the 18–24 age group, the attainment rate at the twelfth level of the system could be permitted to rise slightly.

Consider the following scenario. At the time of this writing (1979), we are in the United States at a peak in the size of the 18–24 age cohort. For the next nine years, the size of that age group will decline between 2 and 3 percent per year. It will bottom out at a point some 20 to 25 percent below its present magnitude. Many colleges will close. Others will survive, but probably at the cost of somewhat lower standards. They will be aided by an extension of the Basic Educational Opportunity Grants Program to make 50 percent of the age group eligible for grants. Thus, we may see within the next five to ten years an unemployment rate as low as 15 percent for the 18–24 age group. That would be a lower rate than we have seen since 1945. At that low rate of unemployment, even with an attainment rate at 70 percent, many non-attainers in the system will have opportunities for employment. A higher attainment rate will then be acceptable and the effects of increasing liabilities for non-attainment will be less severely felt. My estimate would be that 70 percent attainment at the twelfth level is probably as large as the system should ever expand and that a 60 percent level is probably as low as it should fall (see Figure C-1).

DEPARTURES

That there is such a thing as the educational system and that it is useful to understand its behavior seems by now a claim that needs no defense. That I have described it fully and completely is a claim that I would not seek to defend. But the theory of the system, as I have been able to discern it, is a formal theory. It is formal in the way that a symbolized argument is formal. It lacks content, but, on the other hand, it provides the structure of an endless succession of arguments when the variables of the arguments are given values. And the arguments that emerge in this way seem to be peculiarly pertinent in formulating the durable problems of educational policy. Educational policy is policy for the educational system. We understand the behavior of the system by understanding the nature of the practical arguments that enter into its behavior. But since policy formulation is also an exercise of practical rationality — a decision about what to do — it is not surprising then that the discernment of those arguments should lend insight to the conduct of policy.

And even though we may say that the theory of the system as outlined is a formal theory, still, it does not lack a consideration of certain values. The principle of fair benefit distribution as well as the best and equal principles are principles of justice. Nevertheless, they are principles that lack specific content just as the theory of the system lacks educational content. The principle of fair benefit distribution, for example, is like a blank check, a mere form which when filled in with payer, payee, and amount, then, and only then, has some cash value.

If I have been able to describe the formal elements of policy for the system and the practical arguments that guide the behavior of the system, then what remains is to describe the essential educational content of policy for the system. If I have concentrated on what makes the system a system, then in a further treatment what remains is to consider what is needed for it to be an *educational* system.

But to take this step is to exceed any reasonable limits of this exposition. Any adequate account of the content of policy for the system must treat the relation of education to work life, and also its relation to civic life. And if that, then it must deal in some depth with the nature of "membership" and, therefore, with the place of history in the formation of a social memory. For without a social memory there is none of that attachment in the present or through time to underwrite either social membership or the existence of the system itself. Dealing with the educational content of the system leads one then to a treatment also of the moral emotions and the problems of public choice in the direction of the system in ways without which it cannot lay claim to be an *educational* system.

In taking such a step one passes not only from the matter of form to content, but also from one kind of rhetoric to another. The coldly analytic frame of mind that produces the theory of the system must yield to the impulse to voice commitments. One moves from the detachment of describing how things work to an involved perspective of what things matter. In a full account of these further questions it may turn out, however, that the kind of practical rationality required to deal with policy for the system is the kind of thinking that also provides the content of moral education for our day. It is enough, however, for this report to end here. These further steps must wait on a subsequent report, one that can more truly conclude in a point of greater finality.

APPENDICES

Appendix A

TABLES

TABLE A-1
Ratio of High School Graduates to 17 Year Olds in Population, 1870–1975

Year of Graduation	Percentage	Year of Graduation	Percentage
1870	2.0	1940	50.8
		1942	51.2
1880	2.5	1944	42.3
		1946	47.9
1890	3.5	1948	54.0
1900	6.4	1950	59.0
1902	6.4	1952	58.6
1904	6.9	1954	60.0
1906	7.4	1956	62.3
1908	7.4	1958	64.8
1910	8.8	1960	65.1
1912	9.8	1962	69.5
1914	11.7	1964	61.3
1916	13.8	1966	75.8
1918	15.8	1968	77.8
1920	16.8	1970	75.6*
1922	17.8	1972	76.0†
1924	23.4	1974	75.1†
1926	25.5	1975	74.6†
1928	26.2		
1930	29.0		
1932	35.5		
1934	39.2		
1936	42.7		
1938	45.6		

SOURCES: Ferris, Abbot L. *Indicators of Trends in American Education* (New York: Russell Sage Foundation, 1969).

*U.S. Department of Commerce, Bureau of the Census. *Historical Statistics of the United States Part I* (Washington, D.C.: USGPO, 1976).

†National Center for Education Statistics (DHEW). *Digest of Education Statistics — 1976* (Washington, D.C.: USGPO, 1977).

TABLE A-2
Ratio of B.A. or First Professional Degrees Conferred to
High School Graduates 4 Years Earlier, 1885–1975

School Year Ending	Percentage	School Year Ending	Percentage
1885	59.0	1940	18.0
		1942	16.0
1890	47.0	1944	10.0
		1946	11.0
1895	56.0	1948	27.0
1900	36.0	1950	40.0
1902	34.0	1952	28.0
1904	32.0	1954	24.0
1906	32.0	1956	26.0
1908	30.0	1958	28.0
1910	30.0	1960	27.0
1912	30.0	1962	27.0
1914	28.0	1964	27.0
1916	25.0	1966	29.0
1918	18.0	1968	29.0
1920	19.0	1970	31.0
1922	22.0	1972	34.4*
1924	27.0	1973	34.3*
1926	27.0	1974	34.0*
1928	22.0	1975	32.6*
1930	22.0		
1932	23.0		
1934	20.0		
1936	17.0		
1938	18.0		

SOURCES: U.S. Department of Commerce. Bureau of the Census. *Historical Statistics of the United States Part I* (Washington, D.C.: USGPO 1976).

*National Center for Education Statistics (DHEW). *Condition of Education —1977*, and *Digest of Education Statistics — 1976* (Washington, D.C.: USGPO, 1977).

TABLE A-3
School Retention Rates:
5th Grade through College Entrance and First Degree, 1924–32 to 1967–75

Year of Entrance to 5th Grade (1)	5th Grade (2)	8th Grade (3)	12th Grade (4)	H.S. Grad. (5)	Year of H.S. Grad. (6)
1924	1,000	741	344	302	1932
1926	1,000	754	400	333	1934
1928	1,000	805	432	378	1936
1930	1,000	824	463	417	1938
1932	1,000	831	510	455	1940
1934	1,000	842	512	467	1942
1936	1,000	849	425	393	1944
1938	1,000	853	444	419	1946
1940	1,000	836	507	481	1948
1942	1,000	847	539	505	1950
1944	1,000	858	549	522	1952
1946	1,000	919	583	553	1954
1948	1,000	929	619	581	1956
1950	1,000	921	632	582	1958
1952	1,000	936	667	621	1960
1954	1,000	948	684	642	1962
1956	1,000	948	728	676	1964
1958	1,000	961	761	732	1966
1960	1,000	967	787	749	1968
1962	1,000	976	793	752	1970
1964	1,000	976	791	748	1972
1965	1,000	980	786	749	1973
1966	1,000	985	783	744	1974
1967	1,000	984	775	743	1975

SOURCES: *Historical Statistics of the United States. Colonial Times to 1970.* Part 1 p. 379. Series H 587–597. *Statistical Abstract of the United States, 1977.* Columns 8, 10, 11 Calculated.

First-Time College Entrance (7)	Rate of First-Time College Entrance to H.S. Grads. (8)	Year of First Degree (9)	First Degree per H.S. Grads 4 Yrs. Earlier (10)	Rate of First Degree to Entry 4 Yrs. Earlier (11)
118	390	1936	17	43.6
129	417	1938	18	43.2
137	362	1940	18	— —
148	355	1942	16	45.0
160	351	1944	10	28.5
129	276	1946	11	39.8
121	308	1948	27	87.6
(NA)	— —	1950	40	— —
(NA)	— —	1952	28	— —
205	406	1954	24	59.1
234	448	1956	26	58.0
283	511	1958	28	56.7
301	518	1960	27	52.1
308	529	1962	27	51.0
328	528	1964	27	51.1
343	534	1966	29	54.3
362	535	1968	29	54.2
384	524	1970	31	59.1
452	603	1972	33	54.7
465	618	1974	33	53.4
433	578	— —	— —	— —
433	578	— —	— —	— —
448	602	— —	— —	— —
452	608	— —	— —	— —

TABLE A-4
Higher Education:
Rates of Degree Attainment, 1885–1975

School Yr. Ending	Bachelor's or First Professional		Masters or 2nd Professional		Doctor's or Equivalent	
	Total	Per 100 H.S. Grads 4 Yrs. Earlier	Total	Per 100 Bachelor's 2 Yrs. Earlier	Total	Per 1,000 Bachelor's X Yrs. Earlier
1885	14,734	59	1,071	7	77	5.8
1886	13,097	48	859	7	84	2.9
1888	15,256	49	987	8	140	6.1
1890	15,539	47	1,015	7	149	9.0
1892	16,802	51	730	5	190	13.0
1894	21,850	50	1,223	7	279	18.5
1896	24,593	46	1,478	7	271	16.0
1898	25,052	37	1,440	6	324	15.2
1900	27,410	36	1,583	6	382	14.2
1902	28,966	34	1,858	7	293	10.2
1904	30,501	32	1,679	6	334	11.8
1906	32,019	32	1,787	6	383	13.0
1908	33,800	30	1,971	6	391	13.8
1910	37,199	30	2,113	6	443	12.5
1912	42,943	30	3,035	8	500	15.9
1914	44,268	28	3,270	8	559	15.7
1916	45,250	25	3,906	9	667	18.1
1918	38,585	18	2,900	7	556	15.0
1920	48,622	19	4,279	9	615	14.2
1922	61,668	22	5,984	16	836	17.6
1924	82,783	27	8,216	17	939	24.8
1926	97,263	27	9,735	16	1,409	37.3
1928	111,161	22	12,387	15	1,447	33.2

School Yr. Ending	Bachelor's or First Professional		Masters or 2nd Professional		Doctor's or Equivalent	
	Total	Per 100 H.S. Grads 4 Yrs. Earlier	Total	Per 100 Bachelor's 2 Yrs. Earlier	Total	Per 1,000 Bachelor's X Yrs. Earlier
1930	122,484	22	14,969	15	2,299	33.4
1932	138,063	23	19,367	17	2,654	29.0
1934	136,156	20	18,293	15	2,830	27.7
1936	143,125	17	18,302	13	2,770	24.7
1938	164,943	18	21,628	16	2,932	22.3
1940	186,500	18	26,731	19	3,290	23.5
1942	185,346	16	24,648	15	3,497	24.9
1944	125,863	10	13,414	7	2,305	13.8
1946	136,174	11	19,209	10	1,966	14.2
1948	271,186	27	42,432	37	3,989	25.3
1950	432,058	40	58,183	22	6,633	34.9
1952	329,986	28	63,534	15	7,683	41.6
1954	291,508	24	56,823	17	8,996	69.2
1956	309,514	26	59,281	20	8,903	62.2
1958	363,502	28	65,586	21	8,942	32.3
1960	389,183	27	77,692	21	9,829	22.4
1962	414,287	27	88,414	23	11,622	34.7
1964	494,153	27	70,339	25	14,490	48.9
1966	551,047	29	140,548	28	18,237	57.4
1968	666,710	29	176,749	32	23,089	59.2
1970	827,234	31	208,291	31	29,866	72.1
1972	894,110*	33	— —	— —	— —	— —
1974	954,376*	33	— —	— —	— —	— —
1975	931,663*	32	293,651*	31	34,086*	— —

SOURCES: *Historical Statistics. Colonial Times to 1970.* Series H 751–65.

  Statistical Abstract of the United States, 1977 Table No. 266, p. 161.

A NOTE ON DATING THE SYSTEM

In the text, the claim is advanced that the system in the American case does not much predate 1910. On what grounds does such an assertion rest? Table A-1 shows that the remarkably regular and unyielding rise in the high school attainment rate that continued to 1965 began about 1910. Table A-2 shows that the ratio of B.A. or First Professional Degree to high school graduates of four years earlier drops precipitously from the late nineteenth century until about 1920, and then it slowly rises some 10 to 15 percent to its present fairly stable level.

    These two facts, taken together, constitute evidence that the high school was transformed from an essentially college preparatory institution to a comprehensive secondary school in the second decade of the present century, and that only then did that institution begin to take its place in a system with a single ladder of progress from grade one through college. In short, the presence of the system began to be felt in the American scene between 1910 and 1920.

Appendix B

ON THE METHOD OF PRACTICAL RATIONALITY: OBJECTIONS

Two things are especially worth noting about practical arguments. The first is that, like all other arguments, they contain an inference. The second is that, unlike most arguments, the conclusion is not a proposition but a directive, command, or act. For example,

Premise:	The school-age population is rapidly expanding.
Therefore:	Expand the school(s) system.

The argument is illicit. What premise would be sufficient to make it a valid argument?

Note: Answering this question does *not* require that we find a set of premises sufficient to guarantee that the system will expand. The claim that the system *will* expand is not the conclusion of a practical argument.

By introducing a premise into the illustrative argument we may get a valid inference even though the decision is not to expand the system. In that case, in the determination of policy for the system, there are likely to have been *other arguments* which were introduced and which prevailed. But this possibility has no bearing on whether the illustrative argument, with the addition of an appropriate premise, is valid.

THREE OBJECTIONS

#1. The premise elicited in transforming an illicit inference into a valid practical argument may not be the only premise that can yield the conclusion. Therefore, in identifying a particular premise as sufficient to yield the conclusion, we cannot be sure that we have identified any particular principle in the behavior of the system. In short, given any proposition, there is no unique set of premises sufficient to yield that proposition as conclusion.

Let K represent the premises and L the conclusion. Suppose we observe that $K \to L$ is invalid, and that $(K \cdot p) \to L$ is valid. It follows that $(K \cdot p \cdot q \cdot r \ldots) \to L$ is also valid.

Conclusion. There is no unique *set* of premises necessary to make $K \to L$ into a valid argument. *Objection granted.*

#2. Suppose we observe that K → L is invalid, and that (K · p) → L is valid. The validity of (K · r) → L remains undetermined.

Conclusion. From the fact that a particular premise added to K → L is sufficient to make it valid, we cannot conclude that that premise is necessary or *uniquely* sufficient. *Objection granted.*

#3. If (K · p) → L is valid, and if (r → p), then (K · r) → L is valid. In short, if an invalid argument K → L is rendered valid by the additional premise p, then it will be rendered valid also by the addition of any *other* premise instead of p, provided that other premise implies p.

Conclusion. If I know that (K → L) is rendered valid by the introduction of p as a premise, and if I know that there is some other proposition that implies p, then I know that there is *at least* one premise other than p that will make (K → L) valid. If we grant further that given *any* proposition, B, there will be some other proposition, A, such that A → B, then we must grant that there is *no* premise uniquely sufficient to render (K → L) valid. *Objection granted.*

REPLIES TO THREE OBJECTIONS

Objection #1. No serious difficulty for the method of practical rationality arises from admitting this objection. Nor would there be any point in refining our approach, if we could, to meet this objection. All that it establishes is that if an argument is valid, it will remain valid after the addition of other premises.

Objection #2. This objection also presents no difficulty for the following reasons. From the fact that a particular premise added to (K → L) will render it valid, we conclude only that the premise is *sufficient* to render the practical argument of the system valid. We must be prepared to entertain the prospect of there being *other* premises that are also sufficient. *If we find others* then the principle or belief included in the structure of the system turns out to be a disjunction each member of which is sufficient to render the practical argument of the system valid and each of which might be appealed to in differing circumstances. If we do *not* find other premises, that does not *prove* that there are none, but it does strengthen our belief that there are no others.

Objection #3. The central claim is that given any proposition, B, there will be another, A, such that A → B. Thus, not only is there no premise uniquely sufficient to render (K → L) valid, but, in fact, there is an infinite (or at least, very large) set of such propositions each one of which will be sufficient.

But observe! Given any two propositions, A, and B, if (A → B), but (B ↛ A), then B is the weaker of the two. It is logically (or epistemically) weaker in the sense that in knowing the truth of A, we may know more than we know in knowing the truth of B. In knowing that A is true, we may know (or discover) all that the truth of A entails including all that B entails; whereas, in knowing the truth of B, we may know (or discover) only what B entails.

Thus, to the method of practical rationality, we must add the following general rule: In seeking the premises sufficient for the validity of the practical arguments of the system, we seek to identify the logically weakest and therefore most indeterminate claim that is sufficient for the practical argument in question to be valid. If we find more than one premise, logically independent in the sense that neither implies the other, then we have discovered a disjunction as a systemic principle. We have no proof that such a disjunction will be small, but neither do we have any proof that it will be large. As a practical matter, I suspect that it would be very small indeed.

Appendix C

BENEFIT AND LIABILITY:
FURTHER INVESTIGATIONS

In setting the system in motion in Chapters V and VI, the arguments rested heavily upon the tautological principle of zero correlation and the contingent claims of the law of last entry. The conclusions, in every case, were provided rational support, yet, without precise definition or illustration drawn from real world experience with the system. A detailed illustration drawn from actual experience will help to make the theory more vivid and its principles more precise. I have already argued that the theory of the system makes understandable what may otherwise be viewed as paradoxical. That is encouraging evidence that the theory of the system reveals dynamics that more conventional approaches might conceal.

For this purpose we may turn to the principle of shifting benefits and liabilities as it applies to attainment at the 12th level of the American system. That principle expresses the claim that as the system expands into the third sector of the uniform growth line, then having a high school diploma will tend to bring no large advantage to those who have them, but that not having one will become a major liability to the rest.

In illustrating this principle it is not my purpose to test the theory of the system. That is a task vastly more difficult than I can undertake. Rather, I wish only to take two steps to *illustrate* one among many other approaches that will help to make the meaning of that principle more explicit. I wish to illustrate one way in which that principle can be given an empirical formulation.

Clearly, the principle of shifting benefits and liabilities presupposes that it is useful to distinguish between the benefit gained by those who graduate from high school and the liability incurred by those who do not. The usual view is that whatever is gained by attainment at a given level of the system is also the magnitude of the liability experienced by those who do not attain that level. For example, if the mean income of those attaining level n is 140 percent of the mean income of those who attain less than n, then the *income* benefit to the higher attaining group is 40 percent, and the liability, or *income forgone*, for the other group is also 40 percent. This is a reasonable view to take, but, as I shall try to show, it is a view that conceals phenomena captured by the principle of shifting benefits and liabilities. The first step, then, is to draw upon actual experience to establish that benefit and liability should be treated as distinct, although associated, phenomena.

The second step, then, is to develop a method by which the distinct magnitudes of declining relative benefits and increasing relative liability can be empirically monitored. The meaning of these two expressions, *taken together* and adequately defined as empirical measures, will express the principle of shifting benefits and liabilities.

DEFINING THE PROBLEM

With these limited aims in mind, let us define the problem as exactly as possible. We are interested in the value of a single second-order benefit for the allocation of a single non-educational social good. We must attempt to isolate these variables. We may isolate the appropriate value of the high school diploma by concentrating upon the different experience of those who have gained four years of high school contrasted with those who have only 1–3 years. Given this decision, however, we must still decide upon a suitable age cohort and a suitable social benefit for study. We may select the group from 18–24 as the cohort, and income, expressed as salary and wages, as the social benefit.

There are problems associated with these decisions, but before turning to them directly let us recall that the principle of shifting benefits and liabilities is intended to express a dynamic of the system between any version of a second-order good and *any* version of non-educational social benefits. Income provides only one application of that principle. It will also apply, for example, to the value of second-order benefits in allocating social status. And we are quite aware of the fact that some persons will sacrifice income for status and others will sacrifice status for greater income. The claim being advanced is that these different social benefits will equally reflect the principle of shifting benefits and liabilities, but that their different expressions of that principle require different sets of data.

However, consider the problems associated with selecting the group 18–24 as an appropriate cohort. In the first place, we desire to discriminate not only between two levels of attainment, but also between second-order educational goods and educational benefits themselves. We may assume that in any decent society, educational attainment may be rewarded at the beginning of one's work life, but will have less long-term effect than ability, initiative, courage, inventiveness, and knowledge. Getting a job may be significantly influenced by educational attainment, but *holding* a job and advancing in it will depend relatively more on other qualities and relatively less on mere educational attainment.[1] By selecting the cohort 18–24, we can attend to the short-term value of high school graduation when it is most important relative to the long-term value of educational goods. In other words, selecting a larger cohort would simply enlarge the effect of educational *achievement* in the data when what we wish to study is the efficacy of educational *attainment*.

In any case, we cannot perfectly isolate the relevant variables. One obvious reason why we cannot is that persons do not all graduate from high school at the same age. For example, in 1970, 10 percent of all 19 year olds and 1.7 percent of all 20 year olds were enrolled in high school.[2] This distribution is not unusual. Although many will graduate from high school in their seventeenth year, most will have done so by the end of their eighteenth year. Still, many will graduate in their nineteenth

1. See Vincent Tinto, "Does Schooling Matter? A Retrospective Assessment," in L. Shulman, ed., *Review of Research in Education*, Vol. 4 (Itasca, Ill.: Peacock, 1977), pp. 201–35.

2. See 1970 Decennial Census, Special Reports, *Educational Enrollment*, Vol. 2, VB, Table #5.

year and a few even in their twentieth. For these reasons, it is impossible to identify any age cohort that will constitute a pure proxy for a single level of educational attainment.

Furthermore, any age cohort that includes, at the lower end, all persons when they graduate from high school and go to work is highly likely also to include, at the upper end, some who have graduated from college. Thus, any age-cohort large enough to reflect the income efficacy of high school graduation will probably also reflect the experience of some persons with a college degree. Therefore, by selecting the 18–24 age cohort, we appear to include the mixed effects of two *different* second-order benefits of the system. In the effort to isolate the income effects of high school graduation, as contrasted with 1–3 years of high school, we will almost certainly include *some* of the effects of college graduation as well.

Furthermore, we know that in the thirty-five years from 1940 to 1975 the high school attainment rate (expressed as a proportion of 17 year olds) increased from about 50 percent to 76 percent, and that, in the same period, the ratio of college entrants (to high school graduates in the same year) rose from about 36 percent to nearly 61 percent (see Tables A-1, A-2, and A-3). Thus, if we divide the 18–24 cohort into two groups — those with 4 years and those with only 1–3 years of high school — then we shall be dealing with two groups of constantly changing composition. The cohort in 1975, compared to the same cohort in 1940, will include proportionately more high school graduates, more college students, probably more college graduates, and, therefore, more part-time workers. And part-time workers are unlikely to earn as much as full-time workers *regardless* of educational attainment. These differences in the composition of the two groups will surely influence their respective experience with income over time.

The data, moreover, are mixed in still another way. I have noted already that any cohort large enough to include all high school graduates is likely to include also some college graduates. Thus, we run the risk of confusing two different second-order benefits of the system. But such a cohort will necessarily include even more college *entrants,* and it will do so increasingly as we compare 1975 income data with 1940. But access to the system, we have seen already, is itself a kind of non-educational social good. Thus, the data will include not only the mixed effects of two different second-order benefits, but also two different non-educational social goods related to those second-order benefits.[3]

These appear to be serious objections to using the 18–24 age cohort in illustrating the principle of shifting benefits and liabilities. No matter what cohort is

---

3. It may be argued that income data for the 18–24 cohort will be mixed in yet another way, since they will reflect also the relative attraction of still another non-educational social good, namely social status. Many may accept the short-term lower income of a part-time worker, in anticipation of longer-term higher status, and therefore, will enter college in pursuit of status rather than income. However, I suspect that if there is anything of importance in this point, then it would have had greater weight in 1940 when "going to college" rates were low, than in 1975 when they were high. When attainment rates at any level are high, then going beyond that level becomes increasingly compulsory and status considerations would become *relatively* less significant.

selected, however, these difficulties are unlikely to be eliminated entirely. The relevant problem is to assess their magnitude. How serious are these problems? We may answer this question by examining the distribution of the 18–24 age cohort in 1970. That year provides a good test for the following reasons. First of all, the ratio of college entrants to high school graduates in 1970 was 61.8 percent, its highest point between 1932 and 1975. Thus, if the data are skewed by the presence of large numbers of college students or college graduates, then that bias is most likely to be apparent in the data for 1970. Secondly, the high school attainment rate in 1970 was about 75 percent, where it had remained since 1965 and has remained to the present. The year 1970, in that respect, is typical for a fifteen-year period. Hence, if there is some distortion of the data resulting from a high attainment rate in high school *together* with a high college entrance rate, then its magnitude should be most evident in 1970.

In Table C-1, the 1970 distribution of the 18–24-year cohort is displayed. The substantial high school graduation rate for 1970 is reflected in the absolute and proportionate sizes of the two groups. Also reflected in Table C-1 is the fact that the 18–24 cohort includes some 18 and 19 year olds who will be, but had not yet, graduated from high school. But the significant points are these. First, in both groups, the proportion not enrolled in *any* school is substantial, and approximately the same. The presence of students among the group of high school graduates will no doubt produce a downward bias in the income data for that group. But, on the other hand, the presence of college graduates, not enrolled in any school, will probably bias it upward even though the proportion is only about 6 percent. It is not clear, to me at least, what bias would be produced by the presence of students in the

TABLE C-1
18–24 Year Olds in 1970 by Educational Attainment
1–3 and 4 Years of High School

1–3 Yrs. of H.S.		4 Yrs. of H.S.			
4,970, 239 (21.2%)		16,903,223 (72.3%)			
Enrolled in H.S. 2–4 Yrs.	Not Enrolled in School	Enrolled in Undergraduate College	Enrolled in Graduate School	Not Enrolled	Completed 4 or More Yrs. College
1,868,121 (37.6%)	3,102,118 (62.4%)	4,868,340 (28.8%)	385,112 (2.28%)	11,649,771 (68.9%)	1,410,253 (8.3%)

SOURCE: Reconstructed from 1970 Decennial Census, Special Reports, VB, Tables # 1 and # 5.

second, third, and fourth years of high school among those with only 1–3 years of high school. In any case, the significant point is that these potential biases in the data both within and between the two groups probably cancel one another about as well as can be expected.[4] In short, the 18–24 cohort divided between high school graduates and those with only 1–3 years of high school constitutes an acceptable population for illustrating the principle of shifting benefits and liabilities at the 12th level of the American system.

BENEFIT AND LIABILITY DISTINGUISHED

Let us turn then to the first step. The relevant data for the period from 1939 to 1975 are presented in Table C-2. There, for each of several years, we find the mean

TABLE C-2
Mean Income, Salary, and Wages, 18–24 Year Olds,
Related to Educational Attainment, Males, 1939–75,
Selected Years, Adjusted Dollars (1967= 100)

Date	H.S. Attainment	Mean Income 1–3 Yrs. (1)	Mean Income 4 Yrs. (2)	Mean Income 18–24 Males (3)	% 2÷1 (4)	(1–3) (5)	(2–3) (6)	(5 + 6) Dispersion (7)
1939	49.0	167.8	185.6	169	111	− 1.2	16.6	17.8
1949		2,416	2,522	2,277	104	+139	245	106
1959	63.4	2,656	3,085	2,806	116	−150	279	429
1964	61.3	2,463	3,293	2,873	134	−410	420	830
1969	75.9	2,638	3,633	3,131	137	−493	502	995
1972	75.9	2,738	3,860	3,414	141	−676	446	1,122
1975	74.4	2,363	3,519	3,133	148	−770	386	1,156

SOURCES: U.S. Bureau of the Census. *Decennial Census Reports* for 1940, 1950, 1960, 1970; *Current Population Reports*. P-60, Nos. 85, 90, 92, 97, 101.

4. It might be argued that to escape these problems of bias, the appropriate population for study is "Full-time Workers" with 1–3 and with 4 years of high school. And, indeed, some data are available on this population. However, The Bureau of the Census defines "year-round full-time worker" as "one who worked primarily at full-time civilian jobs (35 hours or more per week) for 50 weeks or more during the preceding calendar year." Under such a definition most so-called full-time employees, even those with advanced rank in the county

income of those with 4 years of high school and those with 1–3 years. Column #3 gives the mean income for all males in the entire age cohort. In column #4 the mean income for those with four years of high school is expressed as a percentage of the mean income of those with 1–3 years. We observe that in 1939 the mean income of those with 4 years of high school was 110 percent of the mean income of those with only 1–3 years. By 1974 that figure had risen to 148 percent.

From the data in this column, one can easily draw the conclusion that the relative value of four years of high school, as opposed to less than four, has steadily increased over the thirty-five-year period, and, as far as we know, is continuing to increase. The figures in column #4 constitute *one* measure of the relative benefit to be gained from attainment at the twelfth level of the system. But this is not the view of benefit and liability implicit in the theory of the system.

If we go on to consider columns #5, #6, and #7, then we shall reach very different conclusions, conclusions that more accurately reflect the principle of shifting benefits and liabilities. In columns #5 and #6, we have not simply a measure of the distance between the mean income of those with 4 years of high school and those with 1–3 years. Instead, these columns display the *distance* between the mean income of each sub-group and the mean income for all males in the entire age-cohort. Column #7 then, is the total dispersion of the means of the two groups above and below the mean income of the entire cohort. This is a more accurate measure of the *relative* position of the two sub-groups.

This information from columns #5 and #6 is graphically presented in Figure C-1. There it is visibly evident that the two curves, though related, are not related as the reciprocal of one another. We cannot say that the increasing benefit of 4 years of high school is the same in magnitude as the increasing liability of those who attain only 1–3 years.

We may view the lower segment of Figure C-1 as one way of representing a liability curve, and the upper segment as one way of expressing a benefit curve. We should note that the visual impression of the benefit curve is precisely the curvilinear function that we have anticipated from the exposition of the system in motion. The relative benefit of high school graduation has not continued unimpeded in its upward path. On the contrary, it rose from 1939 to 1969 and has now begun to decline. But secondly, we should note that the liability curve falls in its downward path (of 909 points) at a rate greater than the rise of the benefit curve (485 points) to its peak in 1969. Finally, we can understand why the relative value of high school graduation, as reflected in the figures of column #4, appears to have continued to increase. It *seems* to have continued its increase because the liability curve has fallen at a rate even greater than the decline of the benefit curve.

The relevant phenomenon to note then, is not the continued advantage of high school graduation, as reflected in the figures of column #4, but the increasing *dis*advantage of *not* graduating from high school *together with the*

---

governments of central New York, would not qualify. Neither would many college professors. Such a definition is likely to produce a population more biased than the one selected and in more indeterminate ways than the one selected.

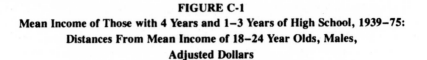

FIGURE C-1
Mean Income of Those with 4 Years and 1–3 Years of High School, 1939–75:
Distances From Mean Income of 18–24 Year Olds, Males,
Adjusted Dollars

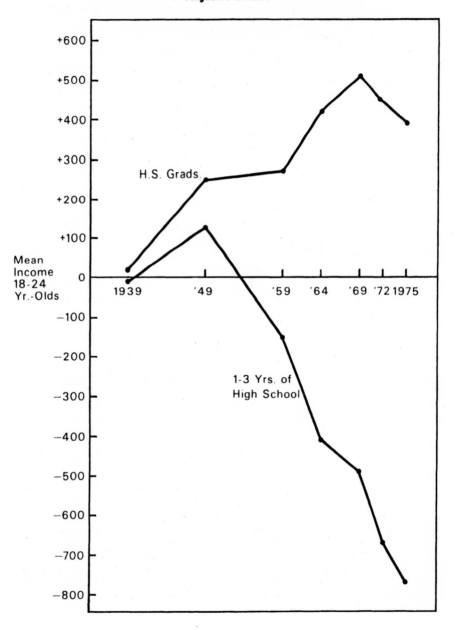

declining benefit of high school graduation to those who graduate.[5] These are precisely the phenomena that are expressed in the principle of shifting benefits and liabilities, and they are concealed in the more conventional approach to the study of these matters. We may take it as established that, from this perspective, there is an important and useful distinction to be drawn between benefits and liabilities when discussing the efficacy of second-order educational goods. Still, the exact rendering of this distinction is not sufficiently clear.

BENEFIT AND LIABILITY, A FREQUENCY ANALYSIS

In addition to examining the mean levels of income gained by the two populations in relation to their age cohort, it may be helpful to consider also how the frequency distribution of income changes for the two groups year by year. In pursuing this illustrative approach, it will be useful to construct an ideal method of arraying the data. We may then view that ideal schema as providing a kind of standard against which to compare the actual record.

Let us array the different levels of income, from $1.00 to some upper limit, on the X-axis, and, on the Y-axis the percent of our two populations falling within each income interval.

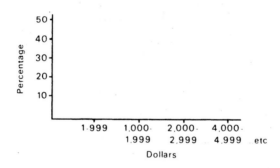

5. I can imagine someone saying, "I know who these people are who suffer the effects of increasing liabilities. They are mostly Blacks, Chicanos and Indians, the racial and ethnic minorities." That is probably true. But it is not relevant to the point being made. The thesis bears repeating that the effects of shifting benefits and liabilities will be felt *no matter what may be the race, color, or ethnic flavor of the declining group of non-attainers.* This is not to deny that, in the United States, there are racial and ethnic effects in determining the composition of that group. It is merely to reaffirm that the group of last entry is not *defined* by race or ethnicity. It would be a racist or jingoistic view that would suppose the group of last entry is *defined* on racial or ethnic grounds. I have claimed otherwise, namely that the effects of shifting benefits and liabilities are systemic. They will be felt no matter what turns out to be the social composition of the group of last entry. The thesis may be mistaken, but it is better that it be mistaken than that it be misconstrued.

The Logic of the Schema

In such a schema, the Y-values are continuous, but the X-values are not. The data points on the X-axis represent income *ranges*. The Y-values, however, are the percentage of the population whose income falls within each range. It follows that in the X-Y plane, we shall have only as many data points as we have income ranges on the X-axis. Those data points can be connected by a line, but we can give no meaning to any part of the line between those data points.

In exploring the logic of this schema, let us assume that the line produced by connecting these data points is always straight; that is, the relationship between the data points is linear rather than curvilinear. Insofar as it is practical to do so, I shall adhere further to the requirement that in each application of the schema the income *intervals* on the X-axis must be uniform — none can be larger than the others — and that the size of those intervals cannot change from one application of the schema to another. This last requirement is essential if we wish to compare frequency distributions for different years. I do not assume, however, that the *number* of data points is the same in each application of the schema.

Given these assumptions, then the schema has several interesting properties. In the first place, it follows that in any of its applications, the total of the Y-values must equal 100 percent. This fact, together with the assumption of linearity, implies that the Y-values for any frequency lines of zero slope will be strictly determined by the number of data points. For n data points, the Y-values of a line of zero slope will be 100/n. If we have five, then the Y-values of a line of zero slope will be 100/5 or 20. If we have four data points, then the Y-values of a line of zero slope will be 100/4 or 25.

But it follows also that if the Y-value at the last data point on a line of zero slope is n, then its maximum decline in a line of non-zero slope will also be n.[6] And if, from one time to another, the Y-value of the last data point declines by n, then the y-value of the first must increase by n, otherwise the assumption of linearity is violated. In other words, given any change in the frequency distribution, the line representing that distribution will rotate around a point located on the line of zero slope.[7] Let us refer to a line of zero slope as the line of origin.

The point of rotation will be that point where any line of plus or minus slope intersects with the line of origin. And that point, if we have an odd number of data points, will be determined by the middle Y-value. And if we have an even number of data points, then it will be determined by the average of the two middle values. For example, given five data points, as in Figure C-2, the Y-value at zero slope will be 100/5 or 20.

6. Actually its maximum decline will be slightly less than n for the following reasons. If we have five data points, $(X_1, Y_1), (X_2, Y_2)....(X_5, Y_5)$, and if the Y-value of the last point is 0, it follows that nobody is in the last income range. Therefore, the population is exhausted by the first four income ranges, not by five. Hence, if the Y-values of a line of zero slope in a schema of five data points is 20, then the maximum decline in the Y-value at (X_5, Y_5) is less than 20. We can give no interpretation to a Y-value of zero. I note this important point, but in exploring the logic of the schema, I shall uniformly ignore it. Ignoring it makes no significant difference to the argument.

7. This point I owe to the critical comments of Robert H. Seidman.

FIGURE C-2
The Frequency Schema Illustrated

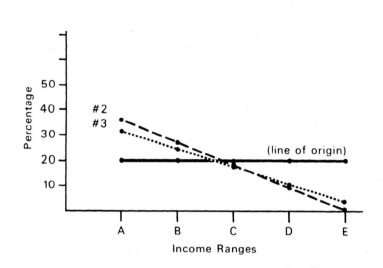

Lines #2 and #3 each have a negative slope. The values of #3 are (A, 30), (B, 25), (C, 20), (D, 15), and (E, 10). The Y-value of the middle data point is 20 on the line of origin. The values for #2 are (A, 35), (B, 27.5), (C, 20), (D, 12.5), (E, 5), and again, 20 is the Y-value of the middle data point on the line of origin.

If we imagine a case with six data points, then their Y-value at zero slope will be 100/6 or 16.66+. On a line with a slope of −4, the middle two data points will be (C, 18.66+) and (D, 14.66+). The average of the two is 16.66+. Thus, such a line will intersect the line of origin when the Y-value is the average of the two middle data points. Changes in the frequency will rotate around that point. We shall see in a moment, however, that the magnitude and direction of that rotation through time is important.

Thus, given any number of data points, we can immediately determine the Y-value at zero slope. From this information, and given the assumption of linearity together with the fact that no values in the schema can be zero or less, we can derive the maximum slope possible, either positive or negative, for any number of data points. And from that information we can determine the value of every intervening data point at maximum slope. The relevant information is presented in Table C-3 for 5, 7, 12, and 14 data points. As the number of data points increases, the maximum possible slope of the frequency distribution declines. This is equivalent to noting that as the range of the income distribution is extended — as opposed to raising the mean level — then the frequency distribution will tend to rotate toward zero slope. To discern the significance of this fact let us consider some theoretical applications of this schema.

TABLE C-3
Maximum Slope and Y-Values for Varying Data Points
in Frequency Distribution of Income

Data Points	Y-Values at Zero Slope	Maximum Y-Value	Maximum Slope
5	20	40	±10
7	14.285	28.57	± 4.761
12	8.333	16.666	± 1.504
14	7.143	14.286	± 1.098

Theoretical Applications

Let us assume that the number of data points is constant in comparing the frequency distribution of income for our two groups over time. Consider then the following four possibilities in the way that distribution might appear.

The theory of the system would lead us to believe that when attainment is low, say, in sector two of the uniform growth line at the nth level, then the difference between the two lines will be slight. They would take on the appearance of Schema #1 where attainment does not imply significantly higher frequencies of greater income for one group over the other. As attainment rises, however, with respect to any level n, we would expect the situation to resemble Schema #2, where higher attainment increases the proportion of the group securing higher income. But we would also anticipate that if the notion of declining relative benefits has any credibility as a function of attainment rates, then the slope of the line for the higher attaining group will tend to decline further as the system expands further. The situation then would resemble that described as Schema #3.

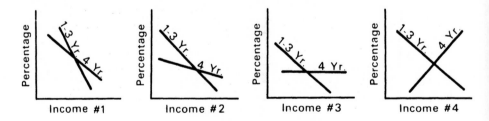

In short, the theory of the system would suggest that as the system expands, the movement is from #1 to #3. The line for the higher attaining group rotates counterclockwise to approach 0. The line for the next lower attaining group, however, would remain fairly stable. Therefore, the arithmetic difference in slope value for the two groups would increase. *This increase is the measure of increasing liability.*

What then is the measure of decreasing relative benefit? Observe that when the line for the attaining group at level n of the system is at zero slope, then merely attaining the nth level determines nothing with respect to one's position on the x-axis. *This is the expression of declining relative benefit* in the sense intended by the principle of shifting benefits and liabilities.

Viewed in this way then, "declining relative benefit" is defined as the rotation of such a frequency distribution line toward zero slope, and "increasing relative liability" is defined as the increasing arithmetic difference between the slopes for the two groups. Thus, the two ideas of "declining relative benefit" and "increasing liability" are conceptually distinct. They are defined independently.

But there is this problem. In the movement from #2 to #3, the graduating group experiences a declining efficacy of educational attainment at a particular level of the system. Nevertheless, the group as a whole is better off than it was before. Fewer are in the low and more are in the higher income ranges. Now it may seem odd to suggest that in the transition from #2 to #3 we have a declining relative benefit of higher attainment, and at the same time, assert that the higher attaining group is better off. Speaking loosely, we may say that, under conditions of Schema #3, a member of the higher attaining group has no better chance of securing a high income than a low one. But we may also say that, in Schema #3, he has a better chance of securing a high income than he would under conditions of Schema #2.

Recall, however, that by "declining relative benefit" we mean to refer to the declining capacity of attainment at level n, to determine the distribution of non-educational social goods to those who attain. In other words, declining relative benefit is a concept that refers to the efficacy of second-order educational benefits for the social allocation of non-educational social goods. It does not imply a declining aggregate welfare for the higher attaining group. Neither does it imply any declining aggregate benefit for the society. Zero correlation is the tautological claim that there is a point where the *efficacy* of education is nil. It does not imply that the society is worse off at zero correlation.

Indeed, it can be argued that, in general, a reduction in the efficacy of educational attainment would be a good thing for *any* society. In a frequency distribution like that in Schema #4, for example, we observe a society that allocates certain of its social benefits almost *exclusively* to those who happen to attain well within the system. This can be viewed as an excessive grant of power to the system. Applied to our sample population, it would mean that high school completion virtually *guarantees* a higher income not only relative to non-attainment, but also absolutely and relative to what attainment would bring under conditions of Schema #3. Under these conditions, the efficacy of education is strongly restored.

We may derive two quite general conclusions: (1) Any rotation of the frequency line toward zero slope at a specific level of the system will constitute a decline in the efficacy of educational attainment *at that level* for the allocation of non-educational social goods; and (2) the direction of that rotation, however, is important. If, for one of the groups, the frequency line rotates (counterclockwise) from a negative slope toward zero, then that group will be better off absolutely than it was before. Whether it is better off in relation to non-attainers remains an independent question. Yet, if the frequency line rotates (clockwise) toward zero from a positive slope, then the group will be worse off. Whether they will be worse off in relation to non-attainers remains again an open question. In short, in both cases "relative benefits" to the attaining group will decline in the sense intended by the principle of shifting benefits and liabilities. But only in the latter case will there be an *absolute* decline in benefits.[8]

We should note that even though a reduction in the social efficacy of educational attainment may be a desirable social goal, still, there are circumstances in which that goal cannot be reached without making certain groups worse off, both absolutely and probably relatively, than they were before. We have here a clue that in the educational system, as in the economy, there may be operating something like Pareto optimality. We are unaccustomed to the idea that there can be such a thing as an optimal state of affairs for the system, that, in other words, it might get too large or too influential in its effects upon the allocation of life chances. Yet that is one implication of the schema. We have here the seeds of a paradigmatic policy problem, that is, a genuine conflict not of interests but of goods.

EMPIRICAL APPLICATIONS

We have yet to determine how these theoretical considerations are reflected in the actual record. The relevant data are presented in Table C-4 where there is displayed the income frequency for each of our two groups within the 18–24 cohort. The frequencies are included for three ten year intervals starting in 1949 and for two three year intervals ending in 1975. It is evident that between 1949 and 1975 the range of income was extended. Therefore, the number of data points increases. In order to keep the income intervals uniform in the different applications of the schema, it will be necessary to use five data points for 1949, then seven, then twelve, and finally fourteen. Hence, the slopes of the lines are not comparable. The lines will necessarily rotate toward zero slope not because of any change in the frequency distribution, but solely because of an increase in the number of data points.

To apply the schema to the case at hand, we shall need some kind of index of benefit and liability not unlike the Consumer Price Index used in adjusting for year to year changes in the purchasing value of the dollar. We may secure that index by first obtaining the actual slope for each year by a linear regression. We may then divide the actual slope by the maximum slope permitted by the number of data points used in the regression. This will yield an index ranging from .00 to 1.00 (or from 0 to 100) that will be comparable for different years. The index then is a ratio

8. We may speculate that if college attainment were to continue increasing, then, at some point to be empirically determined, the frequency distribution for college attainers at the 14th and 16th levels of the system would be related to the curve for high school attainers in the way that currently the frequency distribution of those with 4 years of high school is related to the distribution of those with only 1–3 years. The phenomena of benefit and liability would reoccur at the next higher level of the system. There must be a ceiling to the constant repetition of these phenomena. How can that ceiling be identified?

TABLE C-4
Frequency Distribution of Income, Wages, and Salaries, Males, 4 and 1–3 Years of High School, 18–24 Year Olds, 1949–75, Selected Years

Total Money Income	1949		1959		1969		1972		1975	
	4 Yrs	1–3 Yrs	4 Yrs	1–3 Yrs	4 Yrs	1–3 Yrs	4 Yrs	1–3 Yrs	4 Yrs	1–3 Yrs
0–999	29.9	32.4	21.2	30.0	14.8	28.0	11.4	27.4	9.4	22.0
1,000–1,999	28.9	30.4	23.1	22.4	15.5	15.4	11.5	17.9	9.2	18
2,000–2,999	27.9	26.0	16.3	16.5	15.5	15.4	10.7	10.5	9.9	13
3,000–3,999	11.0	10.0	15.6	13.4	12.1	10.2	11.7	9.0	8.3	10.2
4,000–4,999	2.0	1.8	12.2	9.3	9.1	8.3	10.2	8.7	10.3	7.0
5,000–5,999			8.0	5.0	8.5	6.5	10.8	7.4	9.4	6.7
6,000–6,999			2.6	1.9	8.5	6.5	8.3	5.5	8.8	5.3
7,000–7,999					4.3	2.7	8.2	5.0	8.2	5.4
8,000–8,999					4.3	2.65	5.2	2.5	7.0	3.7
9,000–9,999					4.3	2.65	5.1	2.4	4.9	2.3
10,000–10,999					.56	.34	1.5	.8	3.9	2.0
11,000–11,999					.54	.34	1.5	.8	3.9	2.0
12,000–14,999							3.0	1.5	4.8	2.3
Total	99.7	99.6	99.0	98.5	98.0	98.98	99.1	99.4	98	99.9
Data Pts	5		7		12		14		14	
R	−.918	−.963	−.965	−.989	−.976	−.909	−.926	−.865	−.866	−.897
Actual Slope	−7.37	−8.16	−3.22	−4.51	−1.48	−2.05	−.89	−1.64	−.51	−1.43
Max slope	±10		±4.761		±1.504		±1.098		±1.098	
% Max slope	73.7	81.6	67.6	94.72	97.75	135.4	81.0	149.3	46.4	130.2
Liability Index	7.9		27.12		37.65		68.3		83.8	

SOURCES: U.S. Bureau of the Census. *Decennial Census Reports*. 1950. 1960. 1970: *Current Population Reports*. P-60. Nos. 90, 105.

Decisions made in compiling this table are as follows: (1) Settle on a number of income groupings so that no more than 2% of the population is excluded. (2) Where the Census Bureau groups the data in income intervals of less than $1,000 aggregate the figures, and where they are grouped in more than $1,000 intervals, then disaggregate. (3) Though the last income interval for 1972 and 1975 is $3,000, the frequency for that interval is entered as data point # 14 in running the regression.

of the actual slope to the maximum possible slope permitted by a varying number of data points. If the index declines toward zero, we have a measure of declining relative benefit, and if the arithmetic difference between the indices for the two groups increases, then we have a measure of increasing relative liability.

In this application of the schema, it is therefore relevant to note whether the assumption of linearity adhered to in exploring the logic of the schema holds also in analyzing the actual data. For this reason, Table C-4, in addition to the frequency distribution, includes also the number of data points used for each year, together with the maximum possible slope, the correlation coefficient of the linear regression, and finally the index of relative benefit for the attaining group each year and the index of liability of the non-attaining group.

The correlation coefficients are all in the range from $-.86$ to $-.98$. In short, the assumption of linearity does no violence to the data. But we may note also that the index of benefit for the higher attaining group declines from 73.7 for 1949 and from 97.75 in 1969 to 46.4 in 1975. This is a significant change not attributable to any variability in the income range. We may note further, however, that the liability index shows a marked and consistent increase from 7.9 in 1949 to 83.8 in 1975, and this change also is not attributable to any change in the income range.

SUMMARY

These are substantial results on which to recommend the theory of the system as so far developed. Still, what has been accomplished is quite limited. I do not claim that this illustrative foray into the domain of historical experience constitutes decisive confirmation of the principle of shifting benefits and liabilities. On the contrary, I have been concerned only to illustrate one way, among many others, that we might transform the principles of the theory into measures that will permit us to monitor the behavior of the system.

But these explorations are limited in another way. The focus has been entirely upon the value of second-order benefits for the allocation of non-educational social goods. I would not claim and have not claimed at any point that the value of educational benefits is their efficacy for the social allocation of non-educational goods. On the contrary, I would hold that such a view about the value of education is not simply false, but absurd. Neither have I been concerned at any point with commenting upon the value of education itself. It bears repeating that the theory of the system is not the theory of education. I have persisted in adhering to the view that for the proper development of educational policy, what we need, and what we most certainly have not had, is a credible theory of the educational system. My purpose in setting the system in motion, beginning with Chapter VI, has been first to explicate the principles that guide its behavior, and secondly, to illustrate in a single and quite limited case that those principles might be translated into hypotheses leading to an almost endless series of historical and empirical investigations.

INDEX